D1563208

THE FATHERS
OF THE CHURCH

A NEW TRANSLATION

VOLUME 100

THE FATHERS
OF THE CHURCH

A NEW TRANSLATION

SAINT JEROME

ON ILLUSTRIOUS MEN

Translated by

THOMAS P. HALTON
The Catholic University of America
Washington, D.C.

THE CATHOLIC UNIVERSITY OF AMERICA PRESS
Washington, D.C.

Copyright © 1999
THE CATHOLIC UNIVERSITY OF AMERICA PRESS
All rights reserved
Printed in the United States of America

The paper used in this publication meets the minimum requirements of the
American National Standards for Information Science—
Permanence of Paper for Printed Library Materials, ANSI z39.48–1984.

∞

LIBRARY OF CONGRESS CATALOGING-IN-PUBLICATION DATA

Jerome, Saint, d. 419 or 20.
    [De viris illustribus.   English]
    On illustrious men / Saint Jerome ; translated by Thomas P. Halton.
      p.   cm. — (Fathers of the church, a new translation : v. 100)
    Includes bibliographical references and indexes.
    1. Fathers of the church Bio-biography.   2. Church history—
Primitive and early church, ca. 30–600.   I. Halton, Thomas P.
(Thomas Patrick)   II. Title.   III. Series: Fathers of the church ; v. 100.
BR60.F3J47   1999
270.1'092'2 — dc21
[B]
99-30556
ISBN 0-8132-0100-4 (alk. paper)

CONTENTS

ON ILLUSTRIOUS MEN

APPENDICES

INDICES

EDITORIAL FOREWORD

In 1947 the first volume of the *Fathers of the Church* series, *The Apostolic Fathers*, carried a General Foreword from Ludwig Schopp, the first Editorial Director:

This series of seventy-two volumes will present outstanding patristic writings and include some works never translated before. . . . Introductions will familiarize the reader with the life and works of the authors. While all annotations will be brief, a select bibliography may serve as means for further study.

As Editorial Director of the Fathers of the Church since 1983, having crossed the "seventy-two volumes" limit, I have finally taken the liberty, with the benign connivance of the other members of the Editorial Board, of intruding a work of my own as Volume 100 in the series. In that this volume departs in format from its predecessors, especially in the directive that "annotations will be brief," a word of explanation is called for.

As it happens, I am concurrently under contract with Hendrickson Publishers of Peabody, Massachusetts, to translate Hubertus R. Drobner's *Lehrbuch der Patrologie* (Freiburg, Basel, Vienna: Herder, 1994), "substituting English translations for German works where possible." So it occurred to me that with so much data at my fingertips, so to speak, I might, in the best spirit of early Christian plagiarism, with trigger-happy (or at least "mouse"-happy) abandon, attempt a sort of updating of Jerome's *Ur-Patrologie* with the help of a *Spät-Patrologie* like Drobner's. I am also preparing for The Catholic University of America Press a *Supplement to Johannes Quasten, Patrology, Volumes I–III, 1950–1960*, on which I have constantly drawn. I have been especially predatory in utilizing my translation of Drobner's section on Jerome for the present Introduction. I wish to thank Professor Drobner and Hendrickson Publishers for permission to indulge in this virtual surgical transplant. My hope is that the resultant expanded annotations in the form of select bibliographies may "serve as means for further study," as Schopp intended.

I also warmly thank my colleagues, David J. McGonagle, Director, and Susan Needham, Managing Editor, of The Catholic University of America Press, and Staff Editors Carole Burnett and Cornelia Horn for meticulous assistance and infinite tolerance and patience.

Thomas Halton
Editorial Director

ABBREVIATIONS

AANLR	*Atti dell'Accademia Nazionale dei Lincei. Memorie. Classe di Scienze Morali, Storiche e Filologiche* (Rome)
ABAW	Abhandlungen der Bayerischen Akademie der Wissenschaften (Munich)
AC	*Antike und Christentum* (Münster, 1929–1950)
ACW	Ancient Christian Writers (New York and Mahwah, New Jersey)
AFLC	*Annali della Facoltà di Lettere e Filosofia della Università di Cagliari*
AHC	*Annuarium Historiae Conciliorum* (Paderborn)
AHP	*Annuarium Historiae Pontificiae* (Rome)
AKG	Archiv zur Kulturgeschichte (Münster)
ALGP	*Annali del Liceo classico G. Garibaldi di Palermo*
AMATosc	*Atti e Memorie dell'Accademi Toscana di Scienze e Lettere* (Florence)
AnBoll	*Analecta Bollandiana* (Brussels)
ANF	Ante-Nicene Fathers (repr. Grand Rapids, Michigan)
AnGr	*Analecta Gregoriana* (Rome)
ANRW	Aufstieg und Niedergang der römischen Welt (Berlin)
AnSE	*Annali di storia dell'esegesi* (Bologna)
ATA	Alttestamentliche Abhandlungen (Munich)
AThD	*Acta Theologica Danica* (Copenhagen and Leiden)
AugR	*Augustinianum* (Rome)
BAC	Biblioteca de Autores Cristianos (Madrid)
BBKL	Biographisch-Bibliographisches Kirchenlexikon
BGBH	Beiträge zur Geschichte der biblischen Hermeneutik (Tübingen)
BGL	Benediktinisches Geistesleben (St. Ottilien)
BHL	Bibliotheca Hagiographica Latina (Brussels)
BHTh	Beiträge zur historischen Theologie (Tübingen)
Bibl	*Biblica* (Rome)
BiblThBull	*Biblical Theology Bulletin* (New York and Albany)

BLE	*Bulletin de littérature ecclésiastique* (Toulouse)
BP	Biblioteca Patristica (Florence)
BTH	Bibliothèque de théologie historique (Paris)
BZNW	*Beihefte zur Zeitschrift für die neutestamentlische Wissenschaft und die Kunde der älteren Kirche* (Berlin)
C. and E.	T. D. Barnes, *Constantine and Eusebius* (Cambridge, Massachusetts, 1981)
CAnt	Christianisme antique (Paris)
Cath	Catholicisme (Paris)
CBQ	*Catholic Biblical Quarterly* (Washington, D.C.)
CCG	Corpus Christianorum, Series Graeca (Turnhout)
CCL	Corpus Christianorum, Series Latina (Turnhout)
Cer.-Gast.	Aldo Ceresa-Gastaldo, ed., *Gerolamo. Gli Uomini Illustri*
ChH	*Church History* (Chicago: American Society of Church History)
ChQR	*Church Quarterly Review* (London)
ClassQ	*Classical Quarterly* (Oxford)
CPG	Clavis Patrum Graecorum (Turnhout)
CPL	Clavis Patrum Latinorum (Steenbrugge, 1995[3])
CR	*Classical Review* (Oxford)
CrSt	*Cristianesimo nella storia* (Bologna)
CSEL	Corpus Scriptorum Ecclesiasticorum Latinorum (Vienna)
CTP	Collana di testi patristici (Rome)
CW	*Classical World* (Pittsburgh, Pennsylvania)
DACL	Dictionnaire d'archéologie chrétienne et de liturgie (Paris)
DHGE	Dictionnaire d'histoire et de géographie ecclésiastiques (Paris)
Dr	H. R. Drobner, *Lehrbuch der Patrologie* (Freiburg, Basel, Vienna: Herder, 1994)
DSp	Dictionnaire de spiritualité ascétique et mystique, doctrine et histoire (Paris)
DT	*Divus Thomas. Commentarium de philosophia et theologia* (Piacenza)
DVI	Jerome, *De viris illustribus*
EBib	*Estudios Bíblicos* (Madrid)
EEC[2]	Encyclopedia of Early Christianity, 2d ed., 2 vols. (New York, 1997)

ABBREVIATIONS

EECh	Encyclopedia of the Early Church (New York, 1992)
EHS.T	Europäische Hochschulschriften. Series 23. Theologie (Frankfurt)
EPRO	*Études préliminaires aux religions orientales dans l'empire romain* (Leiden)
ESH	*Ecumenical Studies in History* (Richmond, Virginia)
EThL	Ephemerides Theologicae Lovanienses (Louvain)
EThSt	*Erfurter Theologische Studien* (Leipzig)
FChLDG	*Forschungen zur Christlichen Literatur- und Dogmengeschichte* (Paderborn)
FKDG	Forschungen zur Kirchen- und Dogmengeschichte (Göttingen)
FOTC	The Fathers of the Church (Washington, D.C.)
GCS	Die Griechischen Christlichen Schriftsteller der ersten drei Jahrhunderte (Leipzig and Berlin)
Gestalten	M. Greschat, ed. *Gestalten der Kirchengeschichte* (Stuttgart, 1981 on)
GiornItalFil	*Giornale Italiano di Filologia* (Rome)
GkOrthThR	*Greek Orthodox Theological Review* (Brookline, Massachusetts)
Greg	*Gregorianum* (Rome)
GS	B. Layton, *The Gnostic Scriptures: A New Translation with Annotations and Introductions* (Garden City, New York, 1987)
HeyJ	*Heythrop Journal* (Oxford)
HLL	Handbuch der lateinischen Literatur der Antike (Munich)
HNT	*Handbuch zum Neuen Testament* (Tübingen)
HThR	*Harvard Theological Review* (Cambridge, Massachusetts)
IMU	*Italia medioevale e umanistica* (Padua)
InvLuc	*Invigilata lucernis. Rivista dell'Istituto di Latino* (Bari)
IP	Instrumenta Patristica (Steenbrugge)
JECS	*Journal of Early Christian Studies* (Baltimore, Maryland)
JEH	*Journal of Ecclesiastical History* (London and New York)
JewQRev	*Jewish Quarterly Review* (Philadelphia)
JfNG	*Jahrbuch für Numismatik und Geldgeschichte* (Munich)
JLH	*Jahrbuch für Liturgik und Hymnologie* (Kassel)
JÖByz	*Jahrbuch der Österreichischen Byzantinistik* (Vienna)
JRS	*Journal of Roman Studies* (London)

JSNT	*Journal for the Study of the New Testament* (Sheffield)
JThS	*Journal of Theological Studies* (Oxford)
Kler	*Kleronomia* (Thessalonica)
KuD	*Kerygma und Dogma* (Göttingen)
LCI	Lexikon der christlichen Ikonographie (Freiburg)
LLW	P. Courcelle, *Late Latin Writers and their Greek Sources*, trans. Wedeck (Cambridge, Massachusetts, 1969)
LThK, LThK³	Lexikon für Theologie und Kirche, 1st and 3d editions (Freiburg, 1957–65 and 1993–)
MAH	Mélanges d'archéologie et d'histoire (Paris)
NCE	New Catholic Encyclopedia (New York, 1967)
NDid	*Nuovo Didaskaleion* (Catania)
NHB	D. M. Scholer, *Nag Hammadi Bibliography 1948–1969* (Leiden, 1971)
NHS	Nag Hammadi Studies (Leiden)
NovTest	*Novum Testamentum* (Leiden)
NPNF	Nicene and Post-Nicene Fathers (repr. Grand Rapids, Michigan)
NRTh	*Nouvelle revue théologique* (Tournai)
NTA	*New Testament Apocrypha* (1991), revised ed. of collection of E. Hennecke, ed. W. Schneemelcher and R. McL. Wilson
NTS	*New Testament Studies* (Cambridge)
OCD³	*Oxford Classical Dictionary*, 3d ed. (1996)
ODP	J. N. D. Kelly, *The Oxford Dictionary of the Popes* (1986)
OECT	Oxford Early Christian Texts
OLD	*Oxford Latin Dictionary*
OrChr	*Oriens Christianus* (Rome)
OrChrP	*Orientalia Christiana Periodica* (Rome)
Orph.	*Orpheus* (Catania)
PatMS	Patristic Monograph Series (Cambridge, Massachusetts)
PBR	*Patristic and Byzantine Review*
PdO	*Parole de l'Orient*
PG	Patrologiae Cursus Completus: Series Graeca, ed. J.-P. Migne (Paris)
PGL	*A Patristic Greek Lexicon*, ed. G. W. H. Lampe (Oxford)
PL	Patrologiae Cursus Completus: Series Latina, ed. J.-P. Migne (Paris)
PLRE	A. H. M. Jones, *The Prosopography of the Later Roman Empire*

PLS	Patrologiae Latinae Supplementum
PRE	Paulys Realenzyklopädie der classischen Alter-tumswissenschaft (Stuttgart)
PrOrChr	*Proche orient chrétien* (Jerusalem)
PTA	Papyrologische Texte und Abhandlungen (Bonn)
PTS	Patristische Texte und Studien (Berlin)
PWK	Pauly-Wissowa-Kroll, *Realencyklopädie der classischen Wissenschaft*
PWRE	Pauly-Wissowa Realencyklopädie
Q	*Patrology.* Vols. 1–3 by Johannes Quasten; Vol. 4, ed. Di Berardino with intro. by Quasten
RAC	Reallexikon für Antike und Christentum (Stuttgart)
RAL	*Rendiconti della Classe di Scienze morali, storiche e filologiche dell' Accademia dei Lincei* (Rome)
RE	Realenzyklopädie für protestantische Theologie und Kirche (Leipzig)
REA	*Revue des études anciennes* (Bordeaux)
REAug	*Revue des études augustiniennes* (Paris)
RechSR	*Recherches de science religieuse* (Paris)
RÉG	*Revue des études grecques* (Paris)
RÉL	*Revue des études latines* (Paris)
Ren.	*Renovatio* (Regensburg)
RevBén	*Revue bénédictine* (Namur)
RevThom	*Revue thomiste* (Soisy-sur-Seine)
RHE	*Revue d'histoire ecclésiastique* (Louvain)
RHPR	*Revue d'histoire et de philosophie religieuse* (Paris)
RHT	*Revue d'histoire des textes* (Paris)
RiCultCM	*Rivista di Cultura Classica e Medioevale*
RPAA	*Rendiconti della Pontificia Accademia di Archeologia* (Rome)
RQ	*Römische Quartalschrift für christliche Altertumskunde und Kirchengeschichte* (Freiburg)
RSLR	*Rivista di Storia e Letteratura Religiosa* (Florence)
RSR	*Revue des sciences religieuses* (Strasbourg)
SC	Sources chrétiennes (Paris)
ScEc	*Sciences ecclésiastiques* (Bruges)
ScrTh	Scripta Theologica (Pamplona)
SD	Scripta et Documenta (Montserrat and Barcelona)
SEAug	*Studia Ephemeridis "Augustinianum"* (Rome)
SecCent	*The Second Century* (Abilene, Texas)

SGLG	*Studia Graeca et Latina Gothoburgensia* (Stockholm)
SHG	Subsidia Hagiographica (Brussels)
SJTh	Scottish Journal of Theology (Edinburgh)
STh	*Studia Theologica* (Lund)
StMiss	*Studia Missionalia* (Rome)
Str Pat	Stromata patristica et mediaevalia (Utrecht)
StudPat	Studia Patristica (Oxford)
TAP	The Apostolic Fathers (London)
TAPA	*Transactions and Proceedings of the American Philological Association* (Decatur, Georgia)
Theoph.	Theophaneia. Beiträge zur Religions- und Kirchengeschichte des Alertums (Bonn)
ThH	Théologie historique (Paris)
ThQ	*Theologische Quartalschrift* (Munich)
ThWNT	*Theologisches Wörterbuch zum Neuen Testament* (Stuttgart and Grand Rapids, Michigan)
TLG	*Thesaurus Linguae Graecae: A Canon of Greek Authors and Works* (Oxford, 1986)
TLL	Thesaurus Linguae Latinae (Leipzig)
TRE	Theologische Realenzyklopädie (Berlin)
TS	*Theological Studies*
TU	Texte und Untersuchungen zur Geschichte der altchristlichen Literatur (Leipzig and Berlin)
VetChr	*Vetera Christianorum* (Bari)
VigChr	*Vigiliae Christianae* (Amsterdam and Leiden)
ViSa	Vite dei Santi (Verona)
WUNT	Wissenschaftliche Untersuchungen zum Neuen Testament (Tübingen)
ZKG	*Zeitschrift für Kirchengeschichte* (Stuttgart)
ZKTh	*Zeitschrift für Katholische Theologie* (Vienna)
ZNW	*Zeitschrift für die Neutestamentliche Wissenschaft und die Kunde der älteren Kirche* (Berlin)

SELECT BIBLIOGRAPHY

Texts and Translations

Donalson, Malcolm D. *A Translation of Jerome's Chronicon with Historical Commentary*. Lewiston, New York: Mellen Press, 1996.

Gerolamo. Gli Uomini Illustri. Ed. Aldo Ceresa-Gastaldo. BP 12. Florence: Nardini Editore, 1988.

Hieronymus. *Die Chronik des Hieronymus*. Ed. R. Helm. Eusebius' Werke VII. GCS 23. 3d ed. Berlin, 1984.

Hieronymus. liber De viris inlustribus. Gennadius. liber De viris inlustribus. Ed. E. C. Richardson. TU 14. Leipzig: J. C. Hinrichs, 1896.

Hieronymus und Gennadius. De viris inlustribus. Ed. Carl Albrecht Bernoulli. Freiburg and Leipzig: Mohr, 1895.

IERWNUMOU. De Viris Illustribus. Ed. K. Siamake. Thessalonica, 1992.

Jerome. *Against Rufinus*. Trans. John N. Hritzu. FOTC 53. Washington, D.C.: The Catholic University of America Press, 1965.

———. *Epistulae*. Ed. I. Hilberg. CSEL 54–56. Vienna: 1910, 1912, 1918.

———. *Letters*. NPNF, 2d series, 6. Edinburgh: T & T Clark, 1892. Reprinted Grand Rapids, Michigan: Wm. B. Eerdmans Publishing Company, 1989.

———. *Letters 1–22*. Trans. C. C. Mierow. ACW 33. Westminster, Maryland: Newman Press, 1963.

———. *The Letters of St. Jerome. A selection to illustrate Roman Christian Life in the 4th Century*. J. Duff. Dublin, 1942.

Secondary Sources

Antin, Paul. *Essai sur saint Jérôme*. Paris: Letouzey & Ané, 1951.

———. *Recueil sur saint Jérôme*. Collection Latomus 95. Brussels, 1968.

Auerbach, Erich. *Literary Language and Its Public in Late Latin Antiquity and in the Middle Ages*. Trans. R. Manheim. New York: Pantheon Books, 1965.

Barnes, Timothy D. *Constantine and Eusebius*. Cambridge, Mass.: Harvard University Press, 1981.

———. *Tertullian: A Historical and Literary Study*. Oxford: Clarendon Press, 1971. Subsequently reissued with corrections and a postscript. New York: Oxford University Press, 1985.

Bellini, Enzo, ed. *Su Cristo. Il Grande Dibattio nel Quarto Secolo.* Milan, 1978.

Berschin, Walter. *Greek Letters and the Latin Middle Ages: From Jerome to Nicholas of Cusa.* Trans. Jerold C. Frakes. Washington, D.C.: The Catholic University of America Press, 1988.

Cantalamessa, R. *Easter in the Early Church.* Trans. J. M. Quigley and J. T. Lienhard. Collegeville, Minn.: Liturgical Press, 1993.

Cavallera, Ferdinand. *Saint Jérôme: sa vie et son œuvre.* Louvain, 1922.

Ceresa-Gastaldo, Aldo. "La tecnica biografica del *De viris illustribus* di Gerolamo." *Renovatio* 14 (1979): 221–26.

Clark, Elizabeth A. *Jerome, Chrysostom, and Friends: Essays and Translations.* New York and Toronto: The Edwin Mellen Press, 1979.

————. *The Origenist Controversy: The Cultural Construction of an Early Christian Debate.* Princeton: The Princeton University Press, 1992.

Courcelle, Pierre. *Late Latin Writers and their Greek Sources.* Trans. Harry E. Wedeck. Cambridge, Mass.: Harvard University Press, 1969.

Cox, Patricia. *Biography in Late Antiquity: A Quest for the Holy Man.* Berkeley: University of California Press, 1983.

Dihle, Albrecht. *Die Entstehung der historischen Biographie.* Heidelberg, 1986.

————. *Greek and Latin Literature of the Roman Empire: From Augustus to Justinian.* Trans. Manfred Malzahn. London and New York: Routledge, 1994.

Duval, Y. M., ed. *Jérôme entre l'Occident et l'Orient. XVIe centennaire du départ de saint Jérôme de Rome et son installation à Bethléem.* Paris, 1988.

Gamble, Harry Y. *Books and Readers in the Early Church: A History of Early Christian Texts.* New Haven: Yale University Press, 1995.

García-Lopez, ed. *Biografías literarias latinas. Suetonio, Valerio Probo, Jerónimo.* Madrid, 1985.

Granfield, P., and J. A. Jungmann, edd. *Kyriakon.* Festschrift Johannes Quasten. 2 vols. Münster, 1970.

Grant, Robert M. *Greek Apologists of the Second Century.* Philadelphia: Westminster Press, 1988.

————. *Eusebius as Church Historian.* Oxford, 1980.

Greschat, Martin, ed. *Gestalten der Kirchengeschichte.* Stuttgart, Berlin, Cologne, and Mainz: Kohlhammer, 1981 on.

Kelly, J. N. D. *Jerome: His Life, Writings, and Controversies.* London: Duckworth, 1975.

Lambert, Bernard. *Bibliotheca Hieronymiana Manuscripta: La tradition manuscrite de saint Jérôme.* 5 vols. Steenbrugge, 1970.

Matthews, John. *Western Aristocracies and Imperial Court, A.D. 364–425.* Oxford: Clarendon Press, 1975.

MacMullen, Ramsay. *Christianity and Paganism in the Fourth to Eighth Centuries.* New Haven: Yale University Press, 1997.

Murphy, F. X. *A Monument to Saint Jerome. Essays on Some Aspects of his Life, Works, and Influence.* New York: Sheed and Ward, 1952.

Nautin, Pierre. *Lettres et écrivains chrétiens des IIe et IIIe siècles.* Paris, 1961.

———. "La date du 'De Viris Inlustribus' de Jérôme, de la mort de Cyrille de Jérusalem, et de celle de Grégoire de Nazianze." *Revue d'histoire ecclésiastique* 56 (1961): 33–35.

———. "Études de chronologie hiéronymienne (393–397)." *Revue des études augustiniennes* 18 (1972): 209–18.

———. *Origène: sa vie et son œuvre.* Paris: Beauchesne, 1977.

———. "La liste des œuvres de Jérôme dans le *De viris inlustribus.*" *Orpheus*, n.s., 5 (1984): 319–34.

Ollivier, Claude. *Jérôme.* Paris: Éditions Ouvrières, 1963.

Opelt, I. "Hieronymus' Leistung als Literarhistoriker in der Schrift *De viris illustribus.*" *Orpheus*, n.s., 1 (1980): 52–75.

———. "Origene visto da san Girolamo." *Augustinianum* 26 (1985): 217–22.

Rebenich, Stefan. *Hieronymus und sein Kreis: prosopographische und sozialgeschichtliche Untersuchungen.* Stuttgart: F. Steiner, 1992.

Rousseau, Philip. *Ascetics, Authority, and the Church in the Age of Jerome and Cassian.* Oxford: Oxford University Press, 1978.

Steinmann, J. *Hieronymus, Ausleger der Bibel. Weg und Werk eines Kirchenvaters.* Cologne, 1961.

Vielhauer, Philipp. *Geschichte der urchristlichen Literatur: Einleitung in das Neue Testament, die Apokryphen und die Apostolischen Väter.* Berlin and New York: Walter de Gruyter, 1975.

INTRODUCTION

Born in 347 or 348 into a prosperous Christian family of the propertied class in Stridon near Emona,[1] Jerome went in 360 to Rome to undertake studies in grammar and rhetoric, where he had Rufinus as his friend and Aelius Donatus, the famous grammarian, as his teacher. During his student days he acquired not just a notable knowledge of Latin literature, but also an extraordinary competence in the Latin language.

An anecdote that he himself relates[2] gives an interesting insight into his mode of life at that time, although he had not yet received baptism:

When I was a boy during my studies in the liberal arts at Rome, a group of us of the same age and interests used on Sundays to go around the tombs which were dug in the depths of the earth, and as we walked along the dark passages, the bodies of the martyrs lay on shelves along the walls . . . It was so dark down there that we seemed to be fulfilling the word of the prophet: "Let the living go down to hell" [Ps. 54:16].

Characteristically, as they return to *terra firma*, Jerome is reminded of a line from Virgil: "Fear and the very silence itself struck terror into our souls."[3]

One of the best-known episodes in the life of Jerome is the personal crisis he experienced over his love of the classics, precipitating his famous dream. "I dreamed, I stood before the judgment seat of God and heard His verdict: 'you are a Ciceronian, not a Christian; *where your treasure is, there is your heart also*' [Mt 6:21]."[4] However, throughout his life the classics never lost their influence on him, as the analysis of his work indicates, even if they took second place to Scripture and Christian doctrine.

Together with Rufinus he frequented the monastic community in Rome and became enthusiastic about the monastic life.

After he was baptized in Rome in 367 or 368 (perhaps by Pope Liberius), he seems to have tried a career in the state administration in Trier, then the imperial residence of Gaul. In his *Confessions* Augustine gives an account[5] of two imperial functionaries in Trier, who during a walk came to a house of monks, and there happened upon the *Vita* of the Egyptian monk Antony (composed by Athanasius soon after Antony's death in 355/356 or 357/358, and translated into Latin by Evagrius of Antioch before 375), and, spontaneously filled with enthusiasm for the monastic life, gave up their careers at court. Even if we do not agree with Pierre Courcelle's identification of the two of them with Jerome and Bonosus,[6] the scene in any event describes the atmosphere in which Jerome's decision (c. 370) soon matured to terminate his secular career, in order to lead a life of asceticism and leisurely erudition in his homestead in Aquileia in communion with his friend Rufinus—comparable, doubtless, with that of the circle around Augustine in Cassiciacum and Thagaste a little later.

The community in Aquileia became unravelled, and both Jerome and Rufinus betook themselves to the Eastern fountains of monasticism—Rufinus in 373 to Egypt, Jerome around 371 *via* Constantinople to Antioch, where he was received by Evagrius, who later became bishop of the old Nicene community of Antioch. He spent a brief period as a recluse in the desert in East Syria in Chalcis, but soon returned to Antioch. In this Antiochene period, which lasted down to 379/380, he acquired a good knowledge of both Greek and Hebrew, which laid the foundations for his later activities in translation. He began intensive study of the Bible, toward which, because of its unpolished style—just like Augustine—he had earlier been lukewarm, and attended (in perhaps 377) the exegetical lectures of Apollinaris of Laodicea, which provided the basis for his later works on the text and interpretation of the Bible.

No doubt Jerome, in the library bequeathed by Eustathius, studied the writings of Origen, many of whose works he translated into Latin. He entered, as a guest of Evagrius, the old Nicene community and was ordained by Paulinus to the priesthood, under the stipulation that he would not have to give up his monastic way of life; then he got started with his literary activity. In this period he definitely composed the first monastic legend of Christian literature, the *Vita* of the Egyptian recluse Paul, and possibly (according to Nautin) even that early also the first translations of Origen (the *Homilies on Isaiah, On Jeremiah,* and *On Ezekiel*).[7] Other scholars, however, date these first translations to his next period in Constantinople, as done at the instigation of Gregory Nazianzus. In 379 or 380 he departed for Constantinople, together with Bishop Paulinus, who wanted to obtain recognition as legitimate Bishop of Antioch from the new "Nicene" emperor, Theodosius. This undertaking, however, proved fruitless, since both Emperor and Council (381) recognized Meletius.

However, in this period Jerome made contact with Gregory of Nazianzus, Patriarch of Constantinople, and two other Cappadocians, Gregory of Nyssa and Amphilochius of Iconium, and began or continued his translation activity. In any case it was in Constantinople that the translation of the *Chronicle* of Eusebius was done, as well as its continuation down to the year 378, both of which would exercise such widespread influence throughout the Middle Ages. From Eusebius's *Onomasticon,* Jerome composed his *Liber locorum* and *Liber nominum.*

After Gregory Nazianzus retired from the bishopric of Constantinople, Paulinus and Jerome returned to Antioch without receiving the desired reward for their efforts: the recognition of the old Nicene community. In spring of 382 they journeyed to Rome with Epiphanius of Constantia (Salamis), Jerome having assumed the role of guide. A Roman synod in 382, in which Ambrose of Milan also participated, recognized Paulinus as the sole legitimate Bishop of Antioch; but in the East its decision remained without effect. Epiphanius and Jerome were guests of the widow Paula (with her daughter Eustochium) and Marcella; they—as had previously the mother and sister of the great Cappadocians, Basil and Gregory of Nyssa—had converted their houses into monasteries: this was for Jerome a return to those contacts with the ascetical circles already established during his student days, which now enabled him to pursue his own inclinations. His hosts were distinguished, well-off, and cultured persons; Marcella even learned Hebrew in order to study the Bible in the original. When, in the summer of 383, Paulinus and Epiphanius returned to the East, Jerome stayed on in Rome, where, as he himself recounts,[8] he became secretary to Bishop Damasus. Here he asked Damasus to excuse him, because of constraints of time and expense, if he only translated Origen's two homilies on the *Canticle of Canticles*, while readily acknowledging that, "in his other works Origen surpassed others, but in his *Canticle of Canticles* he surpassed himself." A *Vita* of the twelfth century reports that Jerome, because of his Roman activity, was named a cardinal, and later iconography portrays him frequently in such a garb.

After the death of his patron and protector Damasus (on December 11, 384), Jerome entertained hopes of becoming his successor.[9] Siricius was chosen, however, in his stead, since Jerome, in his ascetical zeal, had made numerous enemies for himself in the city, by sharply denouncing the deplorable ecclesiastical and moral conditions there. On this occasion Jerome's peculiar characteristics emerged for the first time, which later, in the controversies with Rufinus, Augustine, and others, became even more pronounced: the attacks directed by him were sharp, but he himself was emotional and an easy target. Such a hostile climate arose around him in Rome that he had to abandon the city; improper relations with the women of his ascetical circle were maliciously hinted at, or at least the charge of being responsible for the death of one of them because of the extremes of his ascetical injunctions. In August 385 he embarked at Ostia for Jerusalem. A letter to Asella, written on board ship at Ostia, is very enlightening on the poisoned climate that he left behind in Rome:

I am said to be an infamous turncoat, a slippery knave, one who lies and deceives others by satanic arts . . . Some kissed my hands, yet attacked me with the tongues of vipers . . . One would attack my gait or my way of laughing; another would suspect the simplicity of my manner. Such is the company in which I have lived for almost three years . . . Before I became acquainted with the family of the saintly Paula, all Rome resounded with my praises. Almost everyone concurred in judging me worthy of the episcopate. Damasus, of blessed memory, spoke no words but mine. Men called me holy, humble, eloquent.[10]

Paula, the alleged *femme fatale*, and her daughter Eustochium, did indeed with other companions follow him, joining him in Reggio di Calabria. From there they journeyed *via* Cyprus and Antioch to Jerusalem, where they arrived at the end of 385, only to set off soon after for Egypt; here they visited various monastic settlements and in Alexandria came in contact with the great connoisseur of Origen, Didymus.

B. THE BETHELEHEM YEARS (386–420)

In spring of 386 they returned again to Palestine, settling finally in Bethlehem, and founding one male and three female monasteries. The following years, during which Jerome made frequent use of the library of Origen and Eusebius in Palestinian Caesarea, were dedicated to intense literary activity. His publications included translations of the Bible; commentaries on the Pauline Epistles to Philemon, the Galatians, the Ephesians, and Titus; commentaries on Ecclesiastes, Micah, Zephaniah, Nahum, Habakkuk, Haggai, Jonah, and Obadiah; translations of Didymus's *De Spiritu Sancto*, Origen's *Homilies on Luke*, and his catalogue of authors, *De viris illustribus*.

With respect to this early work of patrology, Johannnes Quasten has identified Jerome as "the first to compose a history of Christian theological literature" and credits the work as

the basic source for the history of ancient Christian literature . . . Through more than a thousand years all historians of ancient Christian literature regarded *De viris illustribus* as the basis of all their studies, and their sole endeavor was to write continuations of this great work.[11]

The idea of such a history, however, is rightly attributed by Quasten to Eusebius of Caesarea, who stated as one of his goals in the introduction to his *Ecclesiastical History:*

to report on the number of those who in each generation were ambassadors of the divine word orally or through written compositions; who and how many and when they were who, driving on to the extreme of error because of yearning for innovation, proclaimed themselves authors of "knowledge falsely so-called."[12]

In pursuing this, Eusebius does not draw a tight line between orthodox and heretical writers; nor does Jerome, who interestingly would draw a mild rebuke from Augustine, in his *ep.* 40: "It would be more useful, I think, if, when you have named those whom you know to be heretical . . . you would indicate also wherein they are not to be followed."[13]

Indeed, conflict was to be a hallmark of Jerome's career. In September 393, after the feast of the consecration of a church in Jerusalem, Jerome intervened in the discussion between Epiphanius of Constantia (Salamis) and John of Jerusalem on the theology of Origen. He sided with Epiphanius, to whom he already had been close for years, while his friend Rufinus took the side of John. A polemic began with Rufinus, destined to last for years, but Jerome also found himself involved in a difficult situation, from a churchly point of view. His brother, Paulinianus, in fact, was ordained a deacon by Epiphanius, without the permission of John, under whose jurisdiction the monastery at Bethlehem was situated, whereupon John excommunicated the monastery. Jerome defended Epiphanius in the work *Contra Ioannem Hierosolymitanum*, and sought the support of Theophilus of Alexandria. After repeated attempts John and Jerome were finally reconciled on Holy Thursday 397, and likewise Jerome and Rufinus.

It is not quite certain that the position of Jerome toward Origen changed substantially because of the polarization over the Origenist quarrel. He valued and translated Origen's works both before it and after. The fact that in the controversy he took the side of Epiphanius could be imputed in the beginning to purely personal motives, just as the polemic against Rufinus arose, not from a difference in evaluating the theology of Origen, but from a judgment on the correctness of Rufinus's translation of *De principiis*, and this was the starting point of other controversies, beginning in 397.

Jerome's relations with other prominent bishops of his era likewise underwent tensions. Since Ambrose in his work *De Spiritu Sancto* had made use of Didymus's work bearing the same name, and, in his *Commentary on Luke*, of the homilies of Origen, Jerome translated both works into Latin, to expose the plagiarisms of Ambrose. It is not, however, certain whether the true motive of such behavior was the result of philological rigorism on Jerome's part, or of his wish to avenge the lack of support from Ambrose for himself and Paulinus at the Synod of Rome in 382.

The years 403–405 were unproductive for Jerome because of Paula's long illness and subsequent death on January 26, 404. In 406 he resumed his composition of Biblical commentaries: *On Zechariah, Malachi, Hosea, Joel,* and *Amos,* in 406; *Daniel* in 407; *Isaiah* in 408/409; *Ezekiel* in 411–414 or 412–415; and *Jeremiah* (from 415). Even in this new period of time there was a pause in publishing activity, occasioned by the conquest of Rome by Alaric on August 24, 410, and the subsequent flow of refugees into Palestine. In the winter of 415/416 the *Dialogus contra Pelagianos* appeared, aimed against those, that is, who found refuge with John of Jerusalem.

Jerome died on September 30, 419 or 420. His reputation in antiquity was legendary. For Sulpicius Severus "he was constantly immersed in study and in books; continually occupied in reading and writing, he permitted himself no rest day or night."[14] For Cassiodorus he was "Latinae linguae dilatator eximius, qui nobis in translatione divinae Scripturae tantum praestitit . . . plurimos libros, copiosas epistolas fecit."[15] The western church has since 1295 venerated him, together with Ambrose, Augustine, and Gregory the Great, as one of the four "great Church teachers of the West." Iconography has frequently portrayed him as "Jerome in a cave," with a lion at his feet; best known is the engraving of Albrecht Dürer. More frequently he has been depicted within his monastic study; the legend of the lion from whose paw he had extracted a thorn, and who in gratitude never abandoned him subsequently, is found for the first time in a ninth-century *Vita.*[16]

The last word can be left to Dom P. Antin:

Fin psychologue, moraliste pénétrant, rigide en théorie, prudent en pratique, peu théologien, Jérôme est plein de contrastes. Il est colère, vindicatif, rancunier, flatteur. Mais quel travailleur! Souvent, quel ami fidèle! . . . Il ne goûte pleinement que la vie monastique, car là seulement on est tout à Jésus. Sa vie mystique tend au Christ qui vit pour nous dans l'Ecriture, autre Eucharistie.[17]

NOTES

1. Present-day Ljubljana/Laibach in Slovenia; the precise location of Stridon is unknown.

2. Jerome, *Comm. on Ezechiel* 12.40, CCL 75, 557.

3. Virgil, *Aen.* 2.755.

4. Jerome, *ep.* 22.30.

5. Augustine, *Conf.* 8.6.15.

6. P. Courcelle, *Recherches sur les Confessions de saint Augustin* (Paris, 1950), 181–85, refuted by J. N. D. Kelly, *Jerome: His Life, Writings, and Controversies,* 30.

7. Johannes Quasten, *Patrology,* Vol. 4, 215.

8. Jerome, *ep.* 123.9.

9. *Ep.* 45.3.

10. *Ep.* 45, NPNF 6, ser. 2, 59.

11. J. Quasten, *Patrology,* Vol. 1, 1–2.

12. Eusebius, *Historia ecclesiastica* 1.1.1; see also R. M. Grant, *Eusebius as Church Historian,* (Oxford: Clarendon Press, 1980), 36.

13. Augustine, *ep.* 40, trans. W. Parsons, FOTC 12, 178.

14. Sulpicius Severus, *Dial.* 1.9, PL 20: 190.

15. Cassiodorus, *Inst.* 1.21, PL 70: 1135.

16. PL 22: 209–212.

17. P. Antin, art., "Jérôme," Catholicisme 6, 704.

ON ILLUSTRIOUS MEN

Dürer, Albrecht (1471–1528)
St. Jerome in his study
The Metropolitan Museum of Art, Fletcher Fund, 1919. (19.73.68)

PREFACE

EXTER,[1] you urge me that I, following the example of Tranquillus,[2] prepare an orderly presentation of the ecclesiastical writers, and do for our writers what he did in chronicling eminent secular authors, that is, that I set forth for you a brief treatment of all those who have published anything memorable on the Holy Scriptures from the time of Christ's passion down to the fourteenth year of the emperor Theodosius.[3]

2. Among the Greeks this same sort of enterprise has been carried out by Hermippus the Peripatetic, Antigonus Carystius, the learned Satyrus, and Aristoxenus the musician, by far the most learned of them all.[4] Among the Latins were Varro,[5] Santra,[6] Nepos,[7] Hyginus,[8] and the one whom you would like me to emulate, Tranquillus.

3. But their working conditions and mine are not quite the same, for they had at their disposal ancient histories and chronicles, and could, as if [gathering] from a great meadow,[9] weave a small crown for their task. As for me, what am I to do, in that I have no predecessor[10] and follow the worst teacher possible, as the saying goes, my own poor self? Still, Eusebius Pamphilus, in the ten books of his *Ecclesiastical History,* has been of the greatest help to me, and the volumes of the individuals about whom I propose to write often provide insights into the lives of their authors.

4. Therefore I invoke the Lord Jesus that by listing the writers of his church I may satisfy your exhortation in a fashion worthy of what your Cicero, who stood at the pinnacle of Roman eloquence, did not disdain to do when weaving a catalogue of Latin writers in his *Brutus.*[11]

5. If, however, some of those who down to the present continue to write have been passed over by me[12] in the present volume, they should blame themselves rather than me.

1

2 ST. JEROME

6. For from what I have not read I could not know the ones
who are hiding their own writings, and what was perhaps known
to others remained unknown to me in this corner of the
earth.[13] Certainly when they become illustrious by their writings
they will not heave any deep sighs because of [any] losses
through my silence.

7. Let Celsus, then, learn, and Porphyry and Julian,[14] those
rabid dogs barking[15] against Christ; let their followers learn—
those who think that the church has had no philosophers, no
orators, no men of learning;[16] let them learn the number and
quality of the men who founded, built, and adorned the
church, and let them stop accusing our faith of such rustic simplicity,[17] and recognize instead their own ignorance. Salutations
to you in the Lord Jesus Christ.

NOTES

1. For Dexter, see Q 4, 135; *PLRE* 1, 251; Stefan Rebenich, *Hieronymus und sein Kreis: prosopographische und sozialgeschichtliche Untersuchungen* (Stuttgart: F. Steiner, 1992), 214f. Dexter (*DVI* 132) was a son of Pacian, bishop of Barcelona (*DVI* 106). For possible literary activity of Dexter, cf. W. Berschin, *Greek Letters and the Latin Middle Ages: from Jerome to Nicholas of Cusa*, trans. J. C. Frakes (Washington, D.C.: The Catholic University of America Press, 1988), 302 n. 25 and 295 n. 41, citing in the latter refer-ence G. Morin, "L'opuscule de soi-disant Hégesippe sur les Machabées," *RevBén* 31 (1914–19): 83–91. See also John Matthews, *Western Aristocracies and Imperial Court*, A.D. *364–425* (Oxford: Clarendon Press, 1975), 133, 149.
2. C. *Suetoni Tranquilli, Praeter Caesarum Libros Reliquiae, Pars Prior De Grammaticis et Rhetoribus*, ed. G. Brugnoli (Leipzig, 1960); *Suétone, Gram-marien et rhéteur*, ed. M.-C. Vacher (Paris, 1993); *Suetonius: De grammaticis et rhetoribus*, ed. and trans. with notes by R. A. Kaster (Oxford: Clarendon Press, 1995); R. A. Kaster, *Guardians of Language: The Grammarian and Soci-ety in Late Antiquity* (Berkeley: University of California Press, 1988); A. Wal-lace-Hadrill, *Suetonius* (London, 1983); W. Steidle, *Sueton und die antike Bi-ographie* (Munich, 1951), 142f.; Augusto Rostagni, *Suetonio, De Poetis e Biografi Minori, Restituzione e Commento* (Turin, 1944), VIII–XVIII; C. *Sueto-nius Tranquillus*, ed. Ceresa-Gastaldo, 21; J. W. Duff, *A Literary History of Rome in the Silver Age* (London, 1967), 631ff., esp. 633.
3. S. Williams and G. Friell, *Theodosius: The Empire at Bay* (New Haven: Yale University Press, 1994), for contemporary setting.
4. P. Courcelle, *Late Latin Writers and their Greek Sources*, trans. H. E. Wedeck (Cambridge, Mass.: Harvard University Press, 1969), 79, a little too severely, says: "He probably borrowed these names from the lost pref-

ace of Suetonius's *De viris illustribus*." At least he shows in *Adv. Iovinianum* 2.14 some familiarity with Satyrus as biographer, with colorful details about the philosopher Diogenes; see NPNF 6, ser. 2, 398. For Hermippus see A. Lesky, *Geschichte der griechischen Literatur* (Bern, 1971), 592, 642, 742; for Antigonus of Carystos see A. Lesky, *op. cit.*, 835, Ἱστοριῶν, παραδόξων, συνάγωη; Ulrich von Wilamowitz-Moellendorff, *Philologische Untersuchungen* (1881), 4; for Satyrus, *PWRE*, Series 2, II, I, 228, in the reign of Ptolemy Philopator; for *Aristoxenus, musicus*, L. Pearson, *Aristoxenus Elementa Rhythmica*, (Oxford, 1990), xxvii; also A. Barker, ed., *Greek Musical Writings, Vol. II: Harmonic and Acoustic Theory* (Cambridge University Press, 1995), chap. 7, "Elementa harmonica," 119ff.; and M. L. West, *Ancient Greek Music* (Oxford, 1992).

5. Varro (116–27 B.C.) did a series of cameo studies of 700 important personages; cf. A. Dihle, *Greek and Latin Literature of the Roman Empire: From Augustus to Justinian,* trans. Manfred Malzahn (London and New York: Routledge, 1994), 24: "possibly the most versatile scholar Rome ever produced"; G. M. A. Grube, *The Greek and Roman Critics* (London, 1965), 160f.; V. Brown, "Varro, Marcus Terentius," in *Catalogus Translationum et Commentariorum*, Vol. 4, ed. F. E. Cranz and P. O. Kristeller (Washington, D.C., 1980), 451–500; G. B. Conte, *Latin Literature: A History*, trans. J. B. Solodow (Baltimore and London: The Johns Hopkins University Press, 1994), 50–51, 210–20.

6. For Santra the grammarian, cf. J. W. Duff, *A Literary History of Rome from the Origins to the Close of the Golden Age*, Vol. 5 (London, 1967), 148, 149, 253.

7. On Cornelius Nepos, a contemporary of Cicero, cf. Dihle, *Greek and Latin*, 66. Elsewhere (PL 23: 365) Jerome pronounces the published version of Cicero's *Pro Milone* identical with the delivered original.

8. On C. Julius Hyginus, the Spaniard, librarian of Augustus, cf. Duff, *A Literary History of Rome from the Origins to the Close of the Golden Age*, Vol. 2, 457.

9. *de ingenti prato:* One of Suetonius's works was actually called *Prata.* The image here doubtless comes from Eusebius, also exaggerating the pioneering aspect of his own work, in *h.e.* 1.1.4: "brought together appropriate passages from the utterances of the ancient writers, culling, so to speak, the flowers of intellectual meadows."

10. *nullum praevium:* cf. Eus., *h.e.* 1.1: "a deserted and untrodden road."

11. Cicero (*Brutus*) and Seneca, he admits elsewhere (*Adv. Rufinum* 3.39, FOTC 53, 208), had been his *vademecum,* a sort of Roget's *Thesaurus* for citations from Pythagoras, Plato, and Empedocles. For *Brutus* see G. V. Sumner, *The Orators in Cicero's "Brutus"; Prosopography and Chronology* (Toronto, 1973). See also N. Adkin, "Cicero's *Orator* and Jerome," *VigChr* 51 (1997): 25–39.

12. "qui usque hodie scriptitant a me praetermissi sunt": cf. *DVI* 124: "[Ambrose] usque in praesentem diem scribit . . . meum iudicium subtraham." Is Jerome already thinking with malicious glee of getting even with Ambrose?

13. *in hoc terrarum angulo:* TLL 2, 57, *s.v.*, cites Jerome, *ep.* 64.16, *ep.* 11,

ep. 17.3, *ep.* 21.39; Prop. 4.9.65: "Angulus hic mundi." Cf. A. La Penna, "*Angulus e arces* nell'ode di Orazio a Settimio (*Carm.* II, 6): due simboli filosofici?" *Studi Italiani di Filologia Classica,* XC Annate, ser. 3, Vol. 15, 1 (1997), 85–90; *Horace: Odes,* Book II, ed. R. G. M. Nisbet and M. Hubbard (Oxford); Jerome, *Pref. to Galatians* (NPNF 6, ser. 2, 498): "How few there are who now read Aristotle! How many are there who know the books, or even the name, of Plato? You may find here and there a few old men who have nothing else to do, who study them in a corner (*in angulis*)"; *idem, Pref. to Book of Hebrew Questions* (NPNF 6, ser. 2, 486): "I am in a corner, remote from the city and the forum and the wranglings of crowded courts."

14. Cf. *ep.* 70.3 (CSEL 54, 703): "Scripserunt contra nos Celsus atque Porphyrius: priori Origenes, alteri Methodius, Eusebius et Apollinaris viginti quinque et triginta volumina responderunt." Celsus, Porphyry, and Julian are also linked in *ep.* 57 (NPNF 6, ser. 2, 116). Celsus wrote his polemic, *True Doctrine,* c. 178 A.D., refuted 70 years later by Origen, *Contra Celsum:* Q 2, 52; cf. Robert M. Grant, *Greek Apologists of the Second Century* (Philadelphia: The Westminster Press, 1988), 133–39; R. J. Hoffmann, trans., *Celsus, On the True Doctrine: A Discourse Against the Christians* (New York: Oxford University Press, 1987); H. Chadwick, *Origen, Contra Celsum* (Cambridge, 1953; repr. 1965); M. Borret, "L'Ecriture d'après le païen Celse," in *Le monde grec et la Bible,* ed. C. Mondésert (Paris, 1984), 171–93. Porphyrius's *Contra Christianos* was apparently well known to Jerome; cf. Courcelle, *LLW,* 74 n. 116. See also R. L. Wilken, *The Christians as the Romans Saw Them* (New Haven, 1984), 137–47. On Julian, cf. *ep.* 70.3 (CSEL 54, 703–4): "Iulianus Augustus septem libros . . . adversum Christum evomuit, et iuxta fabulas poetarum suo se ense laceravit"; see also Dihle, *Greek and Latin,* 453–56; W. J. Malley, "Hellenism and Christianity. The Conflict between Hellenic and Christian Wisdom in the *Contra Galilaeos* of Julian and the *Contra Julianum* of St. Cyril of Alexandria," *AnGr* (Rome, 1978); G. W. Bowersock, *Julian the Apostate* (Cambridge, Mass., 1978); Robert Browning, *The Emperor Julian* (Berkeley: University of California Press, 1976); P. Athanasakkis-Fowden, *Julian and Hellenism. An Intellectual Biography* (Oxford, 1981).

15. *rabidae canes:* a recurring image in Jerome; see *ep.* 33.4 (NPNF 6, ser. 2, 46), speaking of Origen's condemnation: "Imperial Rome consents to his condemnation, and even convenes a senate to censure him, not—as the rabid hounds who now pursue him cry—because of the novelty or heterodoxy of his doctrines . . ."; *ep.* 50.1 (CSEL 54, 388): "libros quos contra Iovinianum scripsi, canino dente rodere, lacerare, convellere"; *Adv. Rufinum* 3.42 (FOTC 53, 215): "Dogs bark in defense of their masters; and do you not want me to bark in defense of Christ?"; Prolog to Book 3 of his *Comm. on Jeremiah:* "Although silent himself, he [the devil?] does his barking through an Alpine [*Alpinum/Albinum?*] dog, huge and corpulent [Pelagius?] who can rave more with his claws than his teeth."

16. "no philosophers, no orators, no men of learning": He is obviously thinking of the categories in Suetonius, described by Dihle, *Greek and Latin,* 259: "a collection of short biographies of famous Romans: its individual sections dealt separately with orators, grammarians, philosophers, poets, and other groups of distinguished intellectuals." Cf. Jerome, *Pref. to*

Comm. on Job (NPNF 6, ser. 2, 491): "as regards Latin, my life, almost from the cradle, has been spent in the company of grammarians, rhetoricians, and philosophers."

17. Initially, Augustine had similar problems with the Bible: see *Conf.* 3.5.9.

I. SIMON PETER

IMON PETER, THE SON OF JOHN,[1] from the village of Bethsaida in the province of Galilee,[2] brother of Andrew the apostle,[3] and himself chief of the apostles, after having been bishop of the church of Antioch[4] and having preached to the ones who are scattered, the believers from the circumcision, in Pontus, Galatia, Cappadocia, Asia, and Bithynia,[5] pushed on to Rome in the second year of Claudius to overthrow Simon Magus[6] and held the sacerdotal chair there for twenty-five years, until the last, that is, the fourteenth, year of Nero.[7]

2. At Nero's hands he received the crown of martyrdom, being nailed to the cross with his head towards the ground and his feet raised on high, asserting that he was unworthy to be crucified in the same manner as his Lord.[8]

3. He wrote two epistles which are called Catholic,[9] the second of which, on account of its difference from the first in style, is considered by many[10] not to be his.

4. Then, too, the Gospel according to Mark, who was his disciple and interpreter, is ascribed to him.[11]

5. On the other hand, the books

of which one is entitled his *Acts*,[12]
another, his *Gospel*,[13]
a third, his *Preaching*,[14]
a fourth, his *Revelation*,[15]
a fifth, his *Judgment*,[16] are rejected as apocryphal.[17]

6. Buried at Rome in the Vatican near the Triumphal Way,[18] he is venerated by the whole world.

NOTES

1. Jn 1.42 and 21.15–17.
2. Jn 1.43–44
3. Jn 1.40–41.
4. Eusebius, *Historia ecclesiastica* 3.36.2.
5. 1 Pt 1.1; cf. Eus., *h.e.* 3.1.
6. On Simon Magus cf. *h.e.* 2.13–14.
7. Eusebius, *Chron.*, A.D. 67–68. Text in *Chronik*, ed. R. Helm, *Eusebius Werke* 7 = GCS 24 (1913; 3d ed., with intro. by U. Treu, Berlin, 1984), 185.
8. *h.e.* 2.25.2, 3.1.2, 3.31.1. See R. J. Bauckham, "The Martyrdom of Peter in Early Christian Literature," ANRW II, 26, 1 (Berlin, 1992), 539–95.
9. *h.e.* 3.3.1; E. Cothenet, "La Première de Pierre: bilan de 35 ans de recherches," ANRW II, 25, 5, 3685–3712; P. J. Achtemeier, *I Peter: A Commentary on First Peter* (Minneapolis, 1996). For the Catholic Epistles, see Eus., *h.e.* 6.14.1.
10. *h.e.* 3.3.1; for the ongoing debate about the Second Epistle, cf. R. J. Bauckham, "2 Peter: An Account of Research," ANRW II, 25, 5, 3713–52; D. Farkasfalvy, "The Ecclesial Setting of Pseudepigraphy in Second Peter and its Role in the Formation of the Canon," *SecCent* 5, 1 (1985–86): 3–29; W. R. Farmer, "Some Critical Reflections on Second Peter: a Response to a Paper on Second Peter by Denis Farkasfalvy," *loc. cit.*, 30–46.
11. *h.e.* 2.15; cf. *DVI* 8.1. Cf. M. Guarducci, "L'apostolo Pietro e l'evangelista Marco," RAL VI (1995), 71–75.
12. W. Schneemelcher, *NTA* 2 (1991), 271–321; C. R. Matthews, "Nicephorus Callistus' physical description of Peter: An original component of the Acts of Peter?" in *Apocrypha* 7 (1996): 135–45.
13. *Gospel of Peter:* see Eus., *h.e.* 6.12, and Jerome, *DVI* 41 (Serapion of Antioch); Vielhauer, *Geschichte*, 641–48; *Evangile de Pierre*, SC 201 (Paris, 1973), ed. M. G. Mara; C. Maurer and W. Schneemelcher, *NTA* 2, 216–22; D. F. Wright, "Papyrus Egerton 2 (the Unknown Gospel)—Part of the *Gospel of Peter?*" *SecCent* 5 (1985–86), 129–50; M. K. Stillman, "The *Gospel of Peter*: A Case for Oral-Only Dependency?" *EphTheolLov* 73, 1 (1997): 114–20.
14. *Kerygma Petri: h.e.* 2.3; cf. Origen, *Praef.* 8 to *De princ.* 1, ed. P. Koetschau, GCS 22 (Leipzig, 1913), 14–15.
15. *Revelation,* or *Apocalypse:* R. J. Bauckham, "*The Apocalypse of Peter:* An Account of Research," ANRW II, 25, 6 (Berlin, 1988), 4712–50; *NTA* 2, 620–38.
16. "Judgment" (*Iudicium*): presumably a translation from Eus., *h.e.* 2.25.7, of κρίμα, which should have been κήρυγμα. For *Kerygma Petri*, see *NTA* 2, 34–41.
17. *h.e.* 3.3, 6.14.6–7, 6.25.4–5.
18. *h.e.* 2.25.7: "For if you are willing to go to the Vatican or to the Ostian Way, you will find the trophies [*tropaia*, cited in PGL, 1412B, 'memorials, monuments'] of those who founded the Church"; M. Guarducci, *Epigrafia Greca*, Vol. 4 (Rome, 1978), 552–56 [554 n. 1: τρόπαιον = *sepolcro glorioso*].

REFERENCES

Q 1, 42, 133–35, 303 — Cath 11, 318–33, Sr. M.-F. Lamau — DSp 12, 1452–86, É. Cothenet — EEC 2², 902–6, D. P. Senior and F. W. Norris — EECh 2, 675–77, V. Saxer — LThK 8, 334–37, K. Hofmann — NCE 11, 200–205, J. J. Castelot — TRE 26, 263–73, O. Böcher — Vielhauer, *Geschichte,* 580–89 (1 Pt), 594–99 (2 Pt) — Dihle, *Greek and Latin,* 208 — Kelly, *ODP,* 5

II. JAMES, THE BROTHER OF THE LORD

AMES, WHO IS CALLED the brother of the Lord,[1] surnamed the Just, the son of Joseph by another wife, as some think,[2] but, as appears to me, the son of Mary, the sister of the mother of the Lord of whom John makes mention in his book,[3] was after the Lord's passion at once ordained bishop of Jerusalem by the apostles.[4]

2. He wrote a single epistle, which is reckoned among the seven Catholic Epistles,[5] and even this is claimed by some to have been published by someone else under his name,[6] and gradually as time went on to have gained authority.

3. Hegesippus, who lived near the apostolic age,[7] in the fifth book of his *Commentaries,* writing of James, says:[8]

"After the apostles, James the brother of the Lord, surnamed the Just, was made head of the Church at Jerusalem. Many indeed were called James.

4. "This one was holy from his mother's womb. He drank neither wine nor strong drink, ate no meat, never shaved or anointed himself with ointment or bathed.

5. "He alone had the privilege of entering the Holy of Holies, since indeed he did not use woolen vestments, but linen, and went alone into the temple and prayed on bended knees on behalf of the people, so much so that his knees were supposed to have acquired the hardness of camels' knees."

He says also many other things, too numerous to narrate.

6. But Josephus also, in his *Antiquities,* Book 20,[9] and Clement

in his Ὑποτυπώσεων, *Outlines,* Book 7,[10] mention that on the death of Festus, who reigned over Judea, Albinus was sent by Nero as his successor.[11]

7. Before he had reached his province, Ananus the high priest, the youthful son of Ananus of the priestly class, taking advantage of the state of anarchy,[12] assembled a council and publicly tried to force James to deny that Christ is the Son of God. When he refused, Ananus ordered him to be stoned.[13]

8. Cast down from a pinnacle of the temple, his legs broken, but still half alive, raising his hands to heaven, he said, "Lord forgive them for they know not what they do."[14] Then, struck on the head by a club, of a kind with which fullers are accustomed to wring out garments, he died.[15]

9. This same Josephus records the tradition that James was of such great sanctity and reputation among the people that the downfall of Jerusalem was believed to be a result of his death.

10. He it is of whom the apostle Paul writes to the Galatians, "No one else of the apostles did I see except James the brother of the Lord,"[16] and shortly after the event the *Acts of the Apostles* bear witness to the matter.

11. Also the gospel which is called the *Gospel according to the Hebrews,*[17] and which I have recently translated into Greek and Latin, and of which also Origen frequently makes use,[18] after the account of the resurrection of the Savior says,[19]

12. "The Lord, however, after he had given his grave clothes to the servant of the priest, appeared to James, for James had sworn that he would not eat bread from that hour in which he drank the cup of the Lord until he should see him rising again from among those that sleep";

13. and again, a little later, it says,[20] " 'Bring a table and bread,' said the Lord." And immediately it is added, "He brought bread and blessed and broke it and gave to James the Just and said to him, 'My brother, eat your bread, for the Son of Man is risen from among those that sleep.'"

14. And so he ruled the church of Jerusalem for thirty years, that is, until the seventh year of Nero, and was buried near the temple from which he had been cast down. His [tombstone with its] inscription was well known until the siege of Titus and

the end of Hadrian's reign.[21] Some of our writers think he was buried on Mount Olivet,[22] but they are mistaken.

NOTES

1. Gal 1.19; cf. Eus., *h.e.* 1.13, 2.1.2. Cf. Zuckschwerdt, "Das Naziräat des Herrenbruders Jakobus nach Hegesipp, Eus. *h.e.* 2, 33, 5–6," *ZNW* 68 (1977), 276–87; S. Lyonnet, "Les témoignages de S. Jean Chrysostome et de S. Jérôme sur Jacques, le frère du Seigneur," *RechSR* 29 (1939): 335–51.

2. *h.e.* 2.1.2.

3. Jn 19.25; *h.e.* 2.23.4–6.

4. *h.e.* 3.5.2, 3.7, 3.23.1, 7.19.

5. *h.e.* 2.23.24–25, 3.25.3; P. H. Davids, "The Epistle of James in Modern Discussion," ANRW II, 25, 5, 3621–45; H.-J. Neudorfer, "Ist Sachkritik nötig: Ammerkungen zu einem Thema der biblischen Hermeneutik am Beispiel des Jakobsbriefs," *KuD* 43 (1997): 279–302.

6. F. Hahn and P. Müller, "Der Jakobsbrief," *TheolRundschau* 63, 1 (1998): 1–73.

7. *h.e.* 2.23.3.

8. *h.e.* 2.23.4–6; cf. also *h.e.* 4.22.4.

9. Josephus, *Ant.* 20.197 and 200; Eus., *h.e.* 2.23.21.

10. Cf. C. Duckworth and E. F. Osborn, "Clement of Alexandria's *Hypotyposeis*," *JThS* 36 (1985): 67–83; E. F. Osborn, "Clement's *Hypotyposeis*: Macarius Revisited," *SecCent* 7, 4 (1989–90): 233–35.

11. *h.e.* 2.23.21 (SC 31, 89 and n. 31).

12. anarchy: ἀναρχία.

13. Josephus, *Ant.* 20. 200–201; *h.e.* 2.23.20–22.

14. Lk 23.34; Acts 7.59–60; *h.e.* 2.23.16 (SC 31, 88 and n. 25).

15. *h.e.* 2.1, 2.23.

16. Gal 1.19.

17. Cf. Jerome, *C. Pelag.* 3.2, FOTC 53, 349 n. 10; *NTA* 1 (1991), 178; C. B. Amphoux, "L'Évangile selon les Hébreux, source de l'Évangile de Luc," *Apocrypha* 6 (1995): 67–77; A. F. J. Klijn, "Das Hebräer- und das Nazoräerevangelium," ANRW II, 25, 5. For the complex questions concerning the *Gospel According to the Hebrews,* cf. *NTA* 1 (1991), 145–46, 172–78.

18. For *testimonia* of Origen, cf. *NTA* 1 (1991): 177.

19. *Evang. Heb.*: cf. Eus., *h.e.* 3.25.5–7 (among νόθοι); 3.27.4 (SC 31, 137), 4.22.8, citing Hegesippus.

20. Eucharistic terminology synthesized from Mt 26.26, Mk 14.12, Lk 22.19.

21. On his burial, see Eus., *h.e.* 2.23.18 (SC 31, 88 and n. 28).

22. This is Jerome's own verdict.

REFERENCES

Q 1, 121, 285–86 — Cath 6, 252–59, J. Cartinat — DHGE 26, 604–8 — EEC 1², 603–5, G. A. Koch — EECh 1, 429–30, E. Perotto — LThK 5,

861–63, J. Blinzler — LThK 5³, 720, L. Oberlinner — TRE 16, 485–88, E. Ruckstuhl; 488–95, H. Paulsen — NCE 7, 805–6, J. A. Lefrancois — Vielhauer, *Geschichte*, 567–80

III. MATTHEW, SURNAMED LEVI

ATTHEW, SURNAMED LEVI, first publican, then apostle,[1] composed a gospel of Christ at first published in Judea in Hebrew for the sake of those of the circumcision who believed, but this was afterwards translated into Greek, though by what author is uncertain.[2]

2. Moreover, the Hebrew itself has been preserved until the present day in the library at Caesarea which Pamphilus the martyr so diligently gathered.[3] I have also had the opportunity of having the volume described to me by the Nazarenes of Beroea,[4] a city of Syria, who use it.

3. In this it is to be noted that wherever the Evangelist, whether on his own account or in the person of our Lord the Savior, quotes the testimonies of the Old Testament, he does not follow the authority of the translators of the Septuagint, but the Hebrew.[5]

4. Wherefore these two forms exist: "Out of Egypt have I called my son,"[6] and "for he shall be called a Nazarene."[7]

NOTES

1. Lk 5.27; Mt 9.9. This is repeated in his *Preface to Comm. on Matthew* (398 A.D.), NPNF 6, ser. 2, 495.

2. Eus., *h.e.* 3.24.6, 3.39.16, 5.8.2 (quoting Irenaeus). See B. T. Viviano, "Where was the Gospel according to St. Matthew written?" *CBQ* 41 (1979): 533–46; A. J. Bellinzoni, "The Gospel of Matthew in the Second Century," *SecCent* 9, 4 (1992): 197–258; A. Stock, *The Method and Message of Matthew* (Collegeville, Minn., 1994).

3. For Pamphilus cf. *DVI* 75. For the library, cf. F. J. Witty, "Libraries, Ancient," NCE 8, 719.

4. For Nazoreans of Beroea, cf. Bellinzoni, *art. cit.*, 220–22; T. D. Barnes, *Constantine and Eusebius* (Cambridge, Mass.: Harvard University Press, 1981), 139 and 352 nn. 108–12. Coelosyrian Beroea near Aleppo was a

center of the Nazoreans; cf. Epiphanius, *Pan.* 29.7, 30.2.7, in *The Panarion of St. Epiphanius, Bishop of Salamis: Selected Passages,* trans. P. R. Amidon (New York: Oxford University Press, 1990), 92–93.

5. See A. Ceresa-Gastaldo, *Il latino dell'antichi versioni bibliche,* 23–28.

6. Hos 11.1, quoted in Mt 2.15.

7. Is 11.1, quoted in Mt 2.23.

REFERENCES

Q 1, 83, 111–12, 306 — Cath 8, 902–29, É. Cothenet — DSp 10, 779–97, J. Radermakers — EEC 2², 738–39, D. P. Senior — EECh 1, 543, E. Romero Pose — LThK 7, 176–79, J. Schmid — LThK 6³, 1477–82, A. Sand — NCE 9, 493–502, J. Quinlan — ANRW II, 25, 3 (1984), 1889–1951 [Scholarship from 1945 to 1980], G. Stanton — Vielhauer, *Geschichte,* 355–65 — Dihle, *Greek and Latin,* 208–10

IV. JUDE, THE BROTHER OF JAMES

UDE, THE BROTHER OF JAMES,[1] left a short epistle which is reckoned among the seven Catholic Epistles,[2] and because in it he quotes from the apocryphal book of Enoch,[3] it is rejected by many.[4]

2. Nevertheless, by age and use[5] it has gained authority and is reckoned among the Holy Scriptures.

NOTES

1. Eus., *h.e.* 3.19, 3.32; R. J. Bauckham, "The Letter of Jude: An Account of Research," ANRW II, 25, 5, 3791–3826; idem, *Jude and the Relatives of Jesus in the Early Church* (Edinburgh, 1990).

2. *h.e.* 2.23.

3. Jude 1.14–15.

4. *h.e.* 3.25

5. *h.e.* 2.23.25, 3.19, 3.32.5.

REFERENCES

Cath 6, 1147–52, J. Cartinat — EEC 1², 638, F. W. Norris — LThK 5, 1154–56, J. Blinzler — LThK 5³, 1026–27, C.-P. März — NCE 8, 16–17, J. A. Lefrancois; 17–18, T. W. Leahy — Vielhauer, *Geschichte,* 589–94

V. PAUL, FORMERLY CALLED SAUL

AUL, FORMERLY CALLED SAUL, an apostle[1] over and above the number of the twelve apostles, was of the tribe of Benjamin and the town of Giscalis in Judea.[2] When this was captured by the Romans he moved with his parents to Tarsus [in Cilicia].[3]

2. Sent by them to Jerusalem to study law, he was educated by Gamaliel, a most learned man, whom Luke mentions.[4]

3. But after he had been present at the death of the martyr Stephen, and had received letters from the high priest of the temple for the persecution of those who believed in Christ, he proceeded to Damascus, where, constrained to faith by a revelation, as it is written in the *Acts of the Apostles,*[5] he was transformed from a persecutor into a vessel of election.[6]

4. As Sergius Paulus, proconsul of Cyprus, was the first to believe in his preaching, he took his name from him[7] because he had subdued him to faith in Christ, and having been joined by Barnabas, after traversing many cities,[8] he returned to Jerusalem, and was ordained apostle to the Gentiles by Peter, James, and John.[9]

5. And because a full account of his life is given in the *Acts of the Apostles,* I only say this: that the twenty-fifth year after our Lord's passion, that is, the second of Nero, at the time when Festus, Procurator of Judea, succeeded Felix,[10] he was sent bound to Rome, and, remaining for two years in free custody, disputed daily with the Jews concerning the coming of Christ.[11]

6. It ought to be understood that at his first defense,[12] the power of Nero having not yet been consolidated, nor his wickedness erupted to such a degree as the histories relate concerning him,[13] Paul was liberated by Nero, that the gospel of Christ might be preached also in the West, as he himself writes in the *Second Epistle to Timothy,* at the time when he was about to be put to death and dictated his epistle while in chains:[14]

7. "At my first defense no one took my part, but all forsook me: may it not be laid to their account. But the Lord stood by

me and strengthened me; that through me the message might be fully proclaimed and that all the Gentiles might hear, and I was delivered out of the mouth of the lion"—clearly indicating Nero as lion on account of his cruelty. And in the following he says, "The Lord delivered me from the mouth of the lion," and again shortly, "The Lord delivered me from every evil work and will save me unto his heavenly kingdom," for indeed he felt within himself that his martyrdom was near at hand;

8. for in the same epistle he announced, "for I am already being offered and the time of my departure is at hand."[15] He then, in the fourteenth year of Nero on the same day as Peter, was beheaded at Rome for Christ's sake[16] and was buried in the Ostian Way, the thirty-seventh year after our Lord's passion.[17]

9. He wrote nine epistles to seven churches:[18]

To the Romans, one,
To the Corinthians, two,
To the Galatians, one,
To the Ephesians, one,
To the Philippians, one,
To the Colossians, one,
To the Thessalonians, two;
and besides, these to his disciples,
To Timothy two,
To Titus, one,
To Philemon, one.

10. The epistle which is called the *Epistle to the Hebrews*[19] is not considered to belong to him, on account of its difference from the others in style and language, but it is reckoned either, according to Tertullian,[20] to be the work of Barnabas, or, according to others,[21] to be by Luke the evangelist or by Clement afterwards bishop of the church at Rome,[22] who, they say, arranged and adorned the ideas of Paul in his own language, though, to be sure, since Paul was writing to Hebrews and was in disrepute among them, he may have omitted his name from the salutation on this account.[23] He being a Hebrew wrote Hebrew, that is, his own tongue and most fluently,

11. while the things which were eloquently written in He-

brew were more eloquently turned into Greek, and this is the reason why it seems to differ from other epistles of Paul. Some read also a letter *To the Laodiceans,* but it is rejected by everyone.[24]

NOTES

1. Rom 1.1; 1 Cor 1.1.
2. Giscalis: in Galilee, not Judea; it was conquered by Titus in 67; cf. Josephus, *Bell. Iud.* 4.2.1 and *Anchor Bible Dictionary, s.v.*
3. Acts 21.39, 22.3.
4. Acts 22.3.
5. Acts 9.1.
6. Acts 9.15.
7. Acts 13.7.
8. Acts 13.14, 14.1.
9. Acts 15.22.
10. Acts 24.27–25.1; Eus., *h.e.* 2.22.1.
11. *h.e.* 2.22.1.
12. *h.e.,* 2.22.2.
13. On Nero's persecution cf. *h.e.* 2.25.1–4, quoting Tertullian, *Apol.* 5.
14. 2 Tm 4.16–18.
15. 2 Tm 4.6.
16. Cf. *DVI* 1.6, and Eus., *h.e.* 2.25.8, quoting Dionysius of Corinth.
17. *h.e.* 2.25.7.
18. For surveys of recent scholarship on the various Epistles, cf. ANRW II, 25, 4. On Colossians, see M. Wolter, LThK 6³, 202–3.
19. Hebrews: Eus., *h.e.* 3.3.5; 3.25.5; 6.20.3; 6.25.11, quoting Origen, *Homilies on Hebrews,* now lost. See also H.-F. Weiss, *Der Brief an die Hebräer* (Göttingen, 1991).
20. Tertullian, *De pudicitia* 20.2.
21. *h.e.* 3.38.2.
22. *h.e.* 3.38.2–3.
23. *h.e.* 6.14.1–3, quoting Clement, *Hypotyposeis;* cf. also *h.e.* 6.25.11–14.
24. Q 1, 154, 271; *ad Laod.:* CPG 305; TRE 3, 349; H. J. Findeis, LThK 6³, 648–49; W. Schneemelcher and R. McL. Wilson, *NTA* 1 (1991), 42–46.

REFERENCES

Dr, 9 — Cath 10, 866–910, M. Hubaut — DSp 12, 1, 487–522, X. Jacques and L. F. Ladaria — EEC 2², 881–85, R. Jewett — EECh 2, 657–58, E. Dassmann — LThK 8, 216–28, J. Schmid, R. Schnackenburg — LThK 7³, 1494ff., J. Eckert, H. Merklein, E. Dassmann, A. De Santos Otero — NCE 11, 1–12, F. Schroeder — TRE 28, 286–307, K. Kertelge — Dihle, *Greek and Latin,* 203–7 — J. Murphy-O'Connor, *Paul: A Critical Life* (Oxford, 1996)

VI. BARNABAS, SURNAMED JOSEPH

ARNABAS FROM CYPRUS, surnamed Joseph the Levite,[1] ordained apostle to the Gentiles with Paul,[2] wrote one *Epistle*,[3] valuable for the edification of the church, which is reckoned among the apocryphal writings.[4]

2. Afterwards he separated from Paul on account of John, a disciple also called Mark,[5] but nonetheless exercised the work of preaching the Gospel laid upon him.

NOTES

1. Acts 4.36.
2. Acts 15.22.
3. A. Lindemann and H. Paulsen, *Die apostolischen Väter* (Tübingen, 1992), 23–75; P. Prigent and R. A. Kraft, edd., SC 172 (Paris, 1971); J. C. Paget, *The Epistle of Barnabas: Outlook and Background* (Tübingen, 1994), 1–27, dating it in Nerva's principate.
4. Eus., *h.e.* 3.25.4.
5. Acts 15.36–40.

REFERENCES

Q 1, 85–92 — Dr, 29–30 — Cath 1, 1256, G. Bardy — DSp 1, 1245–47, J. Lebreton — EEC 1², 167–68, E. Ferguson — EECh 1, 111–12, F. Scorza Barcellona — LThK 1, 1256–57, B. Kraft — LThK 2³, 18, F. R. Prostmeier — NCE 2, 103, J. P. Audet — RAC 1, 1212–17, J. Schmid — ANRW II, 27, 1, 159–207, L. W. Barnard — TRE 5, 238–41, K. Wengst — Vielhauer, *Geschichte*, 599–612

VII. LUKE THE EVANGELIST

UKE, A PHYSICIAN of Antioch,[1] as his writings indicate, was not unskilled in the Greek language.[2] An adherent of the apostle Paul and companion of all his journeying, he wrote a *Gospel*, concerning whom the same Paul says, "We send with him a brother whose praise in the gospel is among all the churches,"[3] and to the Colossians, "Luke, the dearly beloved physician, salutes you,"[4] and to Timothy, "Luke only is with me."[5]

2. He also wrote another excellent volume to which he prefixed the title, Acts, πράξεων, of the Apostles,[6] a history which extends to the second year of Paul's sojourn at Rome, that is, to the fourth year of Nero, from which we learn that the book was composed in that same city.[7]

3. Therefore, the Acts of Paul and Thecla[8] and the whole fable about the lion having been baptized by him we reckon among the apocryphal writings,[9] for how is it possible that the inseparable companion of the Apostle in his other affairs should have been ignorant of this thing alone. Moreover, Tertullian, who lived close to those times, mentions a certain presbyter in Asia, an adherent[10] of the apostle Paul, who was convicted by John of having been the author of the book, and who, having confessed that he had done this for love of Paul, resigned his office of presbyter.[11]

4. Some suppose that whenever Paul in his epistle says, "according to my gospel,"[12] he means the book of Luke and that Luke not only had learned the gospel from the apostle Paul, who had not been with the Lord in the flesh, but also from the other apostles.

5. He declares this also at the beginning of his work, saying,[13] "Even as they delivered unto us, who from the beginning were eye-witnesses and ministers of the word." So he wrote the Gospel as he had heard it, but composed the Acts of the Apostles as he himself had seen.

6. He was buried at Constantinople, to which city, in the twentieth year of Constantius, his bones, together with the remains of Andrew the apostle, were transferred.[14]

NOTES

1. Eus., h.e. 3.4.6; Luke is similarly described in Jerome's Preface to Comm. on Matthew, with the added detail that he composed his Gospel in Achaia and Boeotia: see NPNF 6, ser. 2, 495.

2. W. C. van Unnik, "Luke-Acts, a Storm Center in Contemporary Schol-

arship," in *Studies in Luke-Acts,* ed. L. E. Keck and J. L. Martyn (Nashville, 1966), 15–32.

3. 2 Cor 8.18.

4. Col 4.14.

5. 2 Tm 4.11.

6. On *Acts,* cf. LThK 1³, 861–63, A. Weiser.

7. Eus., *Chron.,* A.D. 357. For the 2-year period, cf. Acts 28.30–31.

8. *Periodoi Pauli et Theclae* = the Greek *Acta Pauli et Theclae,* reading *Praxeis* instead of *Periodoi.* See *NTA* 2 (1991), 239–46; cf. B. M. Metzger, "St. Paul and the Baptized Lion," *Princeton Seminary Bulletin* 39, 2 (1945): 11–21.

9. Cf. Q 1, 131; Dr, 26–28. For the lioness episode, see *NTA* 2 (1991), 221f.

10. σπουδαστήν: Liddell, Scott, and Jones, *s.v.,* "well-wisher, supporter, partisan."

11. Tertullian, *De Baptismo* 17.5, CCL 1, 291–92.

12. Eus., *h.e.* 3.4.7; cf. Rom 2.16, 16.25; 2 Tm 2.8.

13. Lk 1.2.

14. *Chron.,* A.D. 357, ed. Helm, 240–41, trans. M. D. Donalson, *A Translation of Jerome's Chronicon with Historical Commentary* (Lewiston, New York: Mellen Press, 1996), 48 (where *a Constantinopolitanis* is mistranslated, *"from* the people of Constantinople"). The information was probably verified during Jerome's stay in Constantinople in 381.

REFERENCES

Q 1, 269, 298, 306 — Cath 7, 1212–33, A. George, J. Duplacy — DSp 9, 1103–21, A. George — EEC 2², 698–99, J. Painter — EECh 1, 509–11, E. Peretto — LThK 6, 1207–11, J. Schmid — LThK 6³, 1109–14, J. Kremer — NCE 8, 1066–73, R. T. A. Murphy — ANRW II, 25, 3, 2258–2328 [*Forschungsbericht*], M. Rese — Vielhauer, *Geschichte,* 366–409 — Dihle, *Greek and Latin,* 211–12

VIII. MARK THE EVANGELIST

ARK, THE DISCIPLE and interpreter of Peter, wrote a short gospel at the request of the brethren at Rome, embodying what he had heard Peter tell.[1] When Peter had heard it, he approved it and issued it to the churches to be read by his authority, as Clement, in the sixth book of his Ὑπο-τυπώσεις, and Papias, bishop of Hierapolis, record.[2]

2. Peter also mentions this Mark in his First Epistle, figuratively indicating Rome under the name of Babylon: "She who is in Babylon, chosen together with you, salutes you; and so does my son Mark."[3]

3. So, taking the *Gospel* which he himself had composed, he went to Egypt, and, first preaching Christ at Alexandria, he formed a church with such great continence in doctrine and life that he constrained all followers of Christ to his example.[4]

4. Philo, then, most eloquent of the Jews, seeing the first church at Alexandria still following Jewish customs, wrote a book on their manner of life[5] as something creditable to his nation, and, as Luke says that "the believers at Jerusalem had all things in common,"[6] so he recorded what he saw was done at Alexandria, under the learned Mark.[7]

5. He died in the eighth year of Nero and was buried at Alexandria, leaving Annianus as his successor.[8]

NOTES

1. The opening phrase is from Irenaeus, *Adv. haer.* 3.1.1, quoted in Eus., *h.e.* 5.8.3. See also *h.e.* 2.15.

2. *h.e.* 2.15.2 and 2.16.1; Clement, *Hypotyp.* 6, Frag. 9, GCS series, *Clemens Alexandrinus,* Band 3, ed. Stählin, xvi; cf. Papias, quoted in Eus., *h.e.* 3.39.15.

3. 1 Pt 5.13, quoted in Eus., *h.e.* 2.15.2.

4. *h.e.* 2.16, stressing asceticism, which supposedly appealed to Philo; H.-M. Schenke, "The Mystery of the Gospel of St. Mark," *SecCent* 4, 2 (1984): 65–82. On the "Secret Gospel of Mark," not even hinted at here, cf. S. Levin, ANRW II, 25, 6, 4270–92.

5. Cf. *h.e.* 2.17.1–6, for excerpts from Philo, *On the Contemplative Life.*

6. Acts 4.32, 34–35, quoted in *h.e.* 2.17.6.

7. Eusebius wrongly identified Philo's account of the *Therapeutai* with the Alexandrian primitive Christian community.

8. *h.e.* 2.24. The year was 62; cf. *Chron.*, ed. Helm, 183.

REFERENCES

Q 1, 83, 306 — *TLG* 0031, 002 — Cath 8, 368–88, S. Légasse — DSp 10, 244–55, P. Lamarche — EEC 2², 719–20, D. P. Senior — EECh 1, 526–27, R. Trevijans — LThK 7, 12–13, J. Blinzler — LThK 6³, 1395–1403, K. Kertelge *et al.* — NCE 9, 233–40, C. P. Ceroke — *NTA* 1, 106–9, "Secret Gospel," H. Merkel — TRE 10, 623–26, W. Schmithals — ANRW II, 25,

3, 1969–2045, "Das Markus-Evangelium. Literarische und theologische Einleitung mit Forschungsbericht," P. Pokorný — Vielhauer, *Geschichte*, 329–55

IX. JOHN, THE APOSTLE AND EVANGELIST

OHN, THE APOSTLE whom Jesus loved most,[1] the son of Zebedee, and brother of the apostle James, whom Herod, after our Lord's passion, beheaded,[2] most recently of all, at the request of the bishops of Asia, wrote a *Gospel*[3] against Cerinthus and other heretics,[4] and especially against the then-arising doctrine of the Ebionites, who assert that Christ did not exist prior to Mary.[5] On this account he was compelled to maintain His divine birth.

2. But there is said to be yet another reason for this work, in that, when he had read the volumes of Matthew, Mark, and Luke, he approved, indeed, the substance of the history and declared that the things they said were true, but that they had given the history of only one year, the one, that is, which follows the imprisonment of John and in which he was put to death.[6]

3. So, skipping this year, the events of which had been set forth by these, he related the events of the earlier period before John was shut up in prison, so that it might be manifest to those who should diligently read the volumes of the four Evangelists.[7] This also takes away the διαφωνία, the discrepancy,[8] which seems to exist between John and the others.

4. He wrote also one *Epistle* which begins as follows: "What was from the beginning, what we have heard and seen with our eyes, what we have explored and (what) our hands have touched concerning the word of life,"[9] which is esteemed by all who are men of the church or of learning.

5. The other two, of which the first is, "The elder to the lady who is elect and to her children,"[10] and the other, "The elder to Gaius, the beloved whom I truly love,"[11] are said to be the work

of John the presbyter in whose memory another sepulchre is shown at Ephesus to the present day,[12] though some think that the two memorials belong to this same John the evangelist. We shall treat of this matter in due course when we come to Papias, his disciple.[13]

6. In the fourteenth year, then, after Nero, Domitian having raised a second persecution,[14] he was banished to the island of Patmos, and wrote there the *Apocalypse*,[15] on which Justin Martyr[16] and Irenaeus[17] wrote commentaries.

7. But after Domitian had been put to death, and his decrees, on account of his excessive cruelty, had been annulled by the senate,[18] John returned to Ephesus under Nerva,[19] and, continuing there until the time of the emperor Trajan, founded and built churches throughout all of Asia, and, worn out by old age, died in the sixty-eighth year after our Lord's passion and was buried in the same city.[20]

NOTES

1. Based on Jn 13.23, and 21.20 ("reposed on Christ's breast"), quoted in Eus., *h.e.* 5.24.3. and 7.25.12.

2. Acts 12.2; Eus., *h.e.* 2.1.5 and 3.5.2.

3. *h.e.* 6.14.7.

4. On Cerinthus: Q 1, 128, 289; LThK 5³, 1402–3, J. Frickel; EECh 1, 158–59, A. F. J. Klijn, citing *Epistula Apostolorum* 1 [12], 7 [18]; Irenaeus, *Adv. haer.* 1.26.1 and 3.3.4; Eus., *h.e.* 3.28.6; Hippolytus, *Philos.* 7.33.1–2; Ps.-Tertullian, *Adv. omn. haer.* 3; Epiphanius, *Pan.* 28.5.1; B. G. Wright III, "Cerinthus *apud* Hippolytus: An Inquiry into the Traditions about Cerinthus's Provenance," *SecCent* 4, 2 (1984): 103–15. *NTA* (1991), 397, corrects Q 1, 128, for the entry "A Gospel of Cerinthus" as follows: "the Gospel used by Cerinthus, and also by Carpocrates, was in fact identical with that of the Ebionites, and apparently only a truncated Gospel of Matthew." On Cerinthus as author of John's *Apocalypse*, cf. Eus., *h.e.* 7.25.10, quoting Dionysius.

5. *h.e.* 3.27.1. On Ebionites see Epiphanius, *Pan.* 30, and G. A. Koch, "A Critical Investigation of Epiphanius's Knowledge of the Ebionites. A Translation and Critical Discussion of *Panarion* 30" (Ph.D. diss., Univ. of Pennsylvania, 1976), xxv–xlix. On Gospel of Ebionites, see *NTA* (1991), 166–71, P. Vielhauer and G. Strecker; ANRW II, 25, 5, 4034–53, G. Howard.

6. *h.e.* 3.24.7–13.

7. *h.e.* 3.24.7–13.

8. διαφωνία: disharmony. See also *DVI* 63.3 and 81.2 (*De Evangeliorum* διαφωνίᾳ).

9. 1 Jn 1.1; *h.e.* 3.24.17 and 7.25.10; R. E. Brown, "John, Epistles of," NCE 7, 1078–80; J. Beutler, "Die Johannesbriefe in der neuesten Literatur (1978–1985)," ANRW II, 25, 5, 3773–90.

10. 2 Jn 1; *h.e.* 3.25.3.

11. 3 Jn 1.

12. On presbyter (πρέσβυς) John, cf. *h.e.* 3.39 and 7.25.11 and *DVI* 18.3 (on Papias). On two tombs, see *h.e.* 3.39 and 7.25.

13. *DVI* 18.

14. Eus., *h.e.* 3.17; cf. *Chron.*, *sub anno* A.D. 94, ed. Helm, 192.

15. *h.e.* 3.18.1 and 5.8.30. On the *Apocalypse*, cf. *h.e.* 3.24.17–18 and 7.25.

16. Incorrect; cf. Courcelle, *LLW*, 96.

17. An erroneous reading of *h.e.* 3.39.12–13.

18. *h.e.* 3.20.

19. *Chron.*, A.D. 96, ed. Helm, 193.

20. *h.e.* 3.31.3 and 5.24.3.

REFERENCES

TLG 0031, 004 — Cath 6, 377–82, J. De Mahuet; 382–409, A. Feuillet — DHGE 26, 1144–51, R. Aubert — DSp 8, 192–247, D. Mollat — EEC 1², 617–21, J. Painter — EECh 1, 158–59, A. F. J. Klijn — LThK 5³, 861–66, J. Beutler — NCE 7, 1080–88 (Gospel), 1078–80 (Epistles), R. E. Brown — TRE 17, 186–200, "Johannesbriefe," H. Thyen; 200–225, "Johannesevangelium," H. Thyen — ANRW II, 25, 3, 2506–68, "The Fourth Gospel. A Report on Recent Research," R. Kysar — Vielhauer, *Geschichte*, 410–84 — J. Beutler, *Literarische Gattungen im Johannesevangelium. Ein Forschungsbericht 1919–1980*

X. HERMAS

ERMAS,[1] whom the apostle Paul mentions in writing to the Romans, "Greetings to Phlegon, Hermes, Patrobas, Hermas, and the brethren that are with them,"[2] is reputed to be the author of the book which is called *The Pastor*[3] and which is also read publicly in some churches of Greece.[4] It is in fact a useful book, and many[5] of the ancient writers quote from it as authority,[6] but among the Latins[7] it is almost unknown.

NOTES

1. Eus., *h.e.* 3.3.6, in a context on Scriptural canonicity, is our chief source of information on the *Shepherd*.

2. The salutation is from Rom 16.14.

3. Editions: R. Joly, *Hermas Le Pasteur,* SC 53 (Paris, 1968); M. Whittaker, *Der Hirt des Hermas,* GCS 48, 2 (1967), 1–98; *NTA* 2 (1991), 592–602; J. J. Ayán Calvo, *Hermas, El Pastor,* with intro., trans., and notes, *Fuentes Patrísticas* 6. See also L. W. Barnard, "The Shepherd of Hermas in Recent Study," *HeyJ* 9 (1968): 29–36; C. Osiek, "The Second Century Through the Eyes of Hermas: Continuity and Change," *BiblThBull* 20 (1990): 116–22; A. Carlini and G. Luigi, *Papyrus Bodmer XXXVIII. Erma: il Pastore (1a–IIIa visione)* (Cologne-Geneva, 1991).

4. *h.e.* 3.3.6. Courcelle, *LLW,* 94–95, concludes that Jerome did not himself read the *Shepherd,* and that he criticized it severely under Origen's influence (n. 29), just as he praised it, following Eusebius. Courcelle says, "Although he mentions it or quotes it in three other passages, there is no assurance that he read it in the original text."

5. Eusebius actually says (*h.e.* 3.3.6): "some [τινές, not *multi*] ancient writers have drawn on it"; at *h.e.* 3.25.4 the *Shepherd* is placed among the νόθοι, "not genuine."

6. Probably based on *h.e.* 5.8.7: "And not only does he [Irenaeus] know, but he also accepts [i.e., as Scripture] the writing of the *Shepherd,* saying: 'Well, then, does Scripture speak which says, . . .'" The quotation is *Shepherd* 2.1. See P. Henne, "Canonicité du Pasteur d'Hermas," *RevThom* 90 (1990): 81–100; C. J. Wilson, "Toward a Reassessment of the Milieu of the *Shepherd of Hermas:* Its Date and its Pneumatology" (Ph.D. diss., Duke University, 1977), abstract in *Dissertation Abstracts International* 39 (1978): 326–27.

7. See Courcelle, *LLW,* 94–95 and n. 25. Tertullian is a big exception: see *De orat.* 16.1, *De pudic.* 10 and 20.2.

REFERENCES

Q 1, 92–105 — Dr, 32–34 — *TLG* 1419 — CPG 1052 — Cath 5, 667–69, P.-Th. Camelot — DHGE 24, 86–87 — DSp 7/1, 320–32, "Hermas. Doctrine Spirituelle," P. Adnès — DSp 7/1, 316–20, 332–34, "Hermas. Questions d'histoire littéraire," J. Paramelle — EEC 1², 521–22, D. E. Aune — EECh 1, 377, P. Nautin — LThK 5, 255, J. Kraus — LThK 4³, 1448–49, N. Brox — NCE 6, 1074 — *NTA* 2, 592–602, P. Vielhauer and G. Strecker — RAC 14, 682–701, A. Hilhorst — TRE 15, 100–108, R. Staats — ANRW II, 27, 1, 524–51, R. Joly — Vielhauer, *Geschichte,* 513–23 — Dihle, *Greek and Latin,* 295, 297–98

XI. PHILO THE JEW

HILO THE JEW, born in Alexandria[1] of a priestly stock,[2] and for that reason included by us among ecclesiastical writers, because, writing a book on the first church in Alexandria of Mark the evangelist, he engaged in praise of us Christians, recalling that they existed, not just there, but in many provinces, and calling their dwellings monasteries.[3]

2. From this it is apparent that the first church of believers in Christ was such as the monks now imitate and emulate, so that nothing is held in private by anyone, not one among them is rich, not one poor, their patrimonies are divided among the needy, they spend their time in prayer and the psalms, in doctrine and continence, just as Luke describes how believers lived at the beginning in Jerusalem.[4]

3. They say that Philo came at great risk to Rome in the reign of Gaius, to whom he had been sent as an ambassador of his people,[5] and that he came a second time in the reign of Claudius and spoke with the apostle Peter in the same city [of Rome] and that he became his friend[6] and that for this reason he embellished with his praises the followers of Mark, a disciple of Peter, at Alexandria.

4. Countless and distinguished works[7] of his survive on the Pentateuch:

On the Confusion of Tongues, one book;[8]
On Nature and Discovery, one book;[9]
On Things Which are Naturally Desired and Execrated, one book;[10]
On Instruction, one book;[11]
On the Heir of Divine Things, one book;
On the Distinction between Odd and Even, one book;[12]
On the Three Virtues, one book;[13]
On Those Whose Names were Changed in the Scriptures and Why, one book;[14]

5. *On Covenants,* one book;[15]

On the Life of the Wise Man, one book;[16]
On Giants, one book;[17]
On the Divine Origin of Dreams, five books;[18]
Questions and Answers on Exodus, five books;[19]
On the Tabernacle and
On the Decalogue, four books;[20]
also *On Sacrificial Victims and Promises or Curses;*[21]
On Providence;[22]
On the Jews;[23]
On the Conduct of Life;[24]
On Alexander, and
That Irrational Animals Have Reason,[25] and
That Every Foolish Man is a Slave.[26]

6. And the book of which we have spoken already, about our life, that is, about men of the apostolic age, which he also called, Περὶ βίου θεωρητικοῦ ἱκετῶν, *On the Contemplative Life of Suppliants,*[27] obviously because they contemplate heavenly things, and always pray to God,

and in other categories,
On Agriculture, two books;
On Drunkenness, two books.

7. There are also other monuments of his genius[28] which have not come into our hands. Concerning him it is commonly said by the Greeks, Ἢ Πλάτων φιλωνίζει ἢ Φίλων πλατωνίζει,[29] that is, "Either Plato follows Philo, or Philo Plato." So great is the similarity of their thought and eloquence.

NOTES

1. Eus., *h.e.* 2.4.2. Cf. Courcelle, *LLW,* 81 and n. 164: "Actually Jerome's remarks . . . are pure plagiarism from Eusebius." See also *h.e.* 2.16.1.
2. "Of a priestly stock" is unsupported in Eusebius or elsewhere. Eus., *h.e.* 2.4.2, merely says, "inferior to none of the magnates in authority."
3. Eusebius, *h.e.* 2.17.8–14, describing the Therapeutae and, in *h.e.* 2.17.19, their female counterparts, the Therapeutridae, a misreading unquestioned by Jerome; μοναστήριον occurs at *h.e.* 2.17.9.
4. Eusebius, in quoting *De vita cont.* 70–73 (in *h.e.* 2.17.16–18), feels he

ON ILLUSTRIOUS MEN 25

has provided irrefutable proofs (ἀναντιρρήτους λέξεις) of the Christian identification; cf. Barnes, *C. and E.*, 130.

5. *h.e.* 2.5.1, 4–5, and 2.18.8. Cf. E. M. Smallwood, *Philonis Alexandrini Legatio ad Gaium* (Leiden, 1961). Eusebius in *h.e.* 2.5.6–7 cites *Legatio* 24.38, and in *h.e.* 2.6.2. quotes *Legatio* 43. See C. Kraus Reggiani, ANRW II, 21, 1, 554–86.

6. *h.e.* 2.17.1. That he met with Peter is repeated in Photius, *Bib. cod.* 105, but is unlikely, and Photius's added detail that Philo converted to Christianity is even more unlikely.

7. What follows is an abbreviated version of *h.e.* 2.18.1–8. Roman numerals in brackets give the volume number in the Loeb Classical Library 10-vol. series *Philo*. See also R. Radice and D. T. Runia, edd., *Philo of Alexandria. An Annotated Bibliography 1937–1986* = Supplements to *VigChr* 8 (1988); D. T. Runia, R. Radice, and D. Satran, "Philo of Alexandria: An Annotated Bibliography, 1986–1987," in *Studies in Hellenistic Judaism* 2, 141–75; R. Arnaldez, "La Bible de Philon d'Alexandrie," in *Le monde grec et la Bible*, ed. C. Mondésert (Paris, 1984), 37–54; D. T. Runia, *Exegesis and Philosophy. Studies in Philo of Alexandria* (Aldershot, 1991); J. Daniélou, *Philon d'Alexandrie* (1958); P. Heinisch, "Der Einfluß Philos auf die älteste christliche Exegese (Barnabas, Justin und Clemens von Alexandria). Ein Beitrag zur Geschichte der allegorisch-mystischen Schriftauslegung im christlichen Altertum," *ATA* 1/2 (1908); J. P. Martín, *Filón de Alejandría y la génesis de la cultura occidental* (Buenos Aires, 1986); P. Borgen, *Philo, John and Paul: New Perspectives on Judaism and Early Christianity* (Atlanta, 1987); J. Ménard, *La gnose de Philon d'Alexandrie* (Paris, 1987); H. Burkhardt, *Die Inspiration heiliger Schriften bei Philo von Alexandrien* (Basel, 1988); R. Radice, *Platonismo e creazionismo in Filone di Alessandria* (1989).

8. *On the Confusion of Tongues*, one book [IV].

9. [V]; a slip on Jerome's part: the title is not *On Nature*, but *On Flight* (περὶ φυγῆς, *not* περὶ φύσεως).

10. *On Things Which are Naturally Desired and Execrated by the Senses*, one book = *De sobrietate* [III].

11. *On [Grouping for] Instruction*, one book [IV].

12. *On the Heir of Divine Things*, one book, and *On the Distinction between Odd and Even*, one book [IV]: Jerome mistakenly divides a single item into two. Cf. *h.e.* 2.18.2.

13. *On the Three Virtues*, one book [VIII]: cf. *h.e.* 2.18.2.

14. *On Those Whose Names were Changed and Why*, one book [V].

15. *On Covenants*, one book: not known.

16. *Life of the Wise Man*, one book: this seems to be a fusion of *De migratione* and *De vita sapientis*; cf. *h.e.* 2.18.4.

17. *On Giants*, one book = *On the Immutability of God*.

18. *On the Divine Origin of Dreams*, five books: only two survive.

19. *On Questions and Solutions in Exodus*, five books: cf. *h.e.* 2.18.5. See also art., "Erotapokriseis," RAC 6, 344.

20. Cf. *h.e.* 2.18.5: *On the Tabernacle* and *On the Decalogue*, four books [VII].

21. Cf. *h.e.* 2.18.5 for full title, *On Victims and Promises or Curses*.

22. Cf. *h.e.* 2.18.6: *On Providence,* cited in Eus., *Praep. Evang.* 7.20 and 8.18.

23. *On the Jews,* cited in Eus., *Praep. Evang.* 8.11.

24. *On the Conduct of Life:* Eus., *h.e.* 2.18.6, ῾Ο Πολιτικός, *The Life of the Citizen,* or *On Joseph.*

25. Cf. *h.e.* 2.18.6: *On Alexander* or *On the Proposition that Irrational Animals Have Reason.*

26. *On the Proposition that Every Foolish Man is a Slave: h.e.* 2.18.7.

27. *On the Contemplative Life of Suppliants: h.e.* 2.18.7 = *De vita contemplativa* [IX]; *Philon d'Alexandrie, De vita contemplativa,* ed. F. Daumas, trans. P. Miguel (Paris, 1963). For relevant bibliography, E. Hilgert, ANRW II, 21, 1 (1984), 62, 63, 79–83.

28. "other monuments of his genius": Eus., *h.e.* 2.18.7, adds *On the Interpretation of Hebrew Names in the Law and Prophets.*

29. "Either Plato Philonizes, or Philo Platonizes": the phrase recurs in Isidore of Pelusium, *ep.* 3.81, PG 78: 788C. Elsewhere (*ep.* 70.3, CSEL 54, 704) Jerome says much the same: "Quid loquar de Philone quem vel alterum vel Iudaeum Platonem critici pronuntiant?"

REFERENCES

Q 2, 1–2 — Dr, 106–7 — *TLG* 0018 — Cath 11, 202–8, J. E. Ménard — DSp 12/1, 1352–74, V. Nikiprowetsky and A. Solignac — EEC 2², 912–14, R. B. Berchman — EECh 2, 682–83, H. Crouzel — LThK 8, 470–71, C. Mondésert — NCE 11, 287–91, R. Arnaldez — TRE 26, 523–31, M. Mach — ANRW II, 21, 1, several articles, esp.: H. Savon, "Ambroise et Jérôme lecteurs de Philon," ANRW II, 21, 1, 2–46; E. Hilgert, "Bibliographia Philoniana, 1935–1981," ANRW II, 21, 1, 47–97 — Dihle, *Greek and Latin,* 161–67

Opera: L. Cohn and P. Wendland, *Philonis Alexandrini Opera quae supersunt,* 8 vols. (1896–1930); R. Arnaldez, C. Mondésert, and J. Pouilloux, edd., *Oeuvres de Philon d'Alexandrie,* 36 vols. (Paris, 1961–88); Eng. trans., *Philo of Alexandria,* Loeb Classical Library. *Biblia Patristica Supplément* (1982) is dedicated to Philo.

XII. LUCIUS ANNAEUS SENECA

UCIUS ANNAEUS SENECA of Cordova,[1] a disciple of the Stoic Sotion,[2] and paternal uncle of the poet Lucan,[3] was a man of very temperate life whom I would not place in a catalogue of saints, were it not that I was prompted to do so by those *Letters from Paul to Seneca* and *from Seneca to Paul*[4] which are very widely read.

2. In these, when Seneca was Nero's teacher and the most influential person of the period,[5] he said that he wished to have the same position among his own [i.e., the pagans] which Paul had among the Christians.[6]

3. Two years before Peter and Paul were crowned with martyrdom, he was put to death by Nero.[7]

NOTES

1. Cordova in Spain.

2. Sotion is in Eus., *Chron.*, A.D. 13, ed. Helm, 171; cf. Dihle, *Greek and Latin*, 88.

3. Lucan: cf. Dihle, *Greek and Latin*, 113–19.

4. F. Corsaro, "Seneca nel 'Catalogo dei Santi' di Gerolamo," *Orpheus* 8 (1987): 264–82; Gamberale, "L. Seneca in catalogo sanctorum: considerazioni su Hier. *vir. ill.* 12," *InvLuc* XI (1989): 203–17; Jannaccone, "S. S. Girolamo e Seneca," *GiornItalFil* 16 (1963): 326–338. Editions: C. W. Barlow, *Papers of American Acad. in Rome* (Rome, 1938) = PLS 1, 673–679; L. Bocciolini Palagi, "Il carteggio apocrifo di Seneca e San Paolo," *BP* 5 (Florence, 1985).

5. Dihle, *Greek and Latin*, 89.

6. Cf. Tertullian, *De anima* 20.1: "Seneca saepe noster." See J. N. Sevenster, *Paul und Seneca* (Leiden, 1961).

7. Eus., *Chron.*, A.D. 66: "L. Ann. Seneca incisione venarum et veneni haustu perit."

REFERENCES

Q 1, 155–156 — Dr, 28 — *TLG* 2431 — PLS 1: 673–678 [Paulus + Seneca] — CAnt 306 — Cath 13, 1078–83, M. Spanneut — DACL 15/1, 1193–98, H. Leclercq — DSp 14, 570–98, M. Spanneut — EEC 2², 1047, L. M. White — EECh 2, 767f., A. Hamman — LThK 9, 664–65, E. Elorduy — NCE 13, 80–81, M. Spanneut — *NTA* 2, 41–70, Schneemelcher — ANRW II, 36, 3 (Berlin, 1989), 1596–97, 1599–1600, F. R. Chaumartin — Dihle, *Greek and Latin*, 88–104, 113–19

XIII. JOSEPHUS, SON OF MATTHEW

JOSEPHUS, son of Matthew, a priest of Jerusalem,[1] made prisoner by Vespasian, was released by Vespasian's son, Titus.[2] Coming to Rome, he offered to the emperors, father and son, his seven books *On the Captivity of the Jews,*[3] which were deposited in the public library, and by the fame of his genius he merited a statue in Rome.[4]

2. He also composed twenty other volumes, *On Antiquities,*[5] from the beginning of the world to the fourteenth year of Domitian Caesar,[6] and two books ἀρχαιότητος, of antiquities, *Against Apion,* an Alexandrian grammarian,[7] who in the reign of Caligula, sent as legate on the part of the pagans, had written a book against Philo[8] which contained calumny of the Jewish race.[9]

3. Another book of his, entitled, Περὶ αὐτοκράτορος λογισμοῦ, *On the Supremacy of Reason,*[10] is regarded as very elegant; it also contains a description of the martyrdom of the Maccabees.[11]

4. Josephus in the eighteenth book of his *Antiquities*[12] most clearly states that Christ was put to death by the Pharisees because of the greatness of his miracles, and that John the Baptist was a true prophet, and that Jerusalem was subjected to destruction because James the apostle had been put to death.[13]

5. He wrote about the Lord, however, as follows:[14]

"About this time there lived Jesus, a wise man, if indeed one ought to call him a man. For he was one who wrought surprising feats and was a teacher of such people as accept the truth gladly. He won over to his side many of the Jews and many of the Gentiles, and he was believed to be the Anointed.

6. "When Pilate, because of the envy of the highest-standing among us, had condemned him to be crucified, those who had in the first place come to love him maintained their affections for him. On the third day he appeared to them restored to life, for the prophecies of the prophets had foretold these and

countless other marvelous things about him. And the tribe of the Christians, named after him, has down to this day not disappeared."

NOTES

1. Eus., *h.e.* 3.9.1 = Josephus, *Bellum Iudaicum* 1.3. Courcelle, *LLW,* 81–86, credits Jerome with reading Josephus's complete works.

2. Titus succeeded Vespasian, June 24, 79, and was succeeded in turn by his brother, Domitian, two years and two months later, Dec. 13, 81; cf. *h.e.* 3.5.1 and 13.1. See Josephus, *Bell. Iud.* 4.653–654.

3. *h.e.* 3.9.3 = *Bell. Iud.* (*BI*) 1.3. Cf. *h.e.* 3.10.9. See also H. Lichtenberger, "Pagans and Christians in Rome in the time of Nero: Josephus and Paul in Rome," ANRW II, 26, 3, 2142–76.

4. *h.e.* 3.9.2.

5. *h.e.* 3.9.3; H. W. Attridge, *The Interpretation of Biblical History in the "Antiquitates Judaicae" of Flavius Josephus* (Missoula, Montana, 1976).

6. Domitian's reign: Dec. 18, 96.

7. A. Dihle, *Greek and Latin,* 168–69, describes Apion as a grammarian from Alexandria whom the Greeks of his native city had sent to Rome in 40 A.D. as the leader of an anti-Jewish delegation and a prolific author on subjects such as the Latin language, Homeric vocabulary, and ancient Egypt. Apion was long dead when Josephus wrote the work, a *post mortem* exercise similar to Origen's *Contra Celsum.* Jerome was especially impressed by it: cf. *ep.* 70 (CSEL 54, 705): "Iosephus antiquitatem approbans Iudaici populi duos libros scripsit contra Appionem, Alexandrinum grammaticum et tanta saecularium profert testimonia ut mihi miraculum subeat quomodo vir Hebraeus et ab infantia sacris litteris eruditus cunctam Graecorum bibliothecam evoluerit." The phrase *antiquitatem . . . Iudaici populi* explains ἀρχαιότητος in the present passage. On Josephus's "secular" learning, cf. R. M. Grant, *Greek Apologists,* 16–18, 153.

8. *h.e.* 2.5.4.

9. Philo's *Legatio* (*h.e.* 2.5.6) and *Virtues* (*h.e.* 2.6.3) detailed the atrocities perpetrated on the Jews.

10. *h.e.* 3.10.6.

11. *h.e.* 3.10.6.

12. *h.e.* 2.5.2.

13. *h.e.* 1.11.2–6.

14. *h.e.* 1.11.7–8. This is the well-known *Testimonium Flavianum* (text: *Ant.* 18.63–64). Eusebius explicitly says, ὁ Χριστὸς οὗτος ἦν. For a *status quaestionis* on this much-discussed text, cf. Feldman, ANRW II, 21, 2, 822; W. A. Bienert, "Test. Flav.," *NTA* (1991), 489–91; D. S. Wallace-Hadrill, "Eusebius of Caesarea and the *Testimonium Flavianum* (Josephus, *Antiquities* XVIII, 63f.)," *JEH* 25 (1974): 353–62; P. Garnet, "If the *Testimonium Flavianum* contains alterations, who originated them?" StudPat 19 (1989), 57.

REFERENCES

Q 1, 2 — Dr, 39–40 — *TLG* 0526 — Cath 6, 1026–27, G. Bizaré — DSp 2, 1, 962–63 — EEC 1², 630–32, H. W. Attridge — EECh 2, 682–83, H. Crouzel — LThK 5, 1141–43, J. Blinzler — LThK 5³, 1005–7, H. Schreckenberg — NCE 7, 1120–23, J. Strugwell — RAC, Lief. 141 (1997), 761–80 — TRE 17, 258–64, G. Mayer — ANRW II, 21, 2, 763–862, L. H. Feldman — Dihle, *Greek and Latin*, 167–71 — Vielhauer, *Geschichte*, 529–40 — L. H. Feldman, *Josephus and Modern Scholarship (1937–1980)* (Berlin and New York, 1984) — L. H. Feldman and G. Hata, edd., *Josephus, Judaism and Christianity* (Detroit: Wayne State University Press, 1987)

XIV. JUSTUS OF TIBERIAS

 USTUS OF TIBERIAS, of the province of Galilee,[1] attempted also to compose *A History of Jewish Events*[2] and certain short commentaries on the Scriptures.[3]

2. Josephus, however, accused him of falsity.[4]

3. And it is well known that he and Josephus wrote at the same time.[5]

NOTES

1. Eus., *h.e.* 3.10.8; T. Rajak, "Justus of Tiberias," *ClassQ* 23 (1973): 345–68. Tiberias, on the Sea of Galilee, was founded by Herod Antipas and named after his friend, the emperor Tiberius.

2. Known from Josephus, *Life* 336–360 and *Against Apion* 34, 36–42, 65, 88, both in Loeb Classical Library Vol. 1 of Josephus, trans. H. St. J. Thackeray, (London and Cambridge, Mass., 1926; repr., 1976); C. R. Holladay, *Fragments from Hellenistic Jewish Authors*, Vol. 1 (Chico, Calif.: Historians, 1983).

3. "commentaries": of dubious existence.

4. *h.e.* 3.10.8.

5. Jerome's personal statement, which "is valueless," according to Courcelle, *LLW*, 95 n. 30.

REFERENCES

TLG 2497 — LThK 5, 1230, J. Schmid — NCE 8, 101–2, R. Krizsky — ANRW II, 20, 1, 337–58, esp. 347f., A. Barzanò — ANRW II, 21, 2, 787–88, L. Feldman — Dihle, *Greek and Latin*, 169

XV. CLEMENT THE BISHOP

LEMENT,[1] OF WHOM THE APOSTLE Paul in his Epistle to the Philippians wrote, "with Clement and my other fellow-workers whose names are written in the book of life,"[2] was the fourth bishop of Rome after Peter, in that Linus was second and Anacletus, third,[3] although the greater part of the Latins[4] think that Clement was second after the apostle.

2. He wrote in the name of the Roman church a most useful *Letter to the Church of Corinth*,[5] which in some places is even read publicly,[6] which seems to me to correspond to the style of the *Epistle to the Hebrews* ascribed to the authorship of Paul,[7] and uses many expressions from that same epistle which not merely agree in sense but even in word order, and there is an altogether great similarity between the two.

3. A second Epistle is also ascribed to his name, which has not been accepted by the ancients,[8]

and a *Disputation of Peter and Apion*,[9] written in a prolix style, which Eusebius rejects in the third book of his *Ecclesiastical History*.[10]

4. He died in the third year of Trajan's reign,[11] and a church built in Rome preserves to this day the memory of his name.

NOTES

1. J. Colson, *Clément de Rome (Église d'hier et d'aujourd'hui)* (Paris, 1960).

2. Phil 4.3, quoted in Eus., *h.e.* 3.15.1.

3. *h.e.* 3.4.9, 3.15.1, 3.21.1, 5.6.1–2; Irenaeus, *Adv. haer.* 3.3.3. This makes Clement the Bishop of Rome in the years 92–101. On Linus see *h.e.* 3.2, 3.4.8, 3.13.1, 5.6.1; Kelly, *ODP*, 6–7; B. Dümler, *LThK* 6³, 946. See also M. Guerra Gomes, "El obispo de Roma y la *regula fidei* en los tres primeros siglos de la Iglesia," *Burgense* 30 (1989): 355–432.

4. See Q 1, 42.

5. *h.e.* 3.16.1, 5.6.3. Text in SC 31, ed. G. Bardy. See B. E. Bowe, *A church in crisis. Ecclesiology and paraenesis in Clement of Rome, Harvard Dissertations in Religion* 23 (Minneapolis, 1988); E. Peretto, "Clemente Romano ai Corinti. Sfida alla violenza," *VetChr* 26 (1989): 89–114; K. Erlemann, "Die Datierung des ersten Klemensbriefes—Anfragen an eine Communis Opinio," *NTS* 44 (1998): 591–607; Q 1, 42–43.

6. *h.e.* 3.16.1, 4.23.11.

7. *Epistle to the Hebrews: h.e.* 3.3.5, 3.38.1–3; H.-F. Weiss, *Der Brief an die Hebräer* (Göttingen, 1991).

8. *h.e.* 3.38.4.

9. *h.e.* 3.38.5, rejecting them on two counts: not referred to by the ancients and not preserving orthodoxy.

10. A belated acknowledgment by Jerome of his sole source. But he seems nonetheless to have read Clement; cf. Courcelle, *LLW,* 93.

11. *h.e.* 3.34; 5.6.4, quoting Irenaeus, *Adv. haer.* 3.3.3.

REFERENCES

Q 1, 42–53 — Dr, 39–40 — *TLG* 1271 — CPG 1, 1001; Spuria, 1003–1022 — Cath 2, 1183–85, G. Bardy — DSp 2, 1, 962–63 — EEC 1², 264–65, G. F. Snyder — EECh 1, 181, P. F. Beatrice — LThK 2, 1222–23, A. Stuiber — NCE 3, 926–28, H. Dressler — LThK 2³, 1227–28, V. Saxer; 1229–31, G. Schöllgen — RAC 3, 188–97, A. Stuiber — TRE 8, 113–20, D. Powell — Kelly, *ODP,* 7–8 — Vielhauer, *Geschichte,* 529–40 — Dihle, *Greek and Latin,* 296, 308

XVI. IGNATIUS THE BISHOP

GNATIUS, THE THIRD BISHOP of the church of Antioch after the apostle Peter,[1] condemned to the beasts in the persecution begun by Trajan,[2] was bound in chains and sent to Rome.[3]

2. When on his voyage he came to Smyrna, where Polycarp, disciple of John, was bishop,[4] he wrote

a *Letter to the Ephesians,*[5]
a second, *To the Magnesians,*[6]
a third, *To the Trallians,*[7]
a fourth, *To the Romans,*[8] and
after he left Smyrna he wrote *To the Philadelphians*[9]
and *To the Smyrnaeans,*[10]

and, personally, *To Polycarp,*[11] commending to him the church of Antioch.

3. In this letter he offers a testimony on the person of Christ concerning the Gospel[12] which has recently been translated by me.

4. "I indeed both saw him in the flesh after the resurrection and believe that he is, and when he came to Peter and to those who were with Peter, he said to them, 'Behold, touch me and see that I am not a phantom without a body.' And immediately they touched him and believed."[13]

5. It seems worthwhile, however, that we make mention of such a great man and that we make a few remarks on his Epistle which he wrote *To the Romans:*

6. "From Syria to Rome I fight with wild beasts by land and by sea, night and day, chained to ten leopards, that is, a company of soldiers, who guard me; and they become worse with kind endearment.

7. "Now I become the more a disciple for their ill deeds, but I am not on that account justified. Would that I could enjoy the beasts which have been prepared for me, and I pray that they may be prompt for me, and I will even entice them to devour me promptly, not as has happened to some other martyrs whom they have not touched from fears. Even if they be unwilling of themselves to come, I will force them to devour me. Pardon me, sons, I know it is expedient for me.

8. "Now I begin to be a disciple, desirous of nothing of visible things, so that I may find Jesus Christ. Fire, cross, beasts, mangling of bones, tearing asunder of limbs, grinding of my whole body, tortures of the devil, let them come upon me, may I but attain the enjoyment of Christ."[14]

9. And when he had been condemned to the beasts and in the ardor of his suffering heard the lions roaring, he said, "I am the Lord's fodder. May I be ground by the teeth of the lions so that I may become pure bread."[15]

10. He suffered martyrdom in the eleventh year of Trajan; his bodily remains lie in Antioch in the cemetery outside the gate of Daphne.[16]

NOTES

1. Eus., *h.e.* 3.36.2; *h.e.* 3.22 mentions Evodius as Ignatius's predecessor.

2. On persecution under Trajan, cf. Eus., *h.e.* 3.33 (the Pliny-Trajan correspondence); Grant, *Greek Apologists*, 28–33.

3. *h.e.* 3.36.3; C. Lucca, "Ignazio di Antiochia e il Martirio, Un'analisi di Romani 2," *Salesianum* 59 (1997): 621–45.

4. *h.e.* 3.36.5.

5. *Letter to the Ephesians:* trans. William R. Schoedel, *Ignatius of Antioch: A Commentary on the Letters of Ignatius of Antioch* (Philadelphia: Fortress Press, 1985), 33–100; cf. *h.e.* 3.36.5.

6. *To the Magnesians:* trans. Schoedel, 101–33; cf. *h.e.* 3.36.5.

7. *To the Trallians:* trans. Schoedel, 135–61; cf. *h.e.* 3.36.5.

8. *To the Romans:* trans. Schoedel, 165–91; cf. *h.e.* 3.36.6.

9. *To the Philadelphians:* trans. Schoedel, 193–215.

10. *To the Smyrnaeans:* trans. Schoedel, 217–53.

11. *To Polycarp:* trans. Schoedel, 255–81; see also *idem,* "Polycarp's Witness to Ignatius of Antioch," *VigChr* 41 (1987): 1–10.

12. "the Gospel": *The Gospel to the Hebrews*; trans. Schoedel, 226–27. Cf. Eus., *h.e.* 3.36.10, and *Chron.,* ed. Helm, 194. Jerome probably knew it by autopsy.

13. Jerome's translation is defective; it should read, "I indeed both know and believe that he was in the flesh"; cf. Schoedel, *op. cit.,* 225. The testimony, which is quoted in *h.e.* 3.36.11, comes not from *Ad Poly.,* but from *Ad Smyrn.* 3.1–2.

14. Cf. *h.e.* 3.36.7–9, quoting *Ad Rom.* 5; cf. Schoedel, *op. cit.,* 178–80.

15. Ignatius, *Ad Rom.* 4.1; Schoedel, *op. cit.,* 175; cf. *h.e.* 3.36 and Iren., *Adv. haer.* 5.28.4. The language may be eucharistic, *pace* Schoedel, *op. cit.,* 176.

16. Jerome probably knew the tomb in Daphne from his own sojourn in Antioch. Cf. *Chron.,* ed. Helm, 205.

REFERENCES

Q 1, 63–76 — Dr, 40–43 — CPG, 1025–36 — Cath 5, 1190–92, C. Ollivier — DHGE 25, 684–86, R. Aubert — DSp 7, 2, 1250–66, P.-Th. Camelot — EEC 1², 559–60, G. F. Snyder — EECh 1, 404–5, P. Nautin — LThK 5, 611–12, O. Perler — LThK 5³, 407–9, F. and R. Prostmeier — NCE 7, 353–54, F. X. Murphy — NTA 1, 143–45 — TRE 16, 40–45, W. R. Schoedel — ANRW II, 27, 1, 386–92 (Polycarp and Ignatius), W. R. Schoedel — H. O. Paulsen, *Gestalten* I, 38–50 — Vielhauer, *Geschichte,* 540–52 — Dihle, *Greek and Latin,* 297 — H. Y. Gamble, *Books,* 109–12 — J. L. Sumney, "Those who 'Ignorantly Deny Him': The Opponents of Ignatius of Antioch," *JECS* 1, 4 (1993): 345–65

For bibliographical survey, see G. Trentin, "Rassegna di studi su Ignazio di Antiochia," Studia Patavina, *Rivista di Scienze Religiose* 19 (1972): 75–87.

XVII. POLYCARP THE BISHOP

OLYCARP, A DISCIPLE of John the apostle,[1] and ordained by him as bishop of Smyrna, was the leader of all of Asia,[2] in that he had seen and had as teachers some of the apostles and of those who had seen the Lord.[3]

2. In the reign of the emperor Antoninus Pius, on account of some questions concerning the day of the Pasch, he came to Rome, where Anicetus was bishop,[4] and he brought back to the faith very many of those believers who had been deceived by the persuasiveness of Marcion[5] and Valentinus.

3. When Marcion happened to meet him and said, "Recognize us," he replied, "I recognize the first-born of the devil."[6]

4. Later on, in the reign of Marcus Antoninus and Lucius Aurelius Commodus, during the fourth persecution after Nero,[7] at Smyrna, before the proconsul seated in judgment and the whole people in the amphitheater howling against him, he was burned alive.[8]

5. He wrote a very useful letter, *To the Philippians,*[9] which, down to this day, is read in the assembly of Asia.[10]

NOTES

1. Eus., *h.e.* 3.36.
2. Cf. *h.e.* 4.14.1–2.
3. *h.e.* 4.14, quoting Iren., *Adv. haer.* 3.3.4.
4. N. Brox, "Der Konflikt zwischen Aniket und Polykarp," *Concilium* 8 (1972): 14–18, 35–42.
5. Marcion: cf. G. May, "Marcione nel suo tempo," *CristStor* 14 (1993): 205–20; A. Orbe, "Hacia la doctrina marcionítica de la redencíon," *Gregorianum* 74 (1993): 45–74.
6. *h.e.* 4.14 (= Iren., *Adv. haer.* 3.3.4); cf. *h.e.* 3.28.
7. Dates of this imperial reign: 138–161. Cf. *h.e.* 4.14–15.
8. Jerome does not mention the *Martyrium Polycarpi* (CPG 1045); on this, cf. B. Dehandschutter, "The *Martyrium Polycarpi:* a Century of Research," ANRW II, 27, 1 (Berlin, 1993), 485–522; V. Saxer, "L'authenticité du Martyre de Polycarpe. Bilan de 25 ans de critique," MAH 94 (1982): 979–1001; H. Musurillo, *Acts* (Tübingen, 1992), 258–85; M. L. Gullaumin, "En marge du *Martyre de Polycarpe.* Le discernement des allusions scrip-

turaires," in *Forma Futuri*, FS M. Pellegrino (Turin, 1975), 462–69; W. R. Schoedel, *Polycarp, Martyrdom of Polycarp, Fragments of Papias*, TAP 5 (London, 1966); and, most recently, G. Buschmann, *Martyrium Polycarpi. Eine formkritische Studie*, BZNW 70 (Berlin and New York, 1994).

9. CPG 1040. See *Die Polykarpbriefe*, trans. with notes by J. B. Bauer, *Komm. zu Apost. Vätern* 5 (Göttingen, 1995); *Die apostolischen Väter. Clemens von Rom, Ignatius von Antiochen, Polykarp von Smyrna*, trans. with intro. by H. U. Von Balthasar, *Christliche Meister* 24 (Einsiedeln, 1984); *Ignacio de Antioquia, Cartas. Policarpo de Esmirna, Carta. Carta de la iglesia de Esmirna a la iglesia de Filomelio*, trans. with intro. and notes by J. J. Ayán Calvo (Madrid, 1991); Paulsen, *HNT* 18 (1985): 109–26; L. W. Barnard, "The Problem of Saint Polycarp's Epistle to the Philippians," *ChQR* 163 (1962): 421–30 [= idem, *Studies in the Apostolic Fathers* (1966), 31–39], on P. N. Harrison's 1936 hypothesis; H. O. Maier, "Purity and Danger in Polycarp's Epistle to the Philippians: The Sin of Valens in Social Perspective," *JECS* 1, 3 (1993): 229–48.

10. See *h.e.* 3.36.

REFERENCES

Q 1, 76–82 — Dr, 43–45, 78–80 — *TLG* 1622 — CPG 1, 1040–42 — Cath 11, 595–97, P.-Th. Camelot — DSp 12, 1902–8, D. van Damme — EEC 2², 933–34, G. F. Snyder — EECh 2, 701, P. Nautin — LThK 8, 597–98, J. A. Fischer — NCE 11, 535–36, F. X. Murphy — TRE 16, 40–45, W. R. Schoedel — ANRW II, 27, 1, 386–92 (Polycarp and Ignatius), W. R. Schoedel — PWRE 21, 2, 1662–93, P. Meinhold — Vielhauer, *Geschichte*, 552–566 — Dihle, *Greek and Latin*, 297, 308 — H. Y. Gamble, *Books*, 110–16 — Paulsen, *Handbuch zum Neuen Testament*, 18

XVIII. PAPIAS THE BISHOP

APIAS, A DISCIPLE of John and bishop of Hierapolis in Asia,[1] wrote only five volumes, entitled *An Explanation of the Discourses of the Lord*.[2] In these, since he is asserting in his preface that he does not follow various opinions but that he has the apostles as witnesses, he says:[3]

2. "I examined what Andrew said, what Peter said, what Philip, Thomas, James, John, Matthew, and any other of the disciples of the Lord said, and what Aristion and the elder John,

the disciples of the Lord, were saying. For I did not suppose that books were useful for me to read so much as the living voice surviving in the authors to the present day."[4]

3. It is obvious from this catalogue of names that the John who is listed among the apostles is not the same as the elder John whom he numbers after Aristion. A further reason for saying this is because of the opinion mentioned earlier,[5] held by very many, that *The Second* and *Third Epistle of John* are the work, not of the Apostle, but of the presbyter.[6]

4. He is said to have published the Jewish opinion of one thousand years [of reign] at the δευτέρωσιν,[7] at the Second Coming, a view shared by Irenaeus,[8] Apollinaris, and others, who claim that after the resurrection the Lord will reign in the flesh with the saints. Tertullian also, in his work *On the Hope of the Faithful*,[9] Victorinus of Pettau,[10] and Lactantius[11] are attracted by this same view.

NOTES

1. Eus., *h.e.* 2.15; U. H. J. Körtner, *Papias von Hierapolis: Ein Beitrag zur Geschichte des frühen Christentums* (Göttingen, 1983); R. M. Grant, "Papias in Eusebius' *Church History*," *Mélanges d'histoire des religions*, FS Henri-Charles Puech (Paris, 1974), 209–14.

2. J. A. Kleist, *The Didache, The Epistle of Barnabas, The Epistles and the Martyrdom of St. Polycarp, The Fragments of Papias, The Epistle to Diognetus*, ACW 6 (1946); W. R. Schoedel, *Polycarp. Fragments of Papias*, Vol. 5 in *The Apostolic Fathers. A New Translation and Commentary* (New York, 1967), 89–130; V. Bartlet, "Papias's *Exposition:* Its Date and Contents," in *Amicitiae Corolla*, FS J. R. Harris (London, 1933), 15–44.

3. *h.e.* 3.39; J.-D. Dubois, "Remarques sur le fragment de Papias cité par Irenée [Iren., *Adv. haer.* 5.33.3–4]," *RHPR* 71 (1991) 3–10; C. M. Nielsen, "Papias. Polemicist against whom?," *TS* 35 (1974): 529–35.

4. J. Kürzinger et al., *Papias von Hierapolis und die Evangelien des Neuen Testaments. Gesammelte Aufsätze, Neuausgabe und Übersetzung der Fragmente, Kommentierte Bibliographie* (Regensburg, 1983); A. Adrien Delclaux, "Deux témoignages de Papias sur la composition de Marc?" *NTS* 27 (1980/81): 401–11; T. Y. Mullins, "Papias on Mark's Gospel," *VigChr* 14 (1960): 216–24; A. Meredith, "The evidence of Papias for the priority of Matthew," in *Synoptic Studies: The Ampleforth Conferences of 1982 and 1983, JSNT* Supplements 7 (Sheffield: JSOT Press, 1984), 187–96.

5. *DVI* 9.5.

6. J. J. Günther, "Early identification of authorship of the Johannine writings," *JEH* 31 (1980): 407–27; R. Bauckham, "Papias and Polycrates on

the Origin of the Fourth Gospel," *JThS* 44, 1 (1993): 24–69; J. Munck, "Presbyters and Disciples of the Lord in Papias," *HThR* 52 (1959): 223–43; *idem*, "Die Tradition über das Matthäusevangelium bei Papias," *Neotestamentica et Patristica*, FS Oscar Cullmann (Leiden, 1962), 249–60; C. E. Hill, "What Papias Said About John (and Luke): A 'New' Papian Fragment," *JThS* 49, 2 (1998): 582–629.

7. On δευτέρωσιν (= Hebrew *mishnah*), see *PGL*, *s.v.:* "secondary literature, oral law and its tradition, as opposed to Scripture"; R. G. Déaut, art., "Mishnah," EECh 1, 563–64; H. Dietenhard, art., "Deuterosis," RAC 3 (1957), 842–49. Jerome uses the word in *ep.* 18B (cf. ACW 33, 100 and 222 n. 17a), and in *ep.* 121.10 he defines it. In his *Comm. on Ezechiel* 36.1–15 (CCL 75, ed. F. Glorie), he defines it more fully: "Neque enim iuxta Iudaicas fabulas, quas illi δευτερώσεις appellant, gemmatum et auream de caelo exspectamus Hierusalem," and goes on to line up the believers in millenarianism in virtually the same terms as here: "quod et multi nostrorum et praecipue Tertulliani liber qui inscribitur *De spe fidelium* et Lactantii *Institutionum* volumen septimum pollicetur et Victorini Pictabionensis episcopi crebrae *Expositiones* et nuper Severus noster in dialogo cui *Gallo* nomen imposuit et, ut Graecos nominem et primum extremumque coniungam, Irenaeus et Apollinaris"; H. J. de Jonge, "ΒΟΤΡΥΣ ΒΟΗΣΕΙ. The Age of Kronos and the Millennium in Papias of Hierapolis," in M. J. Vermaseren, ed., *Studies in Hellenistic Religions*, EPRO 78 (Leiden, 1979): 37–49; S. Heid, *Chiliasmus und Antichrist-Mythos. Eine frühchristliche Kontroverse und das Heilige Land* (Bonn, 1993).

8. Irenaeus, *Adv. haer.* 5, SC 153, ed. A. Rousseau.

9. C. Tibiletti, "Inizi del millenarismo di Tertulliano," *Annali della Facoltà di lettere e filosofia dell'Università di Macerata* 1 (1968): 195–213.

10. See Q 2, 411–13; *DVI* 74.

11. Lactantius, *Inst. div.* 7.24.

REFERENCES

Q 1, 82–85 — Dr, 38, 45 — *TLG* 1558 — CPG 1047 — CAnt, 208 — Cath 10, 563–65, J. Liébaert — EEC 2², 866, E. Ferguson — EECh 2, 647, L. Vanyó — LThK 8, 34–36 — LThK 7³, 1325–26, P. Bruns — NCE 10, 979–80, F. X. Murphy — *NTA* 1, 137–39; 2, 23–24 — TRE 15, 641–44, H. J. Körtner — ANRW II, 27, 1, 235–70, W. R. Schoedel — *PRE* 18/2 (1949), 966–76 — *ThWNT* 6, 651–83, G. Bornkamm — Vielhauer, *Geschichte*, 757–65

XIX. QUADRATUS THE BISHOP

 UADRATUS, A DISCIPLE of the apostles, was named bishop of Athens as successor to Publius,[1] when the latter was crowned with martyrdom for Christ. By his faith and zeal he reunited the church, which was in terror and disarray.

2. When Hadrian spent the winter in Athens, and visited Eleusis[2] and, initiated into almost all the Greek mysteries,[3] presented an opportunity to those who hated the Christians to harass the believers without a decree of the emperor,[4] Quadratus presented a treatise to him composed *In defense of our religion,* very useful, and full of reasoning and of faith, worthy of the teaching of the apostles.[5]

3. In it he also revealed his own venerable old age, in saying that many had been seen by him in the time of the Lord in Judea who were oppressed by various infirmities, and who had been cured, and others who were raised from the dead.[6]

NOTES

1. "bishop of Athens": Eus., *h.e.* 4.23.3. Possibly a different Quadratus, "with a prophetic gift," is mentioned in Eus., *h.e.* 3.37.

2. Hadrian succeeded Trajan in 117. Cf. R. M. Grant, *Greek Apologists,* Chap. 4; D. Kienast, "Hadrian, Augustus und die eleusinischen Mysterien," *JfNG* 10 (1959–1960): 61–69.

3. K. Clinton, "The Eleusinian Mysteries: Roman Initiates and Benefactors, Second Century B.C. to A.D. 267," ANRW II, 18, 2 (Berlin, 1989), 1516–25.

4. Eus., *h.e.* 4.8.6; P. Keresztes, "The Imperial Roman Government and the Christian Church; I. From Nero to the Severi; III. Hadrian's Rescript on the Christians," ANRW II, 23, 1, 287f.

5. *h.e.* 4.3.1–2, with a quotation from the *Apology;* this may be a third Quadratus (cf. n. 1 above); R. M. Grant, "Quadratus, the first Christian Apologist," in R. H. Fischer, ed., *A Tribute to A. Vööbus* (1977), 152–64 [= *idem, Greek Apologists,* 35–36, 184].

6. *h.e.* 4.3.2.

REFERENCES

Q 1, 190–91 — Dr, 38, 55 — *TLG,* 1652 — CPG 1, 1060 — Cath 12, 332–33, P.-Th. Camelot — EEC 2², 767, D. M. Scholer — EECh 2, 727, V. Zangara — NCE 12, 1–2, F. X. Murphy — ANRW II, 27, 2, P. F. Barton

XX. ARISTIDES THE PHILOSOPHER

RISTIDES OF ATHENS,[1] a most eloquent philosopher who became a disciple of Christ without relinquishing his philosopher's gown, was a contemporary of Quadratus.[2]

Like Quadratus, he presented to the emperor Hadrian a volume containing an account of our teaching, namely, the *Apology for Christians,*[3] which, surviving down to the present day, is a proof of his talent among philologists.[4]

NOTES

1. = Eus., *h.e.* 4.3.3, expanded.

2. There are three different people named Quadratus in Eusebius; cf. *DVI* 19, nn. 1 and 5.

3. *h.e.* 4.3.3; cf. R. M. Grant, *Greek Apologists,* 35–39, and, on the text, 195. For a recent edition, cf. *Aristide di Atene, Apologia,* ed. C. Alpigiano, BP 11 (Florence, 1988); BAC 116 (Madrid, 1954); L. Alfonsi, "La teologia della storia nell'*Apologia di Aristide,*" *AugR* 16 (1976): 37–40; K.-G. Essig, "Erwägungen zum geschichtlichen Ort der Apologie des Aristides," *ZKG* 97 (1986): 163–188; G. C. O'Ceallaigh, "'Marcianus' Aristides, on the Worship of God," *HThR* 51 (1958): 227–54.

4. *philologoi,* scholars : *OLD, s.v.,* cites Suet., *Gram.* 10, Referscheid ed. (Leipzig, 1860), 108.

REFERENCES

Q 1, 191–95 — Dr, 39–40 — *TLG* 1184 — CPG 1062–67 — Cath 1, 822, G. Bardy — DHGE 4, 187–91, P. de Labriolle — DSp 2, 1, 962–63 — EEC 1², 111–12, E. Ferguson — EECh 1, 72–73, P. Siniscalco — LThK 1, 852–53, H. Rahner — LThK 1³, 973, G. Scholten — NCE 1, 798, F. X. Murphy — RAC 1, 652–54, B. Altaner — *Der Neue Pauly* 1, 1100 — Dihle, *Greek and Latin,* 300–301

XXI. AGRIPPA CASTOR

GRIPPA, SURNAMED CASTOR,[1] a very learned man, refuted with great effectiveness the twenty-four volumes of the heretic Basilides,[2] which the latter had composed against the Gospel,

2. in which he disclosed all his mysteries and named his prophets, Bar Cochebas and Bar Coph,[3] and other barbarous names, which cause terror to his hearers, and Abraxas,[4] his supreme deity, a name which occupies about the space of a year in the numerical system of the Greeks.

3. Now Basilides, from whom the Gnostics had their origin, lived in Alexandria in the time of Hadrian,[5] at the very time that Bar Kochba,[6] the leader of the Jewish faction, slaughtered the Christians with various punishments.

NOTES

1. = Eus., *h.e.* 4.7.6; Jerome's *Castoris* is an epexegetic genitive.

2. On Basilides (c. 100–160): Q 1, 257–59; Dr, 88–89; CPG 1127; F. W. Norris, EEC 1², 176–77; A. Monaci Castagno, EECh 1, 113; W. A. Löhr, LThK 2³, 59; Scholer, *NHB*, 50; J. H. Waszink, RAC 1 (1950), 1217–25; E. Muhlenberg, TRE 5, 296–301; B. Layton, *GS*, 417–44; W. A. Löhr, *Basilides und seine Schule. Eine Studie zur Theologie und Kirchengeschichte des zweiten Jahrhunderts*, WUNT 83 (Tübingen, 1996); R. M. Grant, "Place de Basilide dans la théologie chrétienne ancienne," *REAug* 25 (1979): 201–16; M. Jufresa, "Basilides, a path to Plotinus," *VigChr* 35 (1981): 1–15; *idem*, "Jewish Christianity at Antioch in the Second Century," *RechScRel* 60 (1972): 97–108.

3. Otherwise unknown.

4. On Abrasax, cf. Irenaeus, *Adv. haer.* 1.24.7: "The ruler of these [heavens] they claim, is Abrasax, and because of this he possesses three hundred and sixty-five numbers in himself," ACW 55, 87, trans. D. J. Unger and J. J. Dillon, and *loc. cit.*, 238, n. 24: "So Abrasax was the name of the ruler of the highest heavens. And Irenaeus is saying the same as Hippolytus, who writes that the ruler of the Ogdoad had this name (*Adv. haer.* 7.26.6 [GCS 26, 205]). The numeric value of the name in Greek letters is 365, namely, 1 plus 2 plus 100 plus 1 plus 200 plus 1 plus 60." See also Hippolytus, *Ref.* 5.3; Epiphanius, *Pan.* 24.7.2–4. See further Courcelle, *LLW*, 97 and n. 49.

5. On Hadrian and Gnosticism, cf. Grant, *Greek Apologists*, 36.

6. P. Schäfer, *Der Bar Kokhba–Aufstand: Studien zum zweiten jüdischen Krieg*

gegen Rom. Texte und Studien zum antiken Judentum, Bd. I (Tübingen, 1981);
H. Mantel, "The Causes of the Bar Kokba Revolt," *JewQRev* 58 (1967–68):
224–42, 274–96.

REFERENCES

Q 1, 284 — DHGE 1, 1029–30, V. Ermoni — EEC 1², 9, F. W. Norris —
EECh 1, 18, G. Ladocsi — LThK 1, 209, H. Rahner — LThK 1³, 251, C.
Scholten

XXII. HEGESIPPUS THE HISTORIAN

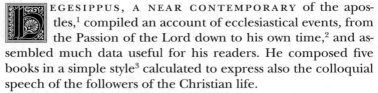 EGESIPPUS, A NEAR CONTEMPORARY of the apos-
tles,¹ compiled an account of ecclesiastical events, from
the Passion of the Lord down to his own time,² and assembled much data useful for his readers. He composed five
books in a simple style³ calculated to express also the colloquial
speech of the followers of the Christian life.

2. He said that he came to Rome in the time of Anicetus,
who was the tenth bishop after Peter,⁴ and that he remained
there down to the episcopacy of Eleutherus, who was formerly a
deacon of Anicetus.⁵

3. Furthermore, in disputations against the idols⁶ he composed a history from the time when they first increased with
their error, indicating by this the age in which he flourished.⁷

4. For he says, "To their dead they raised cenotaphs and
shrines as we see until the present day, and among them is Antinous, a slave of Hadrian Caesar, in whose honor the Antinoan
Games are held, and he also built a city called after Antinous,
and instituted prophets for him in the temple."⁸

5. Records show that Hadrian Caesar numbered Antinous
among his favorites.⁹

NOTES

1. Eus., *h.e.* 2.23.3: ἐπὶ τῆς πρώτης τῶν ἀποστόλων γενόμενος διαδοχῆς;
h.e. 4.8.1–2, 4.8.22. See L. Abramowski, "διαδοχή und ὄρθος λόγος bei He-

gesipp," *ZKG* 87 (1976): 321–27; T. Halton, "Hegesippus in Eusebius," StudPat 17, 2 (Oxford, 1982), 688–93; N. Hyldahl, "Hegesipps *Hypomnemata*," *STh* 14 (1960): 70–113.

2. Not in Eusebius.

3. *h.e.* 4.8.2: ἐν πέντε δ᾿ οὖν συγγράμμασιν . . . ἁπλουστάτῃ συντάξει γραφῆς ὑπομνηματισάμενος; cf. M. Durst, "Hegesipps *Hypomnemata*: Titel oder Gattungsbezeichnung? Untersuchungen zum literarischen Gebrauch von Hypomnema-Hypomnemata," *RQ* 84 (1989): 299–330. Cf. *h.e.* 4.22.1: ἐν πέντε τοῖς . . . ὑπομνήμασιν.

4. *h.e.* 4.11.7, 4.22.3; for Anicetus, see Kelly, *ODP*, 157–68; *Chron.*, A.D. 157, ed. Helm, 203.

5. *h.e.* 4.22.3. For Eleutherus, see Kelly, *ODP*, 177–93; *Chron.*, A.D. 177, ed. Helm, 207.

6. *h.e.* 3.32.

7. This is not a separate treatise.

8. *h.e.* 4.8. On the death of Antinous, see *Chron.*, A.D. 129, ed. Helm, 200.

9. See R. Lambert, *Beloved and God: The Story of Hadrian and Antinous* (London, 1984).

REFERENCES

Q 1, 284–85 — *TLG* 1398 — CPG 1, 1302 — Cath 5, 568–69, P.-Th. Camelot — EEC 1², 515, T. Halton — EECh 1, 371, F. Scorza Barcellona — LThK 5, 60–61, J. Lenzenweger — LThK 4³, 1244, F. Mali — NCE 6, 994, H. Dressler — TRE 14, 560–62, T. Halton

XXIII. JUSTIN THE PHILOSOPHER

USTIN THE PHILOSOPHER,[1] who continued to wear the philosopher's garb, was born in Neapolis, a city of Palestine; his father was Priscus, son of Bacchius.[2] He accomplished great feats for the religion of Christ, to the point of presenting to Antoninus Pius and his sons and the senate a book entitled, *Against the Pagans*,[3] without being ashamed of the ignominy of the cross.[4] He presented another book to the successors of the same Antoninus, Marcus Antoninus Verus and Lucius Aurelius Commodus.[5]

2. A third book of his survives, *Against the Pagans*,[6] where he discourses about the nature of demons;

and a fourth, *Against the Pagans*, to which he gave the title,
Ἔλεγχος, *A Confutation;*[7]

another one, called *On the Monarchy of God;*[8]

and another book, entitled by him, the Ψάλτην, the
Psalmist;[9]

another, *On the Soul;*[10]

and a *Dialog against the Jews*, which he had with Trypho,[11] a
Jewish leader.

He also composed important volumes, *Against Marcion,* of
which Irenaeus makes mention in the fifth book of his *Against
Heresies,*[12]

and another book, *Against All Heresies,*[13] of which he makes
mention in the *Apology* presented to Antoninus Pius.

3. After he had held διατριβαί, debates,[14] in the city of Rome
and had reprimanded the Cynic Crescens,[15] who had uttered
many calumnies against the Christians, for being gluttonous,
and afraid of death, and given to luxury and pleasures, finally
by the efforts and deviousness of Crescens he was accused of being a Christian and poured out his blood for Christ.[16]

NOTES

1. Recent studies include the following: L. W. Barnard, *Justin Martyr. His
Life and Thought* (Cambridge, 1967); *idem,* "Justin Martyr in Recent Study,"
SJTh 22 (1969): 152–64; E. F. Osborn, *Justin Martyr*, BHTh 47 (Tübingen,
1973); E. Robillard, *Justin. L'itinéraire philosophique* (Montreal and Paris,
1989); M. J. Edward, "On the Platonic Schooling of Justin Martyr," *JThS*,
n.s., 42 (1991): 17–34; G. Girgenti, *Giustino Martire. Il primo cristiano platon-
ico* (Milan, 1995); B. Wildermuth, BBKL 3 (1992): 888–95; R. M. Grant,
Greek Apologists, chaps. 6, 7, 8; R. Joly, *Christianisme et philosophie. Études sur
Justin et les Apologistes grecs du deuxième siècle* (Brüges, 1973); A. Davids, *Iusti-
nus philosophus et martyr. Bibliographie 1923–1973* (Nijmegen, 1983); J.
Morales, "La investigación sobre San Justino y sus escritos," *ScrTh* 16
(1984): 869–96.

2. Eus., *h.e.* 4.11.8, 4.8.3. For Neapolis see "Nablus" ("Schechem") in J.
Murphy-O'Connor, *The Holy Land* (Oxford Univ. Press, 1998), 372–73. On
Priscus and Bacchius, cf. *1 Apol.* 1.1.

3. *h.e.* 4.17.1. For text: A. Wartelle, ed., *Saint Justin Martyr. Apologies*
(Paris, 1987); M. Marcovich, ed., *Iustini Martyris Apologiae pro Christianis*
(Berlin and New York, 1994). For translation: *Justin Martyr. The First and
Second Apologies,* trans. L. W. Barnard, ACW 56 (Mahwah, N.J., 1996). See

also A. J. Guerra, "The Conversion of Marcus Aurelius and Justin Martyr. The purpose, genre and content of the *First Apology*," *SecCent* 9 (1992): 171–87.

4. "Ignominy of the cross" seems to be related to Eus., *h.e.* 4.16.3: "I expect to be stretched out on the cross (ἐπὶ ξύλῳ)."

5. *Second Apology*: FOTC 6, 115–35. Cf. P. Keresztes, "The So-called *Second Apology* of Justin," *Latomus* 24 (1965): 858–69. See further CPG 1, 1073, notes.

6. Justin speaks of demons in *1 Apol.* 26, quoted in *h.e.* 4.11. On demons cf. E. Ferguson, "The Demons According to Justin Martyr," in *The Man of the Messianic Reign and Other Essays*, FS Elza Huffard (Wichita Falls, 1980), 103–12.

7. Ἔλεγχος: CPG 1082. See also C. Riedweg, "A Christian Middle-Platonic Document: Ps.-Justin's *Ad Graecos de vera religione*, hitherto known as *Cohortatio ad Graecos*," StudPat 26 (Leuven, 1993): 177ff.; *idem*, *Ps.-Justin (Markell von Ankyra?), "Ad Graecos de vera religione" (bisher "Cohortatio ad Graecos"): Einleitung und Kommentar*, 2 vols. (Basel, 1994).

8. CPG 1084; *h.e.* 4.18.4; FOTC 6, 437–55.

9. Lost work; ψσάλτης: PGL, *s.v.*, "one who sings praises in church, cantor."

10. Lost work.

11. CPG 1076. Text: M. Marcovich, *PTS* 47 (1997). N. Hyldahl, "Philosophie und Christentum. Eine Interpretation der Einleitung zum Dialog Justins," *AThD* 9 (Arhus, 1966); J. C. M. van Winden, *An Early Christian Philosopher. Justin Martyr's Dialogue with Trypho, Chapters One to Nine*, Philosophia Patrum 1 (Leiden, 1971); J. Nilson, "To Whom Is Justin's *Dialogue with Trypho* Addressed?" *TS* 38 (1977): 538–46.

12. *h.e.* 4.18.9. Justin's work has not survived, although a fragment of it is quoted in Irenaeus, *Adv. haer.* 4.6.2, and a possible second fragment in *Adv. haer.* 5.26.2; see CPG 1078.

13. *h.e.* 4.11.10, otherwise unknown.

14. διατριβαί, hinted at in *2 Apol.* 3.

15. Crescens: *h.e.* 4.16.1–9 (quoting Justin, *2 Apol.* 3, which paints a merciless portrait); see FOTC 19, 243ff. and n. 3). Cf. Tatian, *Apol.* 19; also, A. G. Hamman, "Essai de chronologie de la vie et des œuvres de Justin," *AugR* 35 (1995): 231–39.

16. See *Acts* of Justin, in H. Musurillo, *The Acts of the Christian Martyrs* (Oxford, 1972), 42–61; G. Lazzati, "Gli atti di S. Giustino martire," *Aevum* 27 (1953): 473–97; G. A. Bisbee, "The *Acts* of Justin Martyr: A Form-Critical Study," *SecCent* 3 (1983): 129–57.

REFERENCES

Q 1, 196–219 — Dr, 55–56, 58–64, 74–76 — *TLG* 0645 — CPG 1078–89 — Cath 6, 1325–28, P.-Th. Camelot — DSp 8, 1640–47, C. Kannengiesser, A. Solignac — EEC 1², 647–50, T. Stylianopoulos — EECh 1, 462–64, R. J.

De Simone — LThK 5, 1225–26, K. Gross — LThK 5³, 1112–13, S. Heid — NCE 8, 94–95, H. Chadwick — TRE 17, 471–78, O. Skarsaune — *Gestalten* 1, 51–68, C. P. Bammel — Dihle, *Greek and Latin*, 300–303

XXIV. MELITO THE BISHOP

ELITO of the province of Asia, bishop of Sardis,[1] presented to the emperor Marcus Antoninus Verus,[2] who was a disciple of the orator Fronto,[3] a volume in defense of Christian dogma.[4]

2. He also wrote other volumes,[5] among which were the following:

> *On the Pasch*,[6] two books;
> *On the Life of the Prophets*,[7] one book;
> *On the Church*, one book;
> *On Sunday*, one book;
> *On Faith*, one book;
> *On Creation*, one book;
> *On the Senses*, one book;
> *On the Soul and the Body*, one book;
> *On Baptism*,[8] one book;
> *On Truth*, one book;
> *On the Birth of Christ*, one book;
> *On His Prophecy*, one book;
> *On* Φιλοξενία, *Hospitality*, one book,
> and another book entitled, *The Key*;
> *On the Devil*, one book;
> *On the Apocalypse of John*, one book,
> and τὸν περὶ ἐνσωμάτου θεοῦ, *On the Incarnation of God*, one book,
> and six books of *Extracts*.[9]

3. Tertullian, in the seven books which he wrote against the church in favor of Montanus,[10] derides his elegant and declama-

tory style, saying that he was thought of as a prophet by most of us Christians.

NOTES

1. See Eus., *h.e.* 4.26. For Sardis, cf. G. M. A. Hanfmann, *Sardis from Prehistoric to Roman Times. Archaeological Exploration, 1958–1975* (Cambridge, Mass., 1983).

2. Usually called Marcus Aurelius; cf. *h.e.* 4.13.8.

3. Cornelius Fronto, consul in 143, and teacher of rhetoric to Marcus Aurelius. He denounced Christian morality (cf. Minucius Felix, *Oct.* 9.6, 31.2). See P. Frassinetti, "L'orazione di Frontone contro i cristiani," *Giorn ItalFil* 2 (1949): 238–54.

4. Defense: CPG 1093 (1–2). Cf. W. Schneemelcher, "Histoire du salut et empire romain. Méliton de Sardes et l'Etat," *BLE* 75 (1974): 81–98; K. Aland, "The Relation between Church and State in Early Times. A Reinterpretation," *JThS* 19 (1968): 115–27.

5. Jerome merely reproduces the list in Eus., *h.e.* 4.26.2, missing one.

6. CPG 1093 (4); *h.e.* 4.26.2 mentions τὰ Περὶ τοῦ Πάσχα δύο, a work known to Clement of Alexandria, according to *h.e.* 6.13.9. For text and trans.: *Melito of Sardis. "On Pascha" and Fragments*, ed. and trans. S. G. Hall, OECT (Oxford, 1979). See also B. Pseutogka, " Ἡ εἰς τὸ ἅγιον πάσχα ὁμιλία τοῦ Ψευδο- ἱππολύτου εἶναι τὸ πρῶτον βιβλίον τοῦ Περὶ Πάσχα διμεροὺς ἔργου τοῦ Μελίτωνος?" *Kler* 3 (1971): 26–65. For bibliographical surveys, cf. H. Drobner, "15 Jahre Forschung zu Melito von Sardes (1965–1980)," *VigChr* 36 (1982): 313–33 (93 titles); M. Frenschkowski, BBKL 5 (1993): 1219–23; R. M. Mainka, "Melito von Sardes. Eine bibliographische Ubersicht," *Claretianum* 5 (1965): 225–55 (101 titles to 1964); F. Mendoza Ruis, "Estato actual de la investigación sobre la Homilia acerca de la Pascua, atribuida a Meliton de Sardes," *Scripta Theol* 1 (1969): 475–82. See also C. Bonner, *The Homily on the Passion by Melito, Bishop of Sardis*, SD 12 (London, 1940; Ann Arbor Microfilms, 1981); *Méliton de Sardes, "Sur la Pâque" et fragments*, ed. O. Perler, SC 123 (1966); M. Testuz, *Papyrus Bodmer XIII. Méliton de Sardes, Homélie sur la Pâque* (Geneva, 1960).

7. *De vita prophetarum* abbreviates *h.e.* 4.26.2: Περὶ πολιτείας καὶ προφήτων, *On Christian Life and the Prophets*.

8. R. M. Grant, "Melito of Sardis on Baptism," *VigChr* 4 (1950): 33–36.

9. *Extracts*: Quoted in *h.e.* 4.26.12. See CPG 1093(3).

10. *De exstasi*, CPL 31b.

REFERENCES

Q 1, 242–48 — Dr, 70–72 — *TLG* 1495 — CPG 1, 1092–98 — CPL: cf. 202; 1658 — Cath 8, 1126–29, J. Liébaert — DHGE 24, 86–87 — DSp 10, 979–90, O. Perler — EEC 2², 745–46, D. M. Scholer — EECh 1, 551, A.

Hamman — LThK 7, 258–59, J. Quasten — LThK 7³, 86–87, S. G. Hall —
NCE 9, 631–32, G. Racle — Dihle, *Greek and Latin*, 302

XXV. THEOPHILUS THE BISHOP

HEOPHILUS, THE SIXTH BISHOP of the church of
Antioch,¹ in the reign of the emperor Marcus Antoninus Verus,² composed a book, *Against Marcion*, which
survives down to the present day.

2. Also ascribed to him are

three volumes, *To Autolycus*,³
one volume, *Against the Heresy of Hermogenes*,⁴
and other short, elegant tracts which pertain to the edification of the church.⁵

3. I also have read *Commentaries on the Gospel*⁶ and on *The
Proverbs of Solomon*⁷ ascribed to his authorship, which do not
seem to me to match the elegance and style of the previous volumes.

NOTES

1. Eus., *h.e.* 4.20, and *Chron.*, A.D. 169. For works of Theophilus, see *h.e.*
4.24; also R. M. Grant, "Theophilus Antiochenus," in *Catalogus translationum et commentariorum: Mediaeval and Renaissance Latin Translations and Commentaries. Annotated Lists and Guides*, Vol. 2, ed. P. Kristeller and F. E. Cranz
(Washington, D.C., 1971), 235–37.
2. On the date, see R. M. Grant, *Greek Apologists*, 143.
3. *Ad Autolycum:* CPG 1107. Editions: G. Bardy (trans. J. Sender, from
Maran), *Théophile d'Antioche: Trois livres à Autolycus*, SC 20 (Paris, 1948). See
also *Theophilus of Antioch. Ad Autolycum*, ed. and trans. R. M. Grant, OECT
(Oxford, 1970); M. Marcovich, *Tatiani Oratio ad Graecos. Theophili Antiocheni ad Autolycum*, PTS 43–44 (Berlin and New York, 1995).
4. *Against Hermogenes:* F. Bolgiani, "Sullo scritto perduto di Teofilo d' Antiochia *Contro Ermogene*," *Paradoxos Politeia*, FS G. Lazzati (1979), 77–118.
5. Eus., *h.e.* 4.24, says, βίβλια κατηχήτικα.
6. CPG 1108: *Fragmenta e Commentariis (apud Hieronymum, Epist. 121)* =
CSEL 56, 25–26.
7. *Prov. Salom.*: Quoted at *h.e.* 1.2.2.

REFERENCES

Q 1, 236–42 — Dr, 55–56 — *TLG* 1725 — EEC 2², 1122, F. W. Norris — CPG 1107–9 — Cath 14, 1113–18, P. M. Humbaert — EECh 2, 831–32, P. Nautin — LThK 10, 88–89, R. Gögler — NCE 14, 72, M. Whittaker — C. Burini, *Gli apologeti Greci*, CTP 50 (Rome) — Dihle, *Greek and Latin*, 302–3

XXVI. APOLLINARIS THE BISHOP

APOLLINARIS, BISHOP of Hierapolis in Asia,[1] lived during the reign of the emperor Marcus Antoninus Verus[2] and presented to him an excellent work, *In Defense of the Faith of the Christians.*[3]

2. There are also extant of his, *Against the Pagans,*[4] five books,

and *On Truth,*[5] two books,

and *Against the Cataphrygians*[6] [one volume], from the time when Montanus was beginning his error, with his crazy prophetesses, Prisca and Maximilla.[7]

NOTES

1. Eus., *h.e.* 4.21, 4.26.1, and 4.27.
2. i.e., Marcus Aurelius, 161–180.
3. *h.e.* 4.26.1, 4.27.1. Its date is 176 or 177. See also *h.e.* 5.5.4 and Barnes, *C. and E.*, 137.
4. *h.e.* 4.27.1; Grant, *Greek Apologists*, 90.
5. *h.e.* 4.27.1, which adds, "Books One and Two, *Against the Jews*"; cf. Grant, *Greek Apologists*, 86–87.
6. *Cataphrygas: h.e.* 4.27.1. On Montanism see D. E. Groh, EEC 2², 778–80, and Williams, "The Origins of the Montanist Movement: A Sociological Analysis," *Religion* 19 (1989): 331–51.
7. *h.e.* 4.27.1, where they are merely "false prophetesses." Cf. Jerome, *Comm. in Naum prophetam, Prol.*: "insanis vatibus," PL 25, 1232; also, *Comm. in Abacuc*, where good sense is contrasted with "nec in morem insanientium feminarum dat sine mente sonum," PL 25, 1274, quoted in R. E. Heine, ed., *The Montanist Oracles and Testimonia*, PatMS 14 (Macon, Georgia: Mercer University Press, 1989), 156. See M. Y. MacDonald, *Early Christian Women and Pagan Opinion: The Power of the Hysterical Woman* (Cambridge University Press, 1996).

50 ST. JEROME

REFERENCES

Q 1, 377–83 — Dr, 55 — *TLG* 1163 — CPG 1103 (*De Pascha, fragmenta*) — Cath 1, 704, G. Bardy — DHGE 3, 959–60, P. de Labriolle — EEC 1[2], 79, E. Ferguson — LThK 1, 713–14, H. Rahner — LThK 1[3], 826, C. Scholten — NCE 1, 667, E. Day — R. M. Grant, *Greek Apologists*, 83–91

XXVII. DIONYSIUS THE BISHOP

 IONYSIUS, BISHOP of the church of Corinth, was a man of such eloquence and zeal that he instructed by letter not only the people of his own city and province, but also of other provinces and cities.

2. Among his letters[1] is one, *To the Spartans,*

a second, *To the Athenians,*

a third, *To the Nicomedians,*

a fourth, *To the Cretans,*

a fifth, *To the Church of Amastri and the other churches of Pontus,*

a sixth, *To the Faithful of Knossos and to Pinytus,* the bishop of that city,

a seventh, *To the Romans,* which he addressed to their bishop, Soter,

an eighth, *To Chrysophora,* a holy woman.

3. He lived in the reign of the emperor Marcus Antoninus Verus and Lucius Aurelius Commodus.[2]

NOTES

1. The letters are no longer extant. See Eus., *h.e.* 4.23, translated in Q 1, 280–82.

2. "in the reign of the emperor Marcus Antoninus Verus and Lucius Aurelius Commodus": 161–192 A.D.; cf. Eus., *h.e.* 4.14, and *Chron.*, ed. Helm, pp. 204–10.

REFERENCES

Q 1, 280–82 — *TLG* 1329 — CPG 1336 — Cath 3, 616–17 — DHGE 14, 261–62 — DSp 3, 449 — EEC 1², 334, M. P. McHugh — EECh 1, 238, P. Nautin — LThK 3, 404, J. A. Fischer — LThK 3³, 245, E. Grünbeck — NCE 4, 877, D. Kelleher — Gamble, *Books*, 116–18 — Nautin, *Lettres et écrivains chrétiens des IIe et IIIe siècles* (Paris, 1961), 13–32

XXVIII. PINYTUS THE BISHOP

INYTUS OF CRETE, bishop of the city of Knossos,[1] wrote a very elegant letter *To Dionysius*, bishop of Corinth,[2] in which he taught that the faithful should not continue to be fed on a milk diet lest they be taken by surprise as children on the last day, but should be fed on solid food[3] so that they might advance to a spirited old age.

2. He also lived under Marcus Antoninus and Aurelius Commodus.

NOTES

1. Eus., *h.e.* 4.21. Knossos was the capital of Crete.
2. *h.e.* 4.23.
3. 1 Cor 3.2; Heb 5.12–14; *h.e.* 4.23, here abbreviated.

REFERENCES

Q 1, 282–83 — DSp 2, 1, 962–63

XXIX. TATIAN THE HERESIARCH

ATIAN,[1] who first as a teacher of eloquence attained no small fame for himself for his rhetorical skill,[2] became a follower of Justin Martyr,[3] and flourished in the church as long as he did not depart from his side.

2. Later, however, inflated with the pride of eloquence, he founded a new heresy which is called the Encratite,[4] which Severus further increased, and after whom the heretics of his party are called Severians[5] down to this present day.

3. Moreover Tatian wrote numerous volumes, one of which, *Against the Pagans*,[6] survives, which is the most famous[7] in repute among all his works.

4. And he lived under the emperor Marcus Antoninus Verus and Lucius Aurelius Commodus.

NOTES

1. R. M. Grant, *Greek Apologists*, Chaps. 13, 14; *idem*, "Studies in the Apologists. 1: Tatian's Theological Method," *HThR* 51 (1958): 123–28; *idem*, "Forms and Occasions of the Greek Apologists," *Studi e Materiali di Storia delle Religioni* 52 (1986): 213–26. For Tatian's life, see L. Leone, "Due date della vita di Taziano," *OrChrP* 27 (1961): 27–37.

2. M. Whittaker, "Tatian's Educational Background," StudPat 13 (1975/76), 57–59; P. Yousif, "Il patrimonio culturale greco secondo Taziano," in *L'eredità classica nelle lingue orientali* (1985), 73–95.

3. = Eus., *h.e.* 4.16. See R. Weijenborg, "Die Berichte über Justin und Crescens bei Tatian," *Antonianum* 47 (1972): 362–90.

4. L. W. Barnard, "The Heresy of Tatian," in *Studies in Church History and Patristics, Analecta Vlatadon* 26 (Thessalonica, 1979), 181–93; *idem*, "The Heresy of Tatian—once again," *JEH* 19 (1968): 1–10. On Encratism see *La tradizione dell'enkrateia* (1985); H. Chadwick, art., "Enkrateia," *RAC* 5.

5. On Severians cf. *h.e.* 4.29, quoting Irenaeus, *Adv. haer.* 1.28.1.

6. CPG 1104. Text: *Tatian. "Oratio ad Graecos" and Fragments*, ed. and trans. M. Whittaker, OECT (Oxford, 1982); M. Marcovich, *Tatiani Oratio ad Graecos. Theophili Antiocheni ad Autolycum*, PTS 43–44 (Berlin and New York, 1995); Ruiz Bueno, BAC 116 (Madrid, 1954), 572–628. See also M. McGehee, "Why Tatian never 'apologised' to the Greeks," *JECS* 1, 2 (1993): 143–58 [not an "apology," but a protreptic]; P. Bernard, "Le catalogue des statues dans le Discours aux Grecs de Tatien: Rhétorique ou Réalité?" [résumé] *REG* 99, 21–22; F. Bolgiani, "Taziano, *Oratio ad Graecos* cap. 30, I," *Kyriakon*, ed. P. Granfield and J. A. Jungmann, FS J. Quasten, 2 vols., Vol. 1 (Münster, 1970), 226–35; S. Di Cristina, "L'idea di *Dunamis* nel *De mundo* e nell'*Oratio ad Graecos* di Taziano," *AugR* 17 (1977): 485–504; G. F. Hawthorne, "Tatian and his Discourse to the Greeks," *HThR* 57 (1964): 161–88; A. E. Osborne, *Tatian's Discourse to the Greeks. A Literary Analysis and Essay in Interpretation* (Ph.D. diss., Univ. of Cincinnati, 1969); R. M. Grant, *Greek Apologists*, Chaps. 13–14 and p. 246; *idem*, R. M. Grant, "Five Apologists and Marcus Aurelius," *VigChr* 42 (1980): 1–17; J. Beaujeu, "Les apologètes et le culte du souverain," *Le culte des souverains dans l'Empire romain*, Fondation Hardt, *Entretiens* 19 (1973): 101–42.

7. See A. J. Droge, *Homer or Moses? Early Christian Interpretations of the History of Culture* (Tübingen, 1989), 82–101; M. Elze, *Tatian und seine Theologie* (Ph.D. diss., Tübingen University, 1958) = FKDG 9 (Göttingen: Vandenhoeck & Ruprecht, 1960). See also R. M. Grant, "Tatian and the Bible," StudPat 1 (1957): 297–306; *idem, HThR* 46 (1953): 99–101; *idem, JThS* 5 (1954): 62–68; *idem,* "Tatian (*Or.* 30) and the Gnostics," *JThS* 15 (1964): 5–69; M. Marcovich, "Codex Arethae and Tatian," *JÖByz* 44 (1994): 307–12; R. Merkelbach, "Tatian 40," *VigChr* 21 (1967): 219–20; M. Naldini, "Dai Papiri della Raccolta Fiorentina. Lettera di Tatianos al padre," *Chairemon* 4 (Athens and Rome, 1967): 163–68; A. Orbe, "A proposito de Gen. 1.3 en la exegesis de Tatien," *Greg* 42 (1961): 401–43.

REFERENCES

Q 1, 220–28 — Dr, 64–67 — CPG 1104–6 — DSp 15, 52–57, A. Solignac — EEC 2², 1105–6, F. W. Norris — EECh 2, 815, F. Bolgiani — Dihle, *Greek and Latin,* 303

XXX. PHILIP THE BISHOP

HILIP, BISHOP of Crete, or rather of the city of Gortyn,[1] of which Dionysius makes mention in the letter which he wrote to the church of that city,[2]

2. published an important work *Against Marcion,*[3] and flourished in the time of Marcus Antoninus Verus and Lucius Aurelius Commodus.[4]

NOTES

1. Cf. Eus., *h.e.* 4.21, which makes Philip a contemporary of Hegesippus. Titus 1.5 tells us that Paul left Titus in Crete "to appoint presbyters in every city." Titus himself is credited with having been first bishop of Gortyn.

2. Dionysius, *ad Cretenses* = *h.e.* 4.23.5; cf. *DVI* 27.2.

3. *Against Marcion,* named in *h.e.* 4.25.1, which describes the work, now lost, as very elaborate, and links Philip with Irenaeus and Modestus as anti-Marcionite writers.

4. *Chron.,* A.D. 204.

REFERENCES

Q 1, 281, 284 — EECh 2, 681, E. Prinzivalli

XXXI. MUSANUS

USANUS,[1] not undistinguished among those who wrote on the doctrine of the church, in the reign of the emperor Marcus Antoninus Verus,[2] composed a work directed at certain brethren who had fallen away from the church into the heresy of the Encratites.[3]

NOTES

1. Eus., *h.e.* 4.21, and *Chron.*, A.D. 204
2. = Marcus Aurelius.
3. Eusebius speaks of an ἐπιστρεπτικώτατος λόγος: Liddell, Scott, Jones, *s.v.*: "likely to turn or alter; reflective"; ἐπίστρεπτος, "versatile." On Encratites, see *h.e.* 4.28 (Gk., ἐγκρατεία = continence, self-control); cf. *DVI* 29.2.

REFERENCES

Q 1, 284 — EECh 2, 576, A. Pollastri — LThK 7, 698 — LThK 7³, 542, J. Kraus

XXXII. MODESTUS

ODESTUS,[1] who also lived in the reign of the emperor Marcus Antoninus and Lucius Aurelius Commodus, wrote a work *Against Marcion*[2] which is still extant.

2. Other compositions are ascribed to him, but scholars reject them as spurious.[3]

NOTES

1. Eus., *h.e.* 4.21. See also A. Le Boulluec, "La Bible chez les marginaux de l'orthodoxie," in *Le monde grec et la Bible*, ed. C. Mondésert, 153–70.

2. *h.e.* 4.25.1.

3. συντάγματα: Liddell, Scott, Jones, *s.v.*, "a collection of writings"; ψευδεπίγραφα: PGL, *s.v.*, "with false superscription or title"; neut. plur, as substantive; see also EEC 2², 961–64, art., "Pseudepigraphy," J. H. Charlesworth.

REFERENCES

Q 1, 284 — CPL: cf. 2246 — EECh 2, 564, G. Ladocsi — LThK 7, 516, J. Kraus — LThK 7³, 370, G. Schöllgen

XXXIII. BARDESANES THE HERESIARCH

 ARDESANES was regarded as famous in Mesopotamia.[1] At first he was a follower of Valentinus,[2] but then became his adversary, and finally started a new heresy.[3] He was held in repute by the Syrians for his passionate character and vehemence in debate.[4]

2. He wrote countless works against almost all heresies which had originated in his time. The most famous and most powerful of his works was *On Fate*,[5] which he presented to Marcus Antoninus,[6] and many other volumes on persecution which his followers translated from Syriac into Greek.[7]

3. If his efficacy is so splendid and great in translation, what do we think it was like in the original![8]

NOTES

1. Bardesanes/Bar Daisan (154–222), a contemporary of Clement of Alexandria; see Eus., *h.e.* 4.30.1; also Epiphanius, *Panarion* 56, in *The Panarion of St. Epiphanius*, trans. P. R. Amidon, 198.

2. *h.e.* 4.30.3; Epiphanius, *Pan.* 56.2.1.

3. *Pan.* 56.1: "the founder of the sect of the Bardesanites."

4. *h.e.* 4.30.5: "very able . . . very eloquent in Syriac," "very strong at arguing."

5. *h.e.* 4.30.2: "a very powerful dialogue addressed to Antoninus, *On Fate* (Περὶ Εἱμαρμένης)." See A. Dihle, "Astrology in the Doctrine of Bardesanes," StudPat 20 (1987), 160–68; H. J. W. Drijvers, *Bardaisan of Edessa* (1977); *idem*, "Edessa und das jüdische Christentum," *VigChr* 24 (1970): 4–33; U. Bianchi, "Le fonti del dualismo di Bardesane," in *Umanita e Storia. Scritti in onore di A. Atisani* (Naples, 1970), 1–15.

6. T. D. Barnes, *C. and E.*, 141: "Eusebius assigned him to the reign of Marcus Aurelius, even though he was born in 154 and died in 222/3." Edessa was the capital of the small kingdom of Osrrhoëne.

7. "many other volumes": *h.e.* 4.30.1–2: "in consequence of the persecution of that time."

8. Cf. Courcelle, *LLW*, 95 n. 35.

REFERENCES

Q 1, 263–64 — *TLG* 1214 — CPG 1, 1152–53 — Cath 1, 1245–46, G. Bardy — DHGE 6, 765–67, G. Bardy — DSp 14, 1430, A. Guillaumont — EEC 1², 167, F. W. Norris — EECh 1, 110, R. Lavenant — LThK 1, 1242–43, J. Quasten — LThK 2³, 3, H. J. W. Drijvers — NCE 2, 97, G. W. MacRae — RAC 1, 1180–86, L. Cerfaux — TRE 5, 206–12, H. J. W. Drijvers — Dihle, *Greek and Latin*, 330–31 — *Nag Hammadi Bibliography, 1948–1969*, NHS 1 (1971), 50, D. M. Scholer

XXXIV. VICTOR THE BISHOP

ICTOR, THIRTEENTH BISHOP of the city of Rome,[1] wrote *On the Question of the Pasch*[2] and certain other works,[3] and ruled the church for ten years in the time of the emperor Severus.[4]

NOTES

1. Eus., *h.e.* 5.22.1, 5.28.3–5; *Chron.*, A.D. 193, A.D. 196.

2. *h.e.* 5.23–24. Cf. Ch. Mohrmann, "Le conflit pascal au IIe siècle," *VigChr* 16 (1962): 154–71.

3. This probably refers to Victor's excommunication of Theodotus; see *h.e.* 5.28.6–7.

4. His death: *Chron.*, A.D 201; see G. La Piana, "The Roman Church at the End of the Second Century," *HThR* 17 (1925): 201–77.

REFERENCES

Q 1, 279 — CPG 1338 — EEC 2², 1159, M. P. McHugh — EECh 2, 867, B.
Studer — LThK 10, 768–69, G. Schwaiger — NCE 14, 646, E. G. Weltin —
Kelly, *ODP*, 12

XXXV. IRENAEUS THE BISHOP

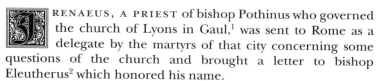RENAEUS, A PRIEST of bishop Pothinus who governed the church of Lyons in Gaul,[1] was sent to Rome as a delegate by the martyrs of that city concerning some questions of the church and brought a letter to bishop Eleutherus[2] which honored his name.

2. Later, when Pothinus attained the crown of martyrdom for Christ when he was nearly ninety years old, Irenaeus replaced him.[3]

3. It is clear that he was a disciple of Polycarp, the bishop and martyr of whom we made mention already.[4]

4. He wrote *Against Heresies*, in five books,[5]

a short work, *Against the Pagans*,[6]
another, *On Knowledge*,[7]
also *To brother Marcianus, The Demonstration of the Apostolic Preaching*,[8]
and a *Book of Various Discourses*,
and *To Blastus, On Schism*,[9]
and *To Florinus, On the Sole Sovereignty* or *That God is not the Author of Evils*,[10]
and a famous σύνταγμα, composition, *On the Ogdoad*,[11] at the end of which, indicating that he was close to the times of the apostles, he concluded thus:[12]

5. "I adjure you who will transcribe this work, by our Lord Jesus Christ, and by his glorious coming, when he comes to judge the living and the dead, that you compare what you have transcribed and correct it most diligently with this copy, and that you shall likewise transcribe this oath and put it in the copy."

6. They say that there are other *Epistles* of his to Victor, bishop of Rome, on the Paschal question,[13] in which he admonishes him that he should not easily sunder the unity of the episcopal college.

7. In fact Victor had believed that many bishops of Asia and the Orient, who celebrated the Pasch with the Jews on the fourteenth of the moon, deserved to be excommunicated. But many who disagreed with them did not go along with Victor in this decision.[14]

8. Irenaeus lived mostly in the reign of Commodus, who had succeeded Marcus Antoninus as emperor.[15]

NOTES

1. Eus., *h.e.* 5.1.1, 5.1.29. For bibliographic and lexicographic aids on Irenaeus, cf. N. Brox, *Irenäus von Lyon. Formalstrukturen seiner Theologie und Forschungsbericht* (1945); M. A. Donovan, "Irenaeus in Recent Scholarship," *SecCent* 4 (1984): 219–41; J. Rouge, L. Doutreleau, B. de Vregille, M. Jourjon, P. Ferlay, "Irénée de Lyon," *Mission* 482 (1986): 183–213. Other studies include M. Jourjon, "Saint Irénée lit la Bible," in *Le monde grec et la Bible*, ed. C. Mondésert, 153–70; K. J. Tortorelli, "Some methods of interpretation in Saint Irenaeus," *VetChr* 30 (1993): 123–32; S. Lundstrom, *Die Überlieferung der lateinischen Irenaeusübersetzung* (Uppsala, 1985).

2. *h.e.* 5.4.1–2.

3. *h.e.* 5.5.8, and *Chron.*, A.D 182, ed. Helm, 208.

4. *DVI* 17.

5. CPG 1306; *St. Irenaeus, Against the Heresies, Book 1*, trans. D. J. Unger and J. J. Dillon, ACW 55 (New York, 1992). Jerome shows a personal knowledge of this work in his *ep.* 75, to Theodora.

6. *h.e.* 5.26.1.

7. *h.e.* 5.26.1. Is this a misunderstanding by Jerome of *h.e.* 5.7.1 (Ἐλέγχου καὶ . . . γνώσεως)?

8. CPG 1307; *Irénée de Lyon, Démonstration de la Prédication Apostolique*, ed. A. Rousseau, SC 400 (Paris, 1995).

9. *h.e.* 5.15 and 5.20.1.

10. CPG 1309; *h.e.* 5.15 and 5.20.

11. σύνταγμα, composition, *On the Ogdoad*: CPG 1308; R. Staats, "Ogdoas als ein Symbol für die Auferstehung," *VigChr* 26 (1972): 29–52.

12. *h.e.* 5.20.2.

13. *Ep. to Victor*: CPG 1310. See *h.e.* 5.24.12–17. This gave him his name, Εἰρηναῖος, "man of peace." See E. Lanne, "S. Irénée de Lyons, artisan de la paix entre les Églises," *Irénikon* 69 (1996): 451–76; H. F. von Campenhausen, "Ostertermin oder Osterfasten? Zum Verständnis des Irenäusbrief an Viktor (Euseb. *Hist. Eccl.* V, 24, 12–17)," *VigChr* 28 (1974): 114–38.

14. *h.e.* 5.24.

15. *h.e.* 5.9.1: "When Antoninus [i.e., Marcus Aurelius] had continued as Emperor for nineteen years [161–180], Commodus took over the sovereignty" (on March 17, 180).

REFERENCES

Q 1, 287–313 — Dr, 43–45, 95–99 — *TLG* 1447 — CPG 1306–21 — CPL 2275 — Cath 6, 81–86, M. Jourjon — DHGE 25, 1477–79, R. Aubert — DSp 7, 2, 1923–69, L. Doutreleau, L. Regnault — EEC 1², 587–89, M. T. Clark — EECh 1, 413–26, A. Orbe — LThK 3, 773–75, P.-Th. Camelot — LThK 5³, 583–85, F. Dünzl — NCE 7, 631–32, H. Dressler — RAC Lief. 142, 820–54, N. Brox — TRE 15, 258–67, H.-J. Jaschke — *Gestalten* 1, 82–96, N. Brox — Vielhauer, *Geschichte*, 529–40 — Dihle, *Greek and Latin*, 303–4

XXXVI. PANTAENUS THE PHILOSOPHER

ANTAENUS, A PHILOSOPHER of the Stoic school,[1] according to a certain ancient custom in Alexandria, where, beginning with Mark the Evangelist, there were always teachers of the church,[2] was endowed with such wisdom and learning both in the Scriptures and in secular literature that he was sent by Demetrius, bishop of Alexandria, into India[3] at the request of legates from this people.

2. And there he found that Bartholomew of the twelve apostles had preached the coming of the Lord Jesus according to the Gospel of Matthew which, written in Hebrew letters, he brought back with him on his return to Alexandria.[4]

3. Indeed many commentaries of his on Holy Scripture survive, but his living voice was more beneficial to the churches.

4. He taught in the reign of the emperors Severus and Antoninus whose surname was Caracalla.[5]

NOTES

1. Eus., *h.e.* 5.10.2, 6.19.13.
2. *h.e.* 2.16 and 5.10.1,3; M. P. Roncaglia, "Pantène et la Didascalée d'Alexandrie," in *A Tribute to Arthur Vööbus* (Chicago, 1977), 211–33.

3. *h.e.* 5.10.2–3; W. H. C. Frend, "Some Cultural Links between India and the West in the early Christian centuries," in *Theoria to Theory* 2 (1968): 306–11.

4. *h.e.* 5.10.3. On Bartholomew cf. R. Trevijano, EECh 1, 112.

5. Severus, 193–211; Caracalla, 211–217. Marrou has very tentatively suggested Pantaenus as the author of *À Diognète*, SC 33² (Paris, 1965; repr., 1997), 266–68.

REFERENCES

Q 2, 42–53 — Dr, 104–7 — Cath 10, 510–11, J. Liébaert — DSp 12, 159–61, A. Méhat — EEC 2², 859, E. Ferguson — EECh 2, 639, S. Lilla — LThK 8, 24, J. A. Fischer — NCE 10, 947, M. Whittaker — Dihle, *Greek and Latin*, 328

XXXVII. RHODO, THE DISCIPLE OF TATIAN

RHODO, AN ASIAN by birth,[1] educated in the Scriptures at Rome by Tatian of whom we have spoken above,[2] composed numerous works, and especially one, *Against Marcion*,[3] in which he shows how also the Marcionites were at variance among themselves.

2. And he said that he had once encountered another heretic, an old man, Apelles[4] and had engaged in a discussion with him and that he, Rhodo, held Apelles up to ridicule because he said that he did not know the God whom he worshipped.[5]

3. In the same book which he wrote to Kallistio he recalled that he was a disciple of Tatian at Rome.[6] He also composed elegant treatises *On the Hexaemeron*,[7] and a distinguished work, *Against the Phrygians*,[8] and his dates were in the reign of Commodus and Severus.[9]

NOTES

1. Eus., *h.e.* 5.13.1.
2. Tatian: *DVI* 29.
3. *plurima*: a mistranslation of Eusebius, διάφορα βίβλια. Cf. CPG 1300,

"Fragmenta (apud Euseb., *H.E.*, V, 13, 2–4, 5, 6–7)." On Marcion, cf. *h.e.* 4.11 and EEC 2², 715–17, H. F. Stander.

4. *h.e.* 5.13.2. Apelles, greatest disciple of Marcion: cf. art., *s.v.*, EECh 1, 54; L. E. Junod, "Les attitudes d'Apelles, disciple de Marcion, à l'égard de l'Ancien Testament," *AugR* 22 (1982): 113–33.

5. What Rhodo said about Apelles was, "As to how there was a single source he said that he did not know"; quoted in *h.e.* 5.13.6–7.

6. *h.e.* 5.13.8.

7. *h.e.* 5.13.8.

8. *Against the Phrygians,* mistakenly assigned to Rhodo by Jerome, who wrongly identifies him with the anonymous anti-Montanist in *h.e.* 5.16 [CPG 1327]; see EECh 1, 150, art., "Cataphrygians," V. Zangara.

9. Commodus, 180–192; Severus, 193–211.

REFERENCES

Q 1, 225, 272–74, 284 — *TLG* 1655 — CPG 1300 — DSp 2, 1, 962–63 — EECh 2, 736, E. Peretto — LThK 8, 1280, H. Rahner

XXXVIII. CLEMENT THE PRESBYTER

LEMENT, A PRIEST of the church of Alexandria,[1] a student of Pantaenus, whom we have discussed already,[2] after the latter's death became director of the [catechetical] school of the church of Alexandria[3] and was a master of κατηχήσεων, catecheses.[4]

2. His distinguished volumes, full of erudition and eloquence, both about the divine Scriptures and the vehicle of secular literature,[5] are well known.

3. Among them are the following:[6]

Στρωματεῖς, *Stromateis*, eight books;[7]
Ὑποτυπώσεων, *Hypotyposeis*, eight books;[8]
Against the Pagans, one book;[9]
Paidagogos, three books;[10]
On the Pasch, one book;[11]
a disquisition, *On Fasting*,[12]
and another work, called *What Rich Man will be Saved*;[13]

On Detraction, one book;[14]

On Ecclesiastical Canons and Against Those who Follow the Error of the Jews, one book, which he dedicated [προσεφώνησεν] in person to Alexander, bishop of Jerusalem.[15]

4. Besides, in his *Stromateis* he makes mention of a work of Tatian, *Against the Pagans,* about which we have already spoken,[16] and of a Χρονογραφία, *Chronography,* of a certain Cassian,[17] a work which I could not find.

Among the Jews he also makes mention of one Aristobulus,[18] and Demetrius and Eupolemus,[19] anti-pagan writers, who, like Josephus,[20] had asserted the greater ἀρχαιογονία, antiquity, of Moses and the Jewish race.[21]

5. From Alexander, bishop of Jerusalem, who later ruled the church with Narcissus,[22] there exists a letter directed to the Antiochenes,[23] congratulating them on the ordination of Asclepiades, the confessor.[24] At the end of the letter it reads:[25]

6. "Brethren of the Lord, I send this letter to you by the hand of Clement, the blessed presbyter, a man illustrious and approved, whom you also know and will now know better, who also when he came here in accordance with the providence and overseership of God consolidated and increased the church of the Lord."

7. It is well known that Origen was his student.[26] He lived in the reign of Severus, and of Antoninus, his son.

NOTES

1. Eus., *h.e.* 5.11.1: Clement is not called a priest by Eusebius.

2. *h.e.* 5.11.1–2; on Pantaenus cf. *DVI* 36.

3. *h.e.* 6.6.1.

4. "and was a master of κατηχήσεων, catecheses": κατηχήσεων, *magister.* EECh 1, 150–51, art., "Catechesis," F. Cocchini.

5. *h.e.* 6.13; "the divine Scriptures": E. Osborn, "La Bible inspiratrice d'une morale chrétienne d'après Clément d'Alexandrie," in *Le monde grec et la Bible,* ed. C. Mondésert, 153–70.

6. Eusebius gives the same list at *h.e.* 6.13. See A. Méhat, "Etat présent des études sur Clément d'Alexandrie. Essai le bilan pour la période 1950–1992," ANRW II, 27, 2; E. Osborn, "Clement of Alexandria: a review of research, 1958–82," *SecCent* 3 (1983): 219–44.

7. *Stromata: h.e.* 6.13.1 gives full title. See also *h.e.* 6.6.1. Jerome also knows the *Stromata* of Origen: cf. *Adv. Rufinum* 1.18.

8. *h.e.* 6.13.2 and 6.14. On Ὑποτυπώσεις, now lost, cf. E. F. Osborn, "Clement of Alexandria's *Hypotyposeis*," *JThS* 36 (1985): 70; *idem*, "Clement's *Hypotyposeis*: Macarius Revisited," *SecCent* 7, 4 (1989–90): 233–35.

9. *Adversus gentes*, called Προτρέπτικος in Eus., *h.e.* 6.13.3.

10. *h.e.* 6.13.3.

11. *h.e.* 6.13.3; cf. R. Cantalamessa, *Easter in the Early Church*, trans. J. M. Quigley and J. T. Lienhard (Collegeville, Minn.: Liturgical Press, 1993), 52–53. See also *h.e.* 4.26.4.

12. *h.e.* 6.13.3.

13. *h.e.* 6.13.3.

14. *h.e.* 6.13.3.

15. *h.e.* 6.13.3.

16. Tatian: *h.e.* 6.13.7 and Clement, *Strom.* 1.21.101.2 (FOTC 85, 99); see also *DVI* 29.

17. "and of a Χρονογραφία, *Chronography*, of a certain Cassian": mentioned with Tatian in *Strom.* 1.21.101.2 (FOTC 85, 99); in Clement the title is ἐξεγήτικα. For Cassian see also *Strom.* 3.13.91.1 (FOTC 85, 313).

18. Aristobulus was a Hellenistic Jewish apologist of the mid-2nd century B. C.; cf. art., "Judaeo-Hellenism," EECh 1, 455, citing N. Walter, *Der Thoraausleger Aristobulus*, TU 86 (Berlin, 1964). Eusebius quotes him in *Praep. evang.* 13.12.1–2 (Clem., *Protrep.* 7.74). See A. van de Bunt and A. van den Hoek, "Aristobulus, Acts, Theophilus, Clement Making Use of Aratus' *Phainomena*: A Peregrination," *Bijdragen* 41 (1980): 290–99.

19. *h.e.* 6.13.7.

20. Josephus: *h.e.* 6.13.7; see also *h.e.* 7.32.16–17. Cf. *DVI* 13.2: "two books ἀρχαιότητος, of antiquities."

21. Clement, *Strom.* 1.15.72.4, FOTC 85, 77 and n. 342. On the priority-of-Moses theme, see D. Ridings, *The Attic Moses. The dependency theme in some early Christian writers* (Gothenburg, 1995); A. J. Droge, *Homer or Moses? Early Christian Interpretations of the History of Culture* (Tübingen, 1989); P. Pilhofer, *Presbyteron kreitton* (Tübingen, 1990).

22. *h.e.* 6.11.1. Alexander was bishop of Jerusalem from 212 to 250.

23. *h.e.* 6.11.5.

24. *h.e.* 6.11.4: Asclepiades succeeded Serapion.

25. *h.e.* 6.11.5.

26. *h.e.* 6.6.1.

REFERENCES

Q 2, 5–36 — Dr, 107–11 — *TLG* 0555 — CPG 1, 1375–99 — Cath 2, 1203–6, G. Bardy — DHGE 2, 1423–28, G. Bardy — DSp 2, 950–61, J. Lebreton — EEC 1², 262–64, W. H. Wagner — EECh 1, 179–81, M. Mees — LThK 6, 331–32, P.-Th. Camelot — LThK 6³, 126–27, E. Früchtel — NCE 3, 943–44, M. Spanneut — RAC 3, 182–88, L. Früchtel — TRE 8, 101–13, A. Méhat — Dihle, *Greek and Latin*, 328–31 — *Gestalten* 1, 121–33, A. M. Ritter — BBKL 1, 1063–66, B. F. W. Bautz

XXXIX. MILTIADES

ILTIADES,[1] of whom Rhodo makes mention in the work which he composed against Montanus, Prisca, and Maximilla, wrote an excellent volume against those same people,[2] and other works against the pagans and the Jews,[3] and he presented an *Apology* to the emperors of his time.[4]

2. He lived in the reign of Marcus Antoninus and Commodus.[5]

NOTES

1. Eus., *h.e.* 5.17.1 (FOTC 19, 320 and n. 1).
2. *h.e.* 5.13.2–7; cf. M. Y. MacDonald, *Early Christian Women*; W. Tabbernee, "Montanist Regional Bishops: New Evidence from Ancient Inscriptions," *JECS* 1, 3 (1993): 249–80.
3. Nothing survives.
4. *h.e.* 5.17.5. See Grant, *Greek Apologists*, 90–91; R. E. Heine, ed., *The Montanist Oracles and Testimonia*, PatMS 14, 154–55.
5. Marcus Antoninus, 161–180; Commodus, 180–192.

REFERENCES

Q 1, 42–53 — Cath 8, 1111, art., "Melchiade ou Miltiade," T. de Morembert — EEC 2², 750, D. M. Scholer — EECh 1, 560, V. Zangara — LThK 7, 421–22, J. A. Fischer — LThK 7³, 261–62, M.-B. v. Stritzky — C. Pietri, *Roma christiana* (Rome, 1976), 160–67

XL. APOLLONIUS

POLLONIUS,[1] a man of great eloquence, wrote against Montanus, Prisca, and Maximilla, a distinguished lengthy work,[2] in which he narrates that Montanus and his insane prophetesses died by hanging themselves,[3] and many other details among which he refers to Prisca and Maximilla as follows:[4]

2. "If they say that they have not accepted gifts, let them confess that those are not prophets who accepted gifts, and I will prove with a thousand proofs that they have. But it is necessary to test a prophet by other fruits. Tell me, does a prophet dye her hair? Does a prophet pencil her eyebrows in black? Does a prophet adorn herself with fine clothes and ornaments? Does a prophet play at the gaming tables and dice? Does she lend money at usury? Let them answer whether it is lawful for these things to be done or not, and it will be my task to prove that they have done these things."

3. He says in the same book that he wrote his book in the fortieth year after the Cataphrygian, κατὰ Φρύγας, heresy[5] had its beginning.

4. Tertullian, having published six books against the church with the title, De ἐκστάσει, On Ecstasy,[6] composed a seventh specifically, Against Apollonius, in which he sought to defend everything which Apollonius had refuted.

5. Apollonius lived in the reign of the emperors Commodus and Severus.

NOTES

1. Eus., h.e. 5.18.1, quoted in Q 2, 317–18.

2. CPG 1328: "Adversus Cataphrygas (apud Euseb., H.E., V,18,2, 3, 4, 5, 6–10, 11)."

3. h.e. 5.18.12: according to Apollonius, "[Montanus] plotted his fictitious prophecy."

4. h.e. 5.18.11.

5. κατὰ Φρύγας: a circumlocution for "a heresy of the Phryges"; see h.e. 5.16.1 and 6.20.3; Epiph., Pan. 49.1 (trans. Amidon, 173); John Dam., Haer. 87; cf. EECh 1, 150, art., "Cataphrygians," E. Peretto.

6. On Ecstasy: now lost; doubtless a work of Tertullian's Montanist period; cf. Q 2, 317; D. Powell, "Tertullianists and Cataphrygians," VigChr 29 (1975): 33–54.

REFERENCES

Q 2, 317–18 — DHGE 3, 1013–14 — EECh 1², 60, F. Scorza Barcellona — LThK 1³, 831, M. Stark — R. E. Heine, The Montanist Oracles and Testimonia, PatMS 14, 154–55

XLI. SERAPION THE BISHOP

ERAPION,[1] ORDAINED BISHOP of Antioch in the eleventh year of the emperor Commodus, wrote a letter to Caricus and Pontius concerning the heresy of Montanus, to which he added the following:[2]

2. "In order that you may know that the folly of this false teaching, that is, of the new prophecy, is abominated by the whole world, I send you the letter of the most blessed Apollinaris, who was bishop of Hierapolis in Asia."[3]

3. He also composed a work directed *To Domnus*, who had lapsed into Judaism[4] in the time of persecution,

and another book, *On the so-called Gospel attributed to Peter*, to the church of Rhossos in Cilicia, which had deviated to heresy as a result of reading it.[5]

4. Certain other short letters of his are read pertaining to the ascetical life.[6]

NOTES

1. Eus., *h.e.* 5.19.1: "bishop after Maximinius."

2. *h.e.* 5.19.2–4, abbreviated here. See R. E. Heine, *The Montanist Oracles and Testimonia*, PatMS 14, 154–55.

3. Apollinaris: *h.e.* 5.19.1; cf. *DVI* 26.

4. *Ad Domnum*: *h.e.* 6.12.1: Jerome has translated as *ad Iudaeos* Eusebius's words, εἰς τὴν Ἰουδαίκην ἐθελοθρῃσκείαν (cf. Col 2.23).

5. See *h.e.* 6.12.2–6, where we get a long excerpt. On *Gospel of Peter*, cf. Q 1, 114; E. Junod, "Eusèbe de Césarée, Serapion d'Antioche et l'Évangile de Pierre. D'un Evangile à un Pseudepigraphe," *RSLR* 24 (1988): 3–16. Marcianus was the leader of a Docetist sect in Rhossos: cf. *h.e.* 6.12.5, not quoted in *DVI*.

6. Based on *h.e.* 6.12.1, which reads: "Now it is likely that other memoirs also, the fruit of Serapion's literary studies (τῆς περὶ λόγου ἀσκήσεως) are preserved by other persons (παρ' ἑτέροις)."

REFERENCES

Q 1, 114, 283–84 — *TLG* 1670 — CPG 1333–34 — Cath 13, 1126–27, G. Mathon — DSp 14, 643–52, D. Dufrasne — EECh 2, 768, A. Hamman — LThK 9, 682, E. Hammerschmidt — NCE 13, 105–6, J. Quasten — NCE

14, 100, art., "Thmuis," M. C. McCarthy — E. Junod, "Observations sur la regulation de la foi dans l'église des IIe et IIIe siècles," *Le Supplément* 133 (1980): 195–213

XLII. APOLLONIUS THE SENATOR, ANOTHER ONE

POLLONIUS,[1] A SENATOR of the city of Rome in the reign of the emperor Commodus, denounced as a Christian by a slave, having been granted his request to render an account of his faith, composed a remarkable work which he read in the Senate.[2]

2. Nevertheless, because of a decree in the senate, he was beheaded as a follower of Christ, on the basis of an old law which was in vogue among them that Christians who had once appeared before them for judgment could not be let off unless they abjured their faith.[3]

NOTES

1. Eus., *h.e.* 5.21.
2. *h.e.* 5.21.4.
3. For the *Acta* of his trial, see T. D. Barnes, *JRS* 58 (1968): 46–48; *idem, Tertullian. A Historical and Literary Study* (1971; reissued with corr. and postscript, Oxford, 1985), 6–7; V. Saxer, *"Martyrium Apollonii Romani*: analyse structurelle et problèmes d'authenticité," *RPAA* 55/56 (1982–84): 265–98; R. Freudenberger, "Die Überlieferung vom Martyrium des römischen Christen Apollonius," *ZNW* 60 (1969): 111–30.

REFERENCES

LThK 1³, 831, T. Baumeister — DHGE 3, 1012–13, J. Kirsch

XLIII. THEOPHILUS, ANOTHER BISHOP

HEOPHILUS, BISHOP of Caesarea in Palestine,[1] formerly called the Tower of Strato,[2] in the reign of the emperor Severus,[3] in conjunction with the other bishops wrote a very helpful synodal letter, *Against Those who Celebrate the Pasch with the Jews on the Fourteenth Day of the Full Moon.*[4]

NOTES

1. Eus., *h.e.* 5.22.1.
2. *Turris Stratonis: h.e.* 2.10.3, quoting Josephus, *Ant.* 19, Loeb Classical Library, Vol. 9 of Josephus, 343–51.
3. Severus: emperor, 193–211.
4. "Synodal Letter": *h.e.* 5.23.3; 5.25.1. Elsewhere (*Adv. Rufinum* 3.16) Jerome tells us: "Within the past two years or so, I have translated two of his letters, one a Synodal, the other a Paschal letter against Origen and his disciples, and other letters against Apollinaris and that same Origen himself," trans. J. N. Hritzu, FOTC 53, 182; see also P. Nautin, *Lettres et écrivains chrétiens des IIe et IIIe siècles* (Paris, 1961), 85–89.

REFERENCES

TLG 1050 — CPG 1340 — EECh 2, 831, G. Ladocsi — LThK 10, 90, K. Baus

XLIV. BACCHYLUS THE BISHOP

ACCHYLUS, BISHOP of Corinth,[1] distinguished during the reign of the same Severus, wrote an elegant synodal treatise, *On the Pasch,*[2] in the name of all the other bishops of Achaia.

NOTES

1. Eus., *h.e.* 5.22; 5.23.4.
2. R. Cantalamessa, *Easter in the Early Church,* 34.

REFERENCES

DHGE 6, 52 — EECh 1, 106, E. Prinzivalli — P. Nautin, *Lettres*, 85–89

XLV. POLYCRATES THE BISHOP

POLYCRATES, BISHOP of Ephesus,[1] along with the other bishops of Asia Minor, who according to ancient usage celebrate the Pasch as do the Jews on the fourteenth of the moon,[2] wrote a synodal letter to Victor, bishop of Rome, in which he declared that he followed the authority of the apostle John and of the ancients.[3] From this we have made these few excerpts:[4]

2. "We therefore keep the precise day, neither adding nor taking away anything. For in Asia great luminaries have fallen asleep and they will rise on the day when the Lord will come in his majesty from the heavens and shall raise up all the saints. I speak of Philip, one of the twelve apostles, who has fallen asleep at Hierapolis, and two of his daughters who grew old as virgins, and another daughter of his who was full of the Holy Spirit and has come to rest at Ephesus.

3. "Moreover, there is also John who reclined on the Lord's breast and was his priest, wearing the golden breastplate, a martyr and master, who has fallen asleep in Ephesus. And Polycarp, bishop and martyr, sleeps in Smyrna. Thraseas also, bishop and martyr of Eumenia, rests in the same Smyrna.

4. "And must I recall Sagaris, bishop and martyr, who sleeps at Laodicea, and Papirius, the blessed, and Melito, a eunuch in the Holy Spirit, who, serving the Lord unceasingly, was laid to rest in Sardis and awaits the resurrection in his coming.

5. "All these celebrated the day of the Pasch on the fourteenth day of the moon according to the gospel tradition, in no way swerving, but always following the rule of the church. And I also, Polycrates, the least of you all, according to the teaching of my kinsmen and some of whom I have followed—for seven of my family were bishops and I am the eighth—have celebrated

the Pasch always when the Jewish people have unleavened bread.

6. "Therefore, brethren, I who have lived sixty-five years of my life in the Lord and have been taught by many brethren from all over the world, having studied all of Scripture, will not fear those who threaten us. For my predecessors have said, 'It is better to obey God rather than men.'"[5]

7. Moreover, I have put down these things that I might demonstrate the talent and authority of the man from a small work. He flourished in the times of the emperor Severus,[6] in the same period that Narcissus was in Jerusalem.

NOTES

1. Eus., *h.e.* 3.31.2–3.
2. *h.e.* 5.23.1.
3. *h.e.* 5.24.1.
4. *h.e.* 5.24.2–8; Cantalamessa, *Easter*, 34–35; see also *h.e.* 3.31.2–3.
5. Acts 5.29.
6. *h.e.* 5.22.

REFERENCES

Q 2, 209 — *TLG* 1626 — CPG 1, 1338 — Cath 11, 598–99, P.-Th. Camelot — EEC 2², 935, E. Ferguson — EECh 2, 701, A. Di Berardino — LThK 8, 598, J. Quasten — Nautin, *Lettres*, 65–104

XLVI. HERACLITUS

N THE REIGN of Commodus and Severus,[1] Heraclitus[2] composed *Commentaries on the Apostle [Paul]*.[3]

NOTES

1. Commodus, 180–192; Septimius Severus, 193–211.
2. See Eus., *h.e.* 5.27, which provides the entire material for the next 5 entries.
3. Not extant; "on the Apostle" invariably means Paul's epistles, not Acts.

REFERENCES

Cath 5, 630 — DHGE 23, 1343, R. Aubert — EECh 1, 375, G. Ladocsi — LThK 5, 238, J. Kraus — LThK 4³, 1430, M. Stark

XLVII. MAXIMUS

N THE REIGN of the same emperors,[1] Maximus,[2] in a distinguished volume, aired a famous question: "What is the origin of evil and was matter made by God?"[3]

NOTES

1. Commodus, 180–192; Septimius Severus, 193–211.
2. Eus., *h.e.* 5.27; work no longer extant.
3. The reference should be to Methodius, *De libero arbitrio;* cf. L. G. Patterson, *Methodius of Olympus: Divine Sovereignty, Human Freedom, and Life in Christ* (Washington, D.C.: The Catholic University of America Press, 1997), 16 and 13 n. 17 ("*De libero arbitrio* . . . may originally have been titled *Maximus: On God, Matter and Free-Will*"). Eusebius quotes it in *Praep. evang.* 7.22, GCS, *Eusebius Werke* 8, 1, 405. See T. D. Barnes, "Methodius, Maximus and Valentinus," *JThS,* n.s., 37 (1979): 353–68.

REFERENCES

EECh 1, 546, C. Gianotto

XLVIII. CANDIDUS

N THE REIGN of the above-mentioned emperors,[1] Candidus[2] published very fine treatises *On the Hexaemeron.*[3]

NOTES

1. Commodus, 180–192; Septimius Severus, 193–211.

2. Eus., *h.e.* 5.27.

3. No longer extant. Eusebius says that he has read it; nothing further is known of the author.

REFERENCES

DHGE 11, 730, G. Bardy

XLIX. APION

N THE REIGN of the emperor Severus,[1] Apion[2] likewise composed a treatise *On the Hexaemeron.*[3]

NOTES

1. Septimius Severus, 193–211.

2. Eus., *h.e.* 5.27.

3. No longer extant.

REFERENCES

DHGE 3, 954–55 — EECh 1, 55, E. Prinzivalli

L. SEXTUS

N THE REIGN of the emperor Severus,[1] Sextus[2] wrote a volume, *On the Resurrection.*[3]

NOTES

1. Septimius Severus, 193–211.

2. Eus., *h.e.* 5.27.

3. No longer extant.

REFERENCES

Q 1, 284 — EECh 2, 775, E. Prinzivalli — LThK 9, 708, J. Kraus

LI. ARABIANUS

NDER THE SAME EMPEROR, Arabianus[1] published certain works concerned with Christian doctrine.

NOTES

1. Eus., *h.e.* 5.27, where he is linked with Sextus (*supra*).

REFERENCES

DHGE 3, 1157–58, R. Aigrain

LII. JUDAS

UDAS[1] DISCOURSED at great length *On the Seventy Weeks in Daniel*[2] and set out a χρονογραφίαν, a *Chronology,*[3] of past ages down to the tenth year of the reign of Severus.[4]

2. In this he was guilty of error because he said that the coming of Anti-Christ would occur in his own time.[5] But this was because the intensity of the persecutions[6] made the threat of the end of the world seem imminent.

NOTES

1. Eus., *h.e.* 6.7, our total information.

2. Dn 9.24–27. For Jerome's commentary on 9.24, cf. CCL 75A, 865–89. See EEC 1, 317–19, art., "Daniel," C. T. McCollough.

3. χρονογραφίαν: in *h.e.* 6.6, immediately preceding 6.7, Eusebius tells of

a similar χρονογραφία in Clement of Alexandria [*Strom.* 1.21]. See Courcelle, *LLW*, 99 n. 62.

4. Septimius Severus reigned, 193–211.

5. For the prevalence of such belief see *Testi Sull'Anticristo Secolo 3*, ed. F.
Shaffoni, Biblioteca Patristica (Florence, 1992).

6. A.D. 202, beginning of the fifth persecution against the Christians.

LIII. TERTULLIAN THE PRESBYTER

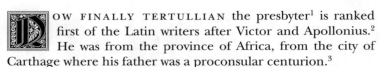 OW FINALLY TERTULLIAN the presbyter[1] is ranked
first of the Latin writers after Victor and Apollonius.[2]
He was from the province of Africa, from the city of
Carthage where his father was a proconsular centurion.[3]

2. A man of impetuous temperament, he was in his prime in
the reign of the emperor Severus and Antoninus Caracalla,[4]
and he wrote many works which I need not name[5] since they are
very widely known.

3. At Concordia, a town in Italy, I saw an old man named
Paul, who said that, when he was still a very young man, he had
seen in Rome a very old man who had been secretary of blessed
Cyprian and had reported to him that Cyprian was accustomed
never to pass a day without reading Tertullian and would frequently say to him, "Hand me the master," meaning, of course,
Tertullian.[6]

4. This one was a presbyter of the church until his middle
years, but later, because of the envy and reproaches of the clerics of the Roman church,[7] he had lapsed into Montanism, and
he makes mention of the new prophecy[8] in many books.

5. In particular, he composed against the church the works

On Modesty;[9]
On Persecution;[10]
On Fasting;[11]
On Monogamy;[12]

six books *On Ecstasy* and a seventh [added] which he composed *Against Apollonius.*[13]

He is said to have lived to a very old age and to have composed many works which are not extant.[14]

NOTES

1. See Eus., *Chron.*, A.D. 208, ed. Helm, 212. Studies of Tertullian include the following: T. D. Barnes, *Tertullian;* R. Braun, "Un nouveau Tertullien. Problèmes de biographie et chronologie," *REL* 50 (1972): 67–84 (on 1970 edition of Barnes's aforementioned book); D. Rankin, *Tertullian and the Church* (Cambridge, 1995), an attempted rehabilitation; E. Osborn, *Tertullian, First Theologian of the West* (Cambridge, 1997); T. D. Barnes, "Tertullian the Antiquarian," StudPat 14, 3 [= TU 117 (1976), 3–20]; R. D. Sider, "Approaches to Tertullian: A Study of Recent Scholarship," *SecCent* 2 (1982): 228–60. See also P. Petitmengin, "Saint Jérôme et Tertullien," in Y. M. Duval, ed., *Jérôme entre l'Occident et l'Orient. XVIe centenaire du départ de saint Jérôme de Rome et son installation à Bethléem* (Paris, 1988), 43–59.

2. Victor: cf. *DVI* 34. Q 1, 279, expresses doubts about Victor being the first to use Latin. For Apollonius cf. *DVI* 40.

3. *patre centurione proconsulari:* see *Chron.*, A.D. 218, ed. Helm, 212.

4. Septimius Severus reigned 193–211; Caracalla, 211–17; *multaque scripsit volumina:* he counseled Eustochium (*ep.* 22.22, CSEL 54, 174–75), "Lege Tertulliani ad amicum philosophum et de virginitate alios libellos." And in *ep.* 70.5 (CSEL 54, 707), "To the orator, Magnus": "Quid Tertulliano eruditius, quid acutius? Apologeticus eius et contra gentes libri cunctam saeculi continent disciplinam," therein extolling his ἐγκύκλιος παιδεία. He is more restrained in writing to Paulinus of Nola (*ep.* 58.10, CSEL 54, 539): "Tertullianus creber est in sententiis, sed difficilis in loquendo."

5. *Praetermittimus:* this kind of *praeteritio* is particularly irritating in a bibliographer (cf. Cyprian, *DVI* 67.2). See Appendix 2.

6. Concordia, birthplace of Rufinus, born c. 345, and of Jerome, a town near Aquileia and Stridon. For the influence of Tertullian on Cyprian, cf. C. B. Daly, *Tertullian the Puritan and His Influence. An Essay in Historical Theology* (Dublin, 1993). On the *Da magistrum* episode Jerome is more restrained in *ep.* 84.2: "The blessed Cyprian takes Tertullian for his master, as his writings prove; yet, delighted as he is with the ability of this learned and zealous writer, he does not join him in following Montanus and Maximilla" (NPNF 6, 176).

7. A retroactive jibe, motivated perhaps by Jerome's own maltreatment by the Roman clergy.

8. On Tertullian's Montanism cf. R. D. Sider, "Approaches to Tertullian," *SecCent* 2 (1982): 233–38; R. Braun, "Tertullien et le montanisme. Église institi et église spirituelle," *RSLR* 21 (1985): 245–57; D. Powell, "Tertullianistae and Cataphrygians," *VigChr* 29 (1975): 33–54; A. Quacquarelli, "L'antimonarchianesimo di Tertulliano e il su presunto montanismo," *VetChr* 10 (1973): 5–45. On *nova prophetia*, cf. V. C. de Clerq, "The Expectation of the Second Coming of Christ in Tertullian," StudPat 11, 2 (= TU 108 [Berlin, 1972]): 146–51; P. C. Atkinson, *A Study of the Development of*

Tertullian's Use and Interpretation of Scripture, with Special Reference to his Involvement in the New Prophecy (Ph.D. diss., Hull University, 1976), not seen by the translator.

9. CPL 30; CCL 2, 1279–1330; C. Micaelli and C. Munier, SC 394–395 (1993); *Tertullian. Treatises on Penance: "On Penitence" and "On Purity"*, trans. W. P. Le Saint, ACW 28 (1959).

10. CPL 25; CCL 2, 1133–55; ANF 4, 116–26.

11. CPL 29; CCL 2, 1255–77; CSEL 20, 274–97; ANF 4, 102–15.

12. CPL 28; CCL 2, 1227–53; *Tertullian: Treatises on Marriage and Remarriage* (including *To his Wife, An Exhortation to Chastity, Monogamy*), trans. W. P. Le Saint, ACW 13 (1951); P. A. Gramaglia, *Il matrimonio nel cristianesimo preniceno. Ad uxorem, De exhortatione castitatis, De monogamia di Tertulliano* (Rome, 1988); R. Uglione, "L'Antico Testamento negli scritti Tertullianei sulle seconde nozze," *AugR* 22 (1982): 165–78; P. Mattei, "Tertullien, *De Monogamia.* Critique textuelle et contenu doctrinale," *RSLR* 22 (1986): 68–88; P. Mattei, "Le divorce chez Tertullien. Examen de la question à la lumière des développements que le *De Monogamia* consacre à ce subjet," *RSR* 60 (1986): 207–34; H. J. Vogt, "Die Ehe ein Sakrament? Hinweise für eine Antwort aus der frühen Kirche," *ThQ* 168 (1988): 16–23; C. Micaelli, "L'influsso di Tertulliano su Girolamo: le opere sul matrimonio e le secondo nozze," *AugR* 19 (1979): 415–29.

13. Cf. Jerome, *DVI* 24.3 and 40.4. For *De extasi*, "Concerning Ecstasy," see CPL 31b; CCL 2, 1334–35. See *Adv. Apelleiacos*, CPL 31a and CCL 2, 1333–34; also J. P. Mahé, "Le traité perdu de Tertullien *Adversus Apelleiacos* et le chronologie de sa triade anti-gnostique," *REAug* 16 (1970): 3–24.

14. Jerome also knows *Scorpiace;* see *Against Vigilantius*, NPNF 6, ser. 2, 420.

REFERENCES

Q 2, 246–340 — Dr, 124–30 — CPL 1–36 — Cath 14, 931–36, C. Munier — DSp 15, 271–95, C. Munier — EEC 2², 1107–9, R. D. Sider — EECh 2, 818–20, P. Siniscalco — LThK 9, 1370–74, B. Kötting — NCE 13, 1019–22, W. LeSaint — Dihle, *Greek and Latin*, 350–59 — Gamble, *Books*, 118–21 — *Gestalten* 1, 97–120, H. von Campenhausen — R. E. Heine, *The Montanist Oracles and Testimonia*, PatMS 14, 154–55

For annual bibliographical surveys of Tertullian, cf. *REAug* 25 (1979): 291–305; also for bibliography cf. R. Braun, J.-C. Fredouille, and P. Petitmengin, "Bibliographia Chronica Tertullianea," in *Chronica Tertullianea* (1975), 1978 on. See also R. W. Sider, *SecCent* 40 (1994): 473–99.

Opera omnia: A. Reifferscheid, G. Wissowa, A. Kroymann, H. Hoppe, V. Bulhart, Ph. Borleffs = CSEL 20, 47, 69, 70, 76 (1890–1957); CCL 1–2 (1954).

More recent editions of individual works include the following:

Ad uxorem: C. Munier, SC 273 (1980);

Adversus Marcionem: R. Braun, SC 365, 368 (1990–91);

Adversus Valentinianos: J.-C. Fredouille, SC 280–281 (1980–81);

De anima: J. H. Waszink (Amsterdam, 1947);

De baptismo: R. F. Refoulé and M. Drouzy, SC 35 (1952);

De carne Christi: J.-P. Mahé, SC 216–217 (1975);

De cultu feminarum: M. Turcan, SC 173 (1971);

De exhortatione castitatis: C. Moreschini and J.-C. Fredouille, SC 319 (1985);

De idololatria: J. H. Waszink and J. C. M. van Winden, *VigChr* Supp. 1 (1987);

De monogamia: P. Mattei, SC 343 (1988).

De paenitentia: C. Munier, SC 316 (1984);

De patientia: J.-C. Fredouille, SC 310 (1984);

De spectaculis: M. Turcan, SC 332 (1986); K.-W. Weber (Stuttgart, 1988);

De virginibus velandis: C. Stücklin, EHS.T 26 (1974); E. Schulz-Flügel and P. Mattei, SC 424 (Paris, 1997).

LIV. ORIGEN, SURNAMED ADAMANTIUS, THE PRESBYTER

RIGEN, SURNAMED ADAMANTIUS,[1] as a result of a persecution raised against the Christians in the tenth year of Severus Pertinax,[2] in which his father Leonidas[3] received the crown of martyrdom for Christ, was left at the age of about seventeen, with his six brothers and widowed mother, in poverty, for their property had been confiscated[4] because of confessing Christ.

2. When only eighteen years old, he undertook the work of conducting the κατηχήσεων, *Catecheses*,[5] in the scattered church of Alexandria.[6] Later, appointed by Demetrius, bishop of this city, as successor to the presbyter Clement,[7] he flourished for many years.

3. When he had already reached middle life, on account of the churches of Achaia, which were torn with many heresies, he undertook a journey to Athens,[8] by way of Palestine,[9] authorized by an ecclesiastical letter, and having been ordained pres-

byter by Theoctistus and Alexander, bishops of Caesarea and Jerusalem,[10] he offended Demetrius, who was so wildly enraged at him that he wrote everywhere to injure his reputation.[11]

4. It is known that before he went to Caesarea, he had been at Rome, under bishop Zephyrinus.[12] Immediately on his return to Alexandria he made Heraclas the presbyter, who continued to wear his philosopher's garb, his assistant in κατηχήσεων, the school for catechetes. Heraclas became bishop of the church of Alexandria after Demetrius.[13]

5. How great Origen's glory was is apparent from the fact that Firmilianus, bishop of Caesarea, with all the Cappadocian bishops,[14] sought a visit from him, and entertained him for a long while. Sometime afterwards, going to Palestine to visit the holy places, he came to Caesarea and was instructed at length by Origen in the Holy Scriptures.[15] But it is also the case that he went to Antioch at the request of Mammaea, mother of the emperor Alexander,[16] and a woman religiously disposed, and was there held in greatest honor, and he sent letters to the emperor Philip, who was the first among the Roman rulers to become a Christian,[17] and to his mother, letters which are still extant.

6. Who does not also know that he was so assiduous in the study of the Holy Scriptures that contrary to the spirit of his time and of his people, he learned the Hebrew language,[18] and, taking the Septuagint[19] translation, he gathered in a single work the other translations also, namely, that of Aquila, the proselyte of Pontus, and Theodotian the Ebionite, and Symmachus,[20] an adherent of the same sect who also wrote commentaries κατὰ Ματθαῖον, on the *Gospel according to Matthew*,[21] from which he tried to establish his doctrine.

7. And besides these, he thought out with great diligence a fifth, sixth, and seventh[22] translation, which we also have from his library, and he compared [them] with the other editions.

8. And since I have given a list of his works, in the volume of letters which I have written to Paula,[23] in a letter which I wrote comparing his to the works of Varro, I pass this by now, not failing, however, to make mention of his immortal genius,[24] that he

understood dialectics,[25] as well as geometry, arithmetic, music, grammar, and rhetoric,[26] and taught all the schools of philosophers,[27] in such wise that he had also diligent students in secular literature, and lectured to them daily,[28] and the crowds which flocked to him were marvelous. These he received in the hope that through the instrumentality of this secular literature, he might establish them in the faith of Christ.[29]

9. It is unnecessary to speak of the cruelty of the persecution which was raised against the Christians under Decius,[30] who was mad against the religion of Philip, whom he had slain, the persecution in which Fabianus, bishop of the Roman church,[31] perished at Rome, and Alexander and Babylas,[32] pontiffs of the churches of Jerusalem and Antioch, were imprisoned for their confession of Christ.

10. If any one wishes to know what was done in regard to the position of Origen, he can clearly learn, first, indeed, from his own epistles,[33] which, after the persecution, were sent to different ones, and secondly, from the sixth book of the *Church History* of Eusebius of Caesarea,[34] and from his six volumes on behalf of the same Origen.[35]

11. He lived until the time of Gallus and Volusianus,[36] that is, until his sixty-ninth year, and died[37] at Tyre, in which city he also was buried.

NOTES

1. Eus., *h.e.* 6.14.10. On "Adamantinos" see *OLD, s.v.*, as well as Liddell, Scott, Jones, and *PGL, s.v.* ἀδαμάντινος; M. Lacore, "L'Homme d'acier—ἀδαμάντινος ἀνήρ de l'Anonyme de Jamblique à Platon," *RÉG* 110, no. 2 (1997): 399–419.

2. *h.e.* 6.2.2.

3. *h.e.* 6.1.1; 6.2.12.

4. *h.e.* 6.2.13.

5. *h.e.* 6.3.3; 6.3.8.

6. *h.e.* 6.3.1; on the persecution in 206, cf. Barnes, *C. and E.*, 83, 327 nn. 18–19.

7. *h.e.* 6.6.1; 6.8.6.

8. *h.e.* 6.23.4; 6.32.2. For Origen in Athens cf. Barnes, *C. and E.*, 84, and P. Nautin, *Origène: sa vie et son œuvre* (Paris: Beauchesne, 1977) 428.

9. *h.e.* 6.23.4.

10. *h.e.* 6.23.4; J. A. McGuckin, "Caesarea Maritima as Origen knew it," *Origeniana Quinta* (1992), 3–25.

11. *h.e.* 6.8.4–5; cf. Barnes, *C. and E.*, 84.

12. *h.e.* 6.14.10.

13. *h.e.* 6.15.1; 6.19.12; 6.26.

14. On Firmilian see *h.e.* 7.14.1; on Origen in Caesarea, A. Knauber, "Das Anliegen der Schule des Origenes zu Cäserea," *MThZ* 19 (1968): 182–203.

15. *h.e.* 6.27.

16. *h.e.* 6.21.3.

17. *h.e.* 6.34; 6.36.3; 6.39.1. On Philip's "Christianity," cf. Barnes, *C. and E.*, 138, and Nautin, *Origène*, 439.

18. *h.e.* 6.16.1. Jerome tells us about his own struggles with learning Hebrew in *epp.* 18.2 and 125.12. Obviously Origen becomes a role-model in this for Jerome; cf. I. Opelt, "Origene visto da san Girolamo," *AugR* 26 (1985): 217–22; M. Vesey, "Jerome's Origen: The Making of a Christian Literary *Persona*," StudPat 28 (1993): 135–45.

19. *h.e.* 6.16.1; P. Lamarche, "La Septante," in *Le monde grec et la Bible*, ed. C. Mondésert, 19–35; E. Ulrich, "Origen's Old Testament Text: the Transmission of the Septuagint to the Third Century C.E.," in *Origen of Alexandria: his World and his Legacy*, ed. C. Kannengiesser and W. L. Petersen (Univ. of Notre Dame Press, 1988), 3–33, esp. 20–33; P. Blowers, "Origen, the Rabbis, and the Bible," *op. cit.*, 96–116.

20. Jerome, *Adv. Rufinum* 2.32, quoting from his own *Praefatio in librum Isaiae:* "I make this one request of my fastidious readers: just as the Greeks read, along with the Septuagint translators, Aquila, and Symmachus, and Theodotion, either because of their zeal for personal information, or that they might better understand the Septuagint, through a comparison of these editions, they, too, in like manner, should deem it an honor to have at least one translator in addition to the earlier ones" (trans. Hritzu, FOTC 53, 157). Aquila was a Jewish proselyte in the reign of Hadrian; cf. Jerome's *ep.* 32: "for some time past I have been comparing Aquila's version of the Old Testament with the scrolls of the Hebrew, to see if from hatred to Christ the synagogue has changed the text; and—to speak frankly to a friend—I have found several variations which confirm our faith" (NPNF 6, 46). On Symmachus cf. *h.e.* 6.17; on Theodotion, *h.e.* 5.8.10, quoting Irenaeus, *Adv. haer.* 3.21.1.

21. *h.e.* 6.17.3–4.

22. *h.e.* 6.16.3–4.

23. Eusebius had a similar thought and a similar solution; see *h.e.* 6.32.3. Cf. Courcelle, *LLW*, 103. The list is in Jerome, *ep.* 33.4.1–20 [*ad Paulam*], written c. 385; on this cf. Appendix 1. See also *h.e.* 6.36.3 and Gamble, *Books*, 156.

24. Courcelle, *LLW*, 100–113, after a balanced view of Jerome's readings in Origen, concludes: "If, therefore, the bulk of Jerome's knowledge of the Fathers of the first two centuries is slight, his debt to Origen on the other hand is very great."

25. *h.e.* 6.19.1–2, 7–8, 11–12.
26. *h.e.* 6.18.3.
27. *h.e.* 6.18.2–4. Surprisingly Jerome does not quote *h.e.* 6.19.3–7 on Porphyry's encounter with Origen. Cf. Courcelle, *LLW*, 127.
28. *h.e.* 6.18.3. Cf. M. Fédou, "L'attitude d'Origène face aux philosophies et religions païennes," *StMiss* 42 (1993): 123–42.
29. *h.e.* 6.3.13.
30. *h.e.* 6.39.1.
31. *h.e.* 6.39.1. On Fabian cf. LThK 3³, 1146–47, G. Schwaiger.
32. *h.e.* 6.39.2–4.
33. *h.e.* 6.2.1; 6.36.3.
34. On "the sixth book of the *Church History*," see Barnes, *C. and E.*, 82–86, 94–101.
35. *h.e.* 6.33.4; cf. Q 2, 145–46; Q 3, 340.
36. *h.e.* 7.1.1. See *Chron.*, A.D. 252, ed. Helm, 218, for Trebonius Gallus (251–253) and his son Volusianus (253).
37. *h.e.* 7.1.1.

REFERENCES

Q 2, 37–101 — Dr, 111–20 — CPG 1410–1525 — Cath 10, 243–56, H. Crouzel — DSp 11, 933–61, H. Crouzel — EEC 2², 835–37, R. J. Daly — EECh 2, 619–23, H. Crouzel — LThK 7, 1230–35, H. Crouzel — LThK 7³, 1131–35, H. J. Vogt — NCE 10, 767–74, H. Crouzel — TRE 25, 397–420, R. Williams — Dihle, *Greek and Latin*, 335–40 — *Gestalten* 1, 134–57, H. Chadwick

See also the following:

H. Crouzel, *Bibliographie critique d'Origène* = IP 8 (1971);

idem, *Bibliographie critique d'Origène, Supplément I* = IP 8A (1982), and *Supplément II* = IP 8B (1996);

idem, "The Literature on Origen 1970–1988," *TS* 49 (1988): 499–516;

idem, "Chronique origènienne," *BLE* 89 (1988): 138–45; 90 (1989): 135–40; 91 (1990): 221–26; 92 (1991): 123–32;

H. G. Hödl, BBKL 6 (1993): 1255–71;

L. Lies, "Zum derzeitigen Stand der Origenesforschung," *ZKTh* 115 (1993): 37–62, 145–71.

LV. AMMONIUS

MMONIUS,[1] a cultured man and very well educated
in philosophy, was famous at Alexandria in the same
period.[2]

2. Among many illustrious products of his talent he composed a work *On the Accord of Moses and Jesus*[3] and he also
worked out *Evangelical Canons*[4] which Eusebius of Caesarea[5] later followed.

3. Porphyry falsely accused him of turning away from Christianity to paganism,[6] although it is well established that he remained a Christian to the end of his life.

NOTES

1. Eus., *h.e.* 6.19.6.

2. *h.e.* 6.19.7. Cf. M. Edwards, "Ammonius, Teacher of Origen," *JEH* 44
(1993): 169–81; E. Elorduy, "Ammonio escriturista," *EBib* 16 (1957):
187–217; J. Reuss, "Der Presbyter Ammonius von Alexandrien und sein
Kommentar zum Joannes-Evangelium," *Bibl* 44 (1963): 159–70.

3. *h.e.* 6.19.10.

4. Cf. CPG 3465 (*s.v.*, "Eusebius Caesariensis") and Q 3, 335; P. H.
Gwilliam, "The Ammonian Sections, Eusebian Canons and Harmonizing
Tables in the Syriac Tetraevangelium," Studia Biblica et Ecclesiastica 2 (Ox-
ford, 1890): 241–71; W. Thiele, "Beobachtungen zu den eusebianischen
Sektionen und Canones der Evangelien," *ZNW* 72 (1981): 100–111; T. D.
Barnes, *C. and E.*, 121–22 and 365 n. 137.

5. H. K. McArthur, "The Eusebian Sections and Canons," *CBQ* 27
(1965): 250–56; J. E. Bruns, "The agreement of Moses and Jesus in the
Demonstratio Evangelica of Eusebius," *VigChr* 31 (1977): 117–25.

6. Eusebius in *h.e.* 6.19.2–9 mistook him for Ammonius Saccas. For Porphyry's two-fold charge against Ammonius and Origen of switching sides,
cf. *h.e.* 6.19.7: πρὸς τὴν κατὰ νόμους πολιτείαν μετεβάλετο; T. D. Barnes, *C.
and E.*, 177–78.

REFERENCES

Q 2, 101 — CPG, 3465 — EECh 1, 31–32, art., "Ammonius Saccas," S. Lilla — LThK 1³, 532, T. Baumeister — RAC 6, 1063, J. Moreau

LVI. AMBROSE THE DEACON

A MBROSE,[1] at first a follower of Marcion, and then converted by Origen,[2] became a deacon of the church and attained great fame through his profession of faith in the Lord. The work of Origen, *On Martyrdom*, was dedicated to him, and to the priest, Protheochtistus,[3] and through the zeal, financial support, and importunity of Ambrose, Origen was able to publish innumerable works.[4]

2. And he himself was a noble man of no inconsiderable talent, as his letters to Origen indicate.[5]

3. He died in the year prior to Origen's death[6] and in this regard he is faulted by many[7] because, dying a rich man, he made no mention in his will of his old, impecunious friend.

NOTES

1. Eus., *h.e.* 6.23.1–2. See also *DVI* 61.3.

2. Cf. *h.e.* 6.18.1, which makes Ambrose a follower of Valentinus.

3. Cf. *h.e.* 6.28, where the name is Protoctetus. See translation of J. J. O'Meara, ACW 19 (1954), 10 and 141. Other works dedicated to him included *Comm. on John, On the Psalms, On Prayer,* and *Contra Celsum.*

4. Cf. *DVI* 61.3 = Eus., *h.e.* 6.23.1–2. Here Eusebius is more explicit: "as [Origen] dictated there were ready at hand more than seven shorthand-writers [ταχυγράφοι], who relieved each other at fixed times, and as many copyists [βιβλιογράφοι], as well as girls skilled in penmanship [κόραις ἐπὶ τὸ καλλιγραφεῖν ἠσκημέναις]; for all of whom Ambrose supplied without stint the necessary means" (trans. J. E. L. Oulton, Loeb Classical Library, Vol. 2 of Eusebius [London and Cambridge, Mass., 1932; reprint, 1980]), 69. See P. Nautin, *Origène,* 57–60. The works of Origen to which Jerome here alludes included *Contra Celsum.*

5. On collections of Origen's letters, cf. Courcelle, *LLW,* 109 and n. 146.

6. The death of Ambrose occurred under Decius in 251 or 252 A.D.; cf. DHGE 2, 1089.

7. Cf. DHGE 2, 1089, quoting Tillemont in Ambrose's defense: "cette prétendue negligence doit être reportée à l'amour qu'Origène avait pour la pauvreté."

REFERENCES

Cath 1, 411, G. Bardy — DHGE 2, 1086–90, S. Salaville — EECh 1, 28, H. Crouzel — LThK 1, 426, H. Crouzel — LThK 1³, 493–94, W. A. Bienert

LVII. TRYPHO, THE PUPIL OF ORIGEN

RYPHO,[1] A DISCIPLE of Origen, to whom he directed some letters which are extant, was very expert in the Scriptures.[2] This is revealed in general in many of his works,[3] but especially a work which he composed *On the Red Heifer in Deuteronomy*[4] and *On the animals cut in half*, which in Genesis are placed by Abraham with the dove and the turtle.[5]

NOTES

1. Not otherwise known; cf. Courcelle, *LLW*, 109 and n. 147
2. Jerome's own comment.
3. *opuscula:* probably letters.
4. Not Deuteronomy, but Numbers 19.1–10.
5. Gn 15.9–10. On διχοτομήματα cf. Liddell, Scott, Jones, *s.v.*, which offers the following references: "LXX *Ex* 29.17, *Le* 1.18." Jerome expatiates on διχοτομήματα in *Hom. in Ps. 84* (FOTC 57, 191–92).

LVIII. MINUCIUS FELIX

 INUCIUS FELIX,[1] a distinguished advocate in Rome, wrote a dialogue, entitled *Octavius*,[2] in which a Christian holds a debate with a pagan.

2. Another work that circulates under his name, *On Fate, or Against the Mathematicians*,[3] although the work of a very learned man, does not seem to me to correspond in style with the work mentioned above.

3. Lactantius also makes mention[4] of this Minucius in his works.

NOTES

1. A. Dihle, *Greek and Latin*, 357–59, adjudicates the Minucius Felix vs. Tertullian priority debate, concluding that it has "been finally settled with a verdict in favour of Tertullian."

2. This is virtually duplicated in *ep.* 70 (*ad Magnum*, CSEL 54, 707), where the apologist gets a high grade for his deployment of secular sources: "Minucius Felix, causidicus Romani fori, in libro, cui titulus *Octavius* est, et in altero contra mathematicos . . ." See text with German translation by B. Kytzler, ed., *Marcus Minucius Felix, Octavius* (Darmstadt, 1993); and Eng. trans. by G. W. Clarke, ACW 39 (1974). Also B. Kytzler et al., *Concordantia in Minuci Felicis Octavium, Alpha-Omega* A 72 (Hildesheim, 1991). Concerning the dialogue form, see P. L. Schmidt, in A. Cameron et al., *Christianisme et formes littéraires de l'antiquité tardive en Occident* (Vandœuvres-Geneva, 1977), 101–90.

3. Promised by Minucius Felix (*Octavius* 36.2), but, if ever written, lost; see J. R. G. Préaux, "À propos du *De fato* (?) de Minucius Felix," *Latomus* 9 (1950): 395–413.

4. Lactantius, *Inst. div.* 5.1.22 (CSEL 19, 402, and FOTC 49, 329).

REFERENCES

Q 2, 155–163 — Dr, 131–132 — CPL 37, 37a — Cath 9, 249–50, P.-Th. Camelot — DSp 10, 1268–72, P. Siniscalco — EEC 2², 753, M. P. McHugh — EECh 1, 562, P. Siniscalco — HLL 4, §475, E. Heck — LThK 7, 434, J. Martin — LThK 7³, 275–76, E. Heck — NCE 9, 883, P. W. Lawler — *PWRE* Supplbd. 81, 952–1002, 1365–78, H. von M. Geisau — TRE 23, 1–3, B. Kytzler — BBKL 5, 1564–67, M. Frenschkowski

LIX. GAIUS

N THE TIME of Zephyrinus, bishop of the city of Rome, that is, in the reign of Antoninus, the son of Severus,[1] Gaius[2] conducted a very significant debate, *Against Proclus,*[3] a follower of Montanus, accusing him of rashness respecting the defense of the new prophecy.[4]

2. In the same volume he enumerates only thirteen epistles of Paul, asserting that the fourteenth, *To the Hebrews,* is not Paul's.[5] It is not regarded as belonging to the apostle Paul among the Romans down to the present day.

NOTES

1. Zephyrinus, 198/9–217; Septimius Severus, 193–211.

2. Eus., *h.e.* 2.25.6; 3.28.1; 6.20.3; R. M. Grant, *Eusebius as Church Historian* (Oxford: Clarendon Press, 1980), 71.

3. Proclus: *h.e.* 2.25.6; 3.31.4; 6.20.3.
4. *h.e.* 6.20.3.
5. *h.e.* 6.20.3; cf. 6.25.11–13.

REFERENCES

CPG 1330–1331 — Cath 2, 367, G. Bardy — DHGE 11, 236–37, G. Bardy — EEC 1², 446, M. P. McHugh — EECh 1, 333, art., "Gaius and the Alogi," E. Prinzivalli — LThK 4, 486, J. A. Fischer — LThK 4³, 262–63, F. Mali — R. E. Heine, *The Montanist Oracles and Testimonia*, PatMS 14, 156–57 — J. D. Smith, *Gaius and the Controversy over the Johannine Literature* (New Haven: Yale University Press, 1979)

LX. BERYLLUS THE BISHOP

ERYLLUS, BISHOP of Bostra in Arabia,[1] after having ruled the church with distinction for some time, finally lapsed into a heresy which asserted that Christ did not exist before the Incarnation.[2] He was straightened out by Origen[3] and wrote various treatises, especially a letter, in which he thanked Origen;[4]

2. there is also a letter of Origen addressed to him.[5] A dialogue of Origen and Beryllus survives[6] in which the latter is accused of heresy.

3. He was famous in the reigns both of Alexander, son of Mammaea,[7] and of his successors as emperors, Maximinus and Gordianus.[8]

NOTES

1. Eus., *h.e.* 6.33.1.
2. *h.e.* 6.33.1; Jerome's phrase *lapsus in haeresim* corresponds to Eusebius's τὸν ἐκκλησιαστικὸν παρεκτρέπων κανόνα. His error was Monarchianism (Drobner, 94–95); he renounced the Patripassian heresy at the Synod of Bostra in 244.
3. *h.e.* 6.33.2.
4. *h.e.* 6.20.2; 6.33.3.
5. *h.e.* 6.33.3.

6. Not extant.

7. *Chron.*, A.D. 222; *h.e.* 6.21.2. For Mammaea cf. *DVI* 54.5.

8. On date cf. *Chron.*, A.D. 236, 238.

REFERENCES

Q 2, 40, 62 — Cath 1, 1516, G. Bardy — DHGE 8, 1136–37, G. Bardy — EEC 1², 181, L. Pittenger — EECh 1, 119–120, P. Nautin — LThK 2, 286, H. Rahner — LThK 2³, 306–7, C. Scholter — P. Nautin, *Lettres*, 135–36, 209–19

LXI. HIPPOLYTUS THE BISHOP

IPPOLYTUS,[1] BISHOP of a church in some city, the name of which I could not discover,[2] in the *Date of the Pasch and the Determination of Times*[3] which he wrote, using the first year of the emperor, Alexander, as his *terminus ad quem*,[4] established a canon of a cycle of sixteen years, which the Greeks call ἐκκαιδεκαετηρίδα,[5] and gave the opportunity to Eusebius, who composed a cycle of nineteen years, that is, ἐννεακαιδεκαετηρίδα,[6] for the same pasch.

2. He wrote various commentaries on the Scriptures, of which I have found the following:[7]

On the Hexaemeron,[8]

On Exodus,

On the Canticle of Canticles,[9]

On Genesis,[10]

On Zechariah,

On the Psalms,[11]

On Isaiah,[12]

On Daniel,[13]

On the Apocalypse,[14]

On Proverbs,[15]

On Ecclesiastes,[16]

On Saul and the Pythoness,[17]

On Antichrist,[18]
On the Resurrection,[19]
Against Marcion,
On the Pascha,[20]
Against All Heresies,[21]

and a homily (προσομιλίαν), *In Praise of the Lord our Savior,* in which he says he delivered it in a church in the presence of Origen.

3. To emulate him, Ambrose, who, as we have said,[22] was converted from the Marcionite heresy to the true faith, exhorted Origen[23] to write commentaries on the Scriptures, providing him with more than seven secretaries, paying their expenses, and an equal number of copyists, and, more important than this, demanding work from him daily with incredible importunity.[24] For this reason, in one of his letters, Origen calls him ἐργοδιώκτην, a task-master.[25]

NOTES

1. See most recently A. Brent, "Hippolytus and the Roman Church in the third century: Communities in tension before the emergence of a monarch bishop," *VigChr* Supp. 31 (Leiden, 1995); on which cf. M. Simonetti, "Una nuovo proposte su Ippolito," *AugR* 36 (1996): 13–46.

2. "some city" = Eus., *h.e.* 6.20.2: "head of another church somewhere."

3. *Date of the Pasch and the Determination of Times:* i. e., the *Chronicon,* CPG 1896; cf. the fragments entitled *Demonstratio temporum Paschatis* in CPG 1895, which makes reference to CPG 1870.

4. *h.e.* 6.22; cf. 6.21.2; *Chron.,* A.D. 223, ed. Helm, 215.

5. "established a canon of a sixteen-year cycle, which the Greeks call ἑκκαιδεκαετηρίδα": Lampe, *PGL, s.v.*

6. ἐννεακαιδεκαετηρίδα: see A. Strobel, *Ursprung und Geschichte des frühchristlichen Osterkalenders* (Berlin, 1977).

7. Missing from the list are *Contra Noetum* (CPG 1902), *Syntagma* (CPG 1897), and *De Universo* (CPG 1898). For a shorter list of his titles (seven, as against nineteen here) cf. Eus., *h.e.* 6.22. See P. Nautin, "Notes sur la catalogue des œuvres d'Hippolyte," *RechSR* 34 (1947): 99–107, 347–59. See also Courcelle, *LLW,* 113–14 and notes.

8. Cf. CPG 1880 (1).

9. CPG 1871.

10. Cf. CPG 1880.

11. CPG 1882, *fragmenta;* A. Whealy, "Prologues on the Psalms. Origen, Hippolytus, Eusebius," *RevBén* 106 (1996): 234–45.

12. CPG 1885.

13. CPG 1873.

14. CPG 1890.

15. CPG 1883.

16. CPG 1884. See A. Labaté, "Sui due frammenti di Ippolito all'Ecclesiaste," *VetChr* 23 (1986): 177–81.

17. *On Saul and the Pythoness:* CPG 1918 (under *Spuria*); cf. 1 Sam 28.3–24. For a translation see McCambley, *GkOrthThR* 35 (1990): 129–37. Similar works survive from Methodius (*DVI* 83.1) and Gregory of Nyssa.

18. CPG 1872; *Ippolito. L'Anticristo,* ed. E. Norelli, Biblioteca Patristica 10 (Florence, 1987).

19. CPG 1900.

20. See note 3 above; also CPG 4611 [1925], under *Spuria*.

21. *Against All Heresies = Philosophoumena;* see CPG 1899 and recent edition by M. Marcovich, PTS 25 (Berlin, 1986). See also Barnes, *C. and E.,* 135 and 349 n. 61, on question of authenticity.

22. Ambrose: *DVI* 56; cf. Eusebius in *h.e.* 6.18, who says, "[from] the heresy of Valentinus."

23. Eus., *h.e.* 6.23.1.

24. Based on a misreading of *h.e.* 6.23.1; ἐξ ἐκείνου means "from that time," not "from that one, him."

25. ἐργοδιώκτης, a taskmaster; Liddell, Scott, Jones, *s.v.* The noun occurs not in a letter of Origen, but in his *Comm. on John* 5.1; see FOTC 80, 160, trans. R. E. Heine. Jerome obviously liked the word: cf. *ep.* 60 (CSEL 54, 549): "ubi est ille ἐργοδιώκτης noster, et cygneo canore vox dulcior?" (said of Nepotian).

REFERENCES

Q 2, 163–206 — Dr, 89–91, 99–103 — E. Ferguson, EEC 1², 531–32 — Cath 5, 755–60, P.-Th. Camelot — DHGE 24, 627–35, V. Saxer — DSp 7, 1, 531–71, M. Richard [= *Opera Minora* 85] — LThK 5, 378–80, R. Gögler — LThK 5³, 147–149, C. Scholten — RAC 15, 492–501, C. Scholten — TRE 15, 381–87, M. Marcovich — Dihle, *Greek and Latin,* 331–34 — *Ricerche su Ippolito,* Studia Ephemeridis Augustinianum 13 (Rome: Institutum Patristicum Augustinianum, 1977)

See also the following:

F. W. Bautz, BBKL 2 (1990): 888–93;

Nuove ricerche su Ippolito, Studia Ephemeridis Augustinianum 30 (Rome: Institutum Patristicum Augustinianum, 1989) [Summary of contents, Geerard, CPG, p. 257];

J. M. Hanssens, "Hippolyte de Rome fut-il novatianiste? Essai d'une biographie," *AHP* 3 (1965): 7–29;

A. Amore, "La personalità dello Scrittore Ippolito," *Antonianum* 36 (1961): 3–28;

P. de Lanversin, "Une belle 'dispute.' Hippolyt est-il d'Occident ou d'Orient?" *PrOrChr* 6 (1956): 118–22;

G. Kretschmar, "Bibliographie zu Hippolyt von Rom," *JLH* 1 (1955): 90–95.

LXII. ALEXANDER THE BISHOP

HEN ALEXANDER, BISHOP of Cappadocia,[1] went to Jerusalem because of a wish to visit the holy places, and when Narcissus, bishop of the same city,[2] already a very old man, was ruling the church, there was an apparition[3] to Narcissus and to many of his clergy that on the morning of the next day a bishop would enter, who should become a coadjutor of the bishop's chair.

2. And so, when the facts turned out just as predicted, with all the bishops of Palestine assembled together, and with Narcissus in particular giving the fullest assent, Alexander jointly undertook with him the government of the church of Jerusalem.[4]

3. At the end of a letter which he wrote *To the Antinoites*,[5] he spoke as follows about the peace of the church:[6]

"Narcissus salutes you, he who before me occupied the episcopal see, and continues to rule the same with me by his prayers. He is around one hundred and sixteen years old and prays that you are of one and the same mind with me."

4. He also wrote another letter, *To the Antiochenes*,[7] by the hand of Clement, a priest of Alexandria, about whom we have spoken earlier,[8] and another letter, *To Origen*,[9] and one in defense of Origen *Against Demetrius*,[10] because according to the testimony of Demetrius, he had ordained Origen as a priest. And there are other letters[11] of his addressed to different persons.

5. In the seventh persecution under Decius,[12] however, at the time when Babylas[13] suffered martyrdom in Antioch, he was conducted to Caesarea, incarcerated, and crowned with martyrdom for confessing Christ.[14]

NOTES

1. Eus., *h.e.* 6.8.7; 6.11; 6.13.3; 6.14.8; 6.19.16–18; 6.20; 6.27–28; 6.39.

2. For Narcissus of Jerusalem, see CPG 1340; EECh 2, 582, M. Spinelli; *h.e.* 5.12.1–2; 5.23.3; 6.8.7; 6.9–11.

3. On the apparition, see *h.e.* 6.11.1.

4. *h.e.* 6.11.1–3.

5. *h.e.* 6.11.3.

6. *h.e.* 6.11.4.

7. *h.e.* 6.11.5.

8. *DVI* 38.

9. *h.e.* 6.14.8.

10. *h.e.* 6.19.17.

11. Available to Origen "in the library at Aelia, equipped by Alexander, then ruling the church there," according to *h.e.* 6.20.1.

12. *h.e.* 6.39.1.

13. *h.e.* 6.29.4; 6.39.4.

14. *h.e.* 6.39.2,3: ἐπὶ τῆς εἰρκτῆς κοινηθέντος; *h.e.* 7.12 reports the death of an Alexander in Caesarea during the persecution of Valerian.

REFERENCES

DHGE 2, 178–79, J.-P. Kirsch — EEC 1², 30, E. Ferguson — EECh 1, 21, H. Crouzel

LXIII. JULIUS THE AFRICAN

ULIUS AFRICANUS,[1] whose *Chronicles* in five volumes[2] are extant, in the reign of the emperor Marcus Aurelius Antoninus, the successor of Macrinus,[3] undertook an embassy for the restoration of the city of Emmaus, which was later called Nicopolis.[4]

2. A letter, *To Origen on the Question of Susanna*[5] is his, in which he says that this narrative is not found in the Hebrew text and that the expression ἀπὸ τοῦ πρίνου πρίσαι καὶ ἀπὸ τοῦ σχίνου σχίσαι[6] does not agree with the Hebrew etymology. Origen wrote a learned letter in reply to him.[7]

3. Another epistle of his, *To Aristides*, survives,[8] in which he discusses at length the apparent discrepancy, διαφωνία,[9] between the genealogies of the Lord in Matthew and Luke.[10]

NOTES

1. Eus., *h.e.* 1.7; 6.31. Background studies include the following: F. C. R. Thee, *Julius Africanus and the Early Christian View of Magic* (Tübingen, 1984); E. Dal Covola, "La politica religiosa di Alessandro Severo. Par una valutazione dei rapporti tra l'ultimo dei Severi e il Cristiani," *Salesianum* 49 (1987): 359–75.

2. Χρονογραφίαι, *Chronicles*, 1–5: CPG 1690; *h.e.* 6.31.2; H. Gelzer, *Sextus Julius Africanus und die byzantinische Chronographie* (Leipzig, 1880–88; reprint, 1978).

3. Marcus Aurelius, 161–180.

4. Emmaus/Nicopolis in southern Judea: Eus., *Chron.*, A.D. 221.

5. *To Origen, On Susanna:* CPG 1692; text: SC 302, 514–73. The episode concerning Susanna is Dn 13.1–65 in the deuterocanonical Scriptures. See EECh 2, 801, art., "Susanna," G. Ladocsi. For the extensive collection of Origen's letters made by Eusebius (*h.e.* 6.36.3), see CPG 1490–1496.

6. For the Hebrew/Greek problem, see SC 302, 516–17.

7. CPG 1494; SC 302, 471ff.

8. CPG 1693; Eus., *h.e.* 6.31.3, 1.7.1. Aristides was a friend of Origen who shared his interest in genealogies; see FOTC 94, 115 n. 2. There is no mention by Jerome of Julius's *Kestoi* (CPG 1691), though Eusebius has it (*h.e.* 6.31.1). See J. R. Vieillefond, *Les Cestes* (Florence and Paris, 1970); H. Chantraine, "Der metrologische Traktat des Sextus Iulius Africanus, seine Zugehörigkeit zu den κεστοί und seine Authentizität," *Hermes* 105 (1977): 422–41.

9. Used elsewhere by Jerome.

10. *h.e.* 6.31.3.

REFERENCES

Q 2, 137–40 — Dr, 191–92 — CPG 1, 1690–1695 — *TLG* 2956 — EEC 1², 644–45, M. P. McHugh — EECh 1, 460, M. Simonetti — LThK 1³, 194, M. Durst — TRE 1, 635–40

LXIV. GEMINUS THE PRESBYTER

EMINUS, A PRIEST of the church of Antioch,[1] composed a few monuments to his genius, living in the reign of the emperor Alexander[2] with Zebennus, bishop of the city,[3] at the precise time when Heraclas[4] was ordained bishop of the church of Alexandria.

NOTES

1. G. Ladocsi, EECh 1, 340, states, "[Geminus] has left us very little evidence of his genius."

2. Eus., *h.e.* 6.28.1, tells us that Alexander (Severus) reigned for 13 years [i.e., until 235].

3. Zebennus succeeded Philetus (*h.e.* 6.23.3) and was succeeded by Babylas (*h.e.* 6.29.4).

4. *h.e.* 6.26. Heraclas, who succeeded Demetrius, is called "our blessed pope" by Dionysius of Alexandria (*h.e.* 7.7.4). See *Chron.*, A.D. 231, ed. Helm, 215.

REFERENCES

EECh 1, 340, G. Ladocsi

LXV. THEODORUS, SURNAMED GREGORY, THE BISHOP

HEODORUS, LATER CALLED Gregory,[1] bishop of Neocaesarea, in Pontus,[2] while still in his youth went along with his brother Athenodorus from Cappadocia to Berytus and from there to Caesarea in Palestine in order to study Greek and Latin literature.[3]

2. When Origen saw their outstanding ability he exhorted them to study philosophy,[4] into which, little by little, he introduced the Christian faith, and made them believers. Having pursued their studies in this way for five years,[5] they were sent back by him to their mother.

3. One of them, Theodore, when departing, wrote a *Panegyric*[6] in thanksgiving to Origen, which he recited before a distinguished assembly, including Origen himself, and which survives down to the present day.

4. He also wrote an *Exposition of Ecclesiastes*,[7] brief but extremely useful, and other letters of his are widely known,[8] but especially the signs and miracles which as a bishop he performed with great glory of the churches.

NOTES

1. Eus., *h.e.* 6.30.1.
2. *h.e.* 7.14.1; 7.28.1.
3. *h.e.* 6.30.1.
4. *h.e.* 6.30.1.
5. *h.e.* 6.30.1.
6. CPG 1763; P. Guyot and R. Klein, *Gregorius Thaumaturgus, Oratio prosphonetica ac panegyrica in Origenem*, Fontes Christiani 24 (Freiburg and New York: Herder, 1996); St. Gregory Thaumaturgus, *Address of Thanksgiving to Origen*, trans. Michael Slusser, FOTC 98, 91–126.
7. CPG 1766; *Metaphrase on the Ecclesiastes of Solomon*, trans. Slusser, FOTC 98, 127–46.
8. Other works: *Canonical Epistle, To Theopompus, On the Impassibility and Passibility of God*, and *To Philagrius [Evagrius], on Consubstantiality*, trans. Slusser, FOTC 98, 147–51, 152–73, and 174–78, respectively.

REFERENCES

Q 2, 123–28 — EEC 1², 499–500, F. W. Norris — EECh 1, 202, A. Quacquarelli — LThK 4³, 1027–29, H. Crouzel — RAC 12, 779–93, H. Crouzel — P. Nautin, *Origène*, 183f.

LXVI. CORNELIUS THE BISHOP

ORNELIUS, BISHOP OF THE CITY OF ROME,[1] to whom Cyprian directed eight letters still in existence,[2] wrote

a letter *To Fabius*, bishop of the church of Antioch,
[also] *On the Synod of Rome, Italy, and Africa*,[3]
another one *On Novatian and on Those Who Lapsed*,
a third, *On the Acts of the synod*,
a fourth, *To the same Fabius*, very lengthy, and including the causes and the condemnation of the heresy of Novatian.

2. He ruled the church for two years during the reign of Gallus and Volusianus,[4] and he was crowned with martyrdom for Christ. He was succeeded by Lucius.[5]

NOTES

1. Eus., *h.e.* 6.39.1; *Chron.*, A.D. 252. Cornelius was bishop of Rome, 251–253.

2. Only two survive: *epp.* 59 (trans. Clarke, ACW 46, 68–88, and notes, 233–264) and 60 (Clarke, *op.cit.*, 88–92, and notes, 265–71).

3. *"To Fabius . . . On the Synod"*: see *h.e.* 6.43.3.

4. Trebonius Gallus (251–253) and his son Volusianus.

5. Lucius, June 25, 253, through March 5, 254. See *h.e.* 7.2.1; LThK 6³, 1085, G. Schwaiger.

REFERENCES

Q 2, 236–37 — DHGE 13, 891–94, G. Bardy — EEC 1², 294, M. P. McHugh — EECh 1, 202, B. Studer — CPG 1850–51 — LThK 2³, 1313–14, G. Schwaiger — Gamble, *Books*, 218f.

LXVII. CYPRIAN THE BISHOP

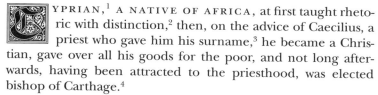 YPRIAN,[1] A NATIVE OF AFRICA, at first taught rhetoric with distinction,[2] then, on the advice of Caecilius, a priest who gave him his surname,[3] he became a Christian, gave over all his goods for the poor, and not long afterwards, having been attracted to the priesthood, was elected bishop of Carthage.[4]

2. It is superfluous to compile an index of his scholarly output since his works are more illustrious than the sun.[5]

3. He endured martyrdom during the eighth persecution in the reign of the emperors Valerian and Gallienus,[6] on the same day, but not in the same year, as Cornelius at Rome.[7]

NOTES

1. Eus., *h.e.* 6.43.3; 7.3. Cyprian was bishop, 247/248–258.

2. Cf. Lactantius: "[Cyprian] had acquired great glory for himself in the profession of the art of oratory . . . he had an ability in speaking, easy, fluent, pleasant . . . you cannot distinguish whether he was more ornate in eloquence, or more successful in explanation, or more powerful in persuasion," from *Inst. div.* 5.1, probably Jerome's source here. Trans. is that of Sister Mary Francis McDonald, FOTC 49, 329.

3. Caecilius: DHGE 11, 130, A. Audollent.

4. M. Bévenot, "Cyprian's platform in the rebaptism controversy," *HeyJ* 19 (1978): 123–42.

5. "superfluum est indicem texere": an odd statement from a bibliographer, but perhaps understandable in this case because of Pontius's list of publications available in the *Vita Cypriani;* cf. *infra, DVI* 68. Jerome singles out for praise Cyprian's *Quod idola dii non sint* in *ep.* 70 (CSEL 54, 707): "qua brevitate, qua historiarum omnium scientia, quo verborum et sensuum splendore perstrinxit!" And in *ep.* 58 (CSEL 54, 539): "beatus Cyprianus instar fontis purissimi dulcis incedit et placidus et, cum totus sit in exhortatione virtutum, occupatus persecutionis angustiis scripturas divinas nequaquam disseruit." For his works, see Appendix 3. See also C. H. Turner, "Two early lists of Cyprian's works," *CR* 6 (1892): 205–9; V. Saxer, *Saints anciens d'Afrique du Nord* (Vatican City, 1979).

6. Valerian, 253–260. On Valerian's persecution, cf. Eus., *h.e.* 7.12, and on Gallienus (260–268), *h.e.* 7.13.1. See Ch. Saumagne, *Saint Cyprien, évêque de Carthage, "pape" d'Afrique (248–258). Contribution à l'étude des "persécutions" de Dèce et de Valérien* (Paris, 1975).

7. Cornelius died in June 253. For Cyprian's death on Sept. 14, 258, cf. Eus., *Chron.*, A.D. 257; LThK 2³, 1366; Kelly, *ODP*, 30.

REFERENCES

Q 2, 340–83 — Dr, 133–39 — CPL 38–51 — DHGE 13, 1149–60, G. Bardy — EEC 1², 306–8, R. D. Sider — EECh 1, 211–12, V. Saxer — LThK 2³, 1364–66, G. W. Clarke — RAC 3, 463–66, A. Stuiber — TRE 8, 246–54, M. Bévenot — Wickert, *Gestalten* 1 (1984), 158–75 — Dihle, *Greek and Latin*, 384–89

For bibliography, see BBKL 1 (1975), 1178–83; for ongoing bibliography, updated annually, *Chronica Cyprianea, REAug* 32 (1986) on.

For *opera omnia*, see G. Hartel, ed., CSEL 3/1–3 (1868–71); R. Weber, M. Bévenot, M. Simonetti, and C. Moreschini, edd., CCL 3–3A (1972–76); *Ad Donatum, De bono patientiae*, J. Molager, ed., SC 291 (1982); *Vita*, Ch. Mohrmann, A. A. R. Bastiaensen, and L. Canali, edd., ViSa 3 (1975): 1–49.

For studies, see St. Cavallotto, "Il magistero episcopale di Cipriano di Cartagine. Aspetti metodologici," *DT* 91 (1988): 375–407; P. Bouet, Ph. Fleury, A. Goulon, M. Zuinghedau, and P. Dufraigne, *Cyprien, Traités. Concordance — Documentation lexicale et grammaticale*, 2 vols. (New York, 1986); J. A. Fischer, "Die Konzilien zu Karthago und Rom im Jahr 251," *AHC* 11 (1979): 263–86; M. Bévenot, "Cyprian's platform in the rebaptism controversy," *HeyJ* 19 (1978): 123–42; Kötting, "Die Stellung des Konfessors in der Alten Kirche," *JAC* 19 (1976): 7–23; M. Sage, *Cyprien*, PatMS 1 (1975); M. A. Fahey, *Cyprian and the Bible: a Study in Third-Century Exegesis*, BGBH 9 (1971); V. Saxer, *Vie liturgique et quotidienne à Carthage vers le milieu du IIIe siècle. Le témoignage de saint Cyprien et de ses contemporains d'Afrique*, Studi di antichità cristiana 29 (1969); G. S. M. Walker, *The Churchmanship of St. Cyprian*, *ESH* 9 (1968); H. Koch, *Cyprianische Untersuchungen*, *AKG* 4 (1926); A. d'Alès, *La théologie de saint Cyprien*, *BTH* (1922); A. von Harnack, *Das Leben Cyprians von Pontius, die erste christliche Biographie*, TU 39/3 (1913); J. Ernst, "Papst Stephan I. und der Ketzertaufstreit," *FChLDG* 5/4 (1905); P. Monceaux, *Histoire littéraire de l'Afrique chrétienne depuis les origines jusqu'à l'invasion arabe, II: Saint Cyprien et son temps* (Paris, 1902); E. W. Benson, *Cyprian, His Life, His Times, His Work* (London, 1897).

The text of *De lapsis* appears in OECT (1971), 1–55, ed. M. Bévenot. For studies, see V. Fattorini and G. Picenardi, "La riconciliazione in Cipriano di Cartagine (*ep.* 55) e Ambrogio di Milano (*De paenitentia*)," *AugR* 27 (1987): 377–406; M. Bévenot, "The Sacrament of Penance and St. Cyprian's *De Lapsis*," *TS* 16 (1955): 175–213; B. Poschmann, "*Paenitentia secunda*. Die kirchliche Buße im ältesten Christentum bis Cyprian und Origenes," *Theoph.* 1 (1940): 368–424.

The text of *De Ecclesiae Unitate* appears in OECT (1971), 56–99, ed. M. Bévenot. For studies, see H. Montgomery, "Subordination or Collegiality? St. Cyprian and the Roman See," *Greek and Latin Studies in Memory of Caius Fabricius*, ed. S.-T. Teodorsson, *SGLG* 54 (1990), 41–54; P. Hinchcliff, *Cyprian of Carthage and the Unity of the Catholic Church* (London, 1974); U. Wickert, "*Sacramentum unitatis." Ein Beitrag zum Verständnis der Kirche bei Cyprian*, *BZNW* 41 (1971); L. Campeau, "Le texte de la Primauté dans le *De Catholicae Ecclesiae Unitate* de S. Cyprien," *ScEc* 19 (1967): 81–110, 255–75; M. Bévenot, "St. Cyprian's *De Unitate* chap. 4 in the Light of the Manuscripts," *AnGr* 11 (1937) [= London, 1938]; O. Perler, "Zur Datierung der beiden Fassungen des vierten Kapitels *De Unitate Ecclesiae*," *RQ* 44 (1936): 1–44; O. Perler, "*De catholicae ecclesiae Unitate* cap. 4–5. Die ursprünglichen Texte, ihre Überlieferung, ihre Datierung," *RQ* 44 (1936): 151–68; B. Poschmann, "*Ecclesia Principalis." Ein kritischer Beitrag zur Frage des Primats bei Cyprian* (Berlin, 1933); H. Koch, "*Cathedra Petri." Neue Untersuchungen über die Anfänge der Primatslehre*," *BZNW* 11 (1930); J. Ernst, *Cyprian und das Papsttum* (Mainz, 1912); H. Koch, *Cyprian und der römische Primat. Eine kirchen- und dogmengeschichtliche Studie*, TU 35/1 (1910).

For studies of the letters of Cyprian, see R. Seagraves, "*Pascentes cum disciplina." A Lexical Study of the Clergy in the Cyprianic Correspondence*, Paradosis 37 (1993); H. Gülzow, *Cyprian und Novatian. Der Briefwechsel zwischen den Gemeinden in Rom und Karthago zur Zeit der Verfolgung des Kaisers Decius*, BHTh 48 (1975); L. Duquenne, *Chronologie des lettres de S. Cyprien. Le dossier de la persécution de Dèce*, SHG 54 (1972).

LXVIII. PONTIUS THE DEACON

ONTIUS, DEACON of Cyprian, endured exile with him up to the day of his death,[1] and left an important volume, *On the Life and Passion of Cyprian.*[2]

NOTES

1. Exiled in 257 to Curubis (Korfa) in Tunisia, Cyprian died by beheading on September 14, 258.

2. *Vita Cypriani auctore Pontio Diacono,* the first Christian biography; see CPL 52; M. Pellegrino, *Vita e Morte,* Verba Seniorum 3 (Alba, 1955); Ch. Mohrmann, A. A. R. Bastiaensen, and L. Canali, edd., ViSa 3 (1975): 1–49; for English trans., see ANF 5, 267–74, and FOTC 15, 3–24, trans. M. M. Müller and R. J. Deferrari. Studies of the *Vita* include J. Aronen, "Indebtedness to *Passio Perpetuae* in Pontius' *Vita Cypriani,*" *VigChr* 38 (1984): 67–76; G. Lomiento, "La Bibbia nella compositio della Vita Cypriani di Ponzio," *VetChr* 5 (1968): 23–60.

REFERENCES

Q 2, 340–41, 345–46, 349 — CPL 52 — EECh 2, 702, V. Saxer — LThK 8, 616, S. Martin

LXIX. DIONYSIUS THE BISHOP

IONYSIUS, bishop of the city of Alexandria,[1] as a presbyter directed the school of catechetics, κατηχήσεων,[2] at the time of Heraclas,[3] and was a most distinguished student of Origen.[4]

2. In agreement with the teaching of Cyprian and of the synod of Africa on baptizing heretics,[5] he sent to various recipients numerous letters, which survive down to the present day.

3. In particular, he wrote *To Fabius,* bishop of the church of Antioch, *On Penance;*[6]

and *To the Romans* through Hippolytus another letter;[7]
To Xystus, who had succeeded Stephen, two letters;[8]
two letters *To Philemon* and *To Dionysius,*[9] priests of the church of Rome;

also *To the same Dionysius,*[10] afterwards bishop of Rome;

and *To Novatian,*[11] who had argued that he had been ordained bishop of Rome against his will, the beginning of which letter was as follows:

4. "Dionysius, to his brother, Novatian, greetings. If, as you say, you were ordained against your will, you will prove it when you leave of your own free will."[12]

5. There is another letter of his *To Dionysius and To Didymus;*[13]

and numerous *Festal Letters [ʿΕορταστικαί] on the Pasch,*[14] written in a declamatory style;

also *To the Church of Alexandria*[15] from exile;

and *To Hierax,* a bishop in Egypt;[16]

and another, *On Mortality;*[17]

and *On the Sabbath;*[18]

and Περὶ γυμνασίου, *Concerning Exercise;*[19]

also *To Hermammon;*[20]

another, *On the Persecution of Decius;*[21]

and two books, *Against Bishop Nepos,*[22] who had in his writings proposed a bodily life of a thousand years,[23] in which books he also discoursed on the Apocalypse of John[24] with great diligence;

6. also, *Against Sabellius;*[25]

and *To Ammon,* bishop of Bernice;[26]

and *To Telesphorus;*[27]

and *To Euphranor;*[28]

and four books *To Dionysius,* bishop of the city of Rome;[29]

To the Laodicaeans, On Penance;[30]

also *To Conon, On Penance;*[31]

To Origen, On Martyrdom;[32]

To the Armenians, On Penance and On the Succession of Faults;[33]

To Timothy, On Nature;[34]

To Euphranor, On Temptations;[35]

also numerous letters *To Basilides,*[36] in one of which he states that he has begun work on *Commentaries on Ecclesiastes.*[37]

Furthermore, an important letter is also attributed to him, *Against Paul of Samosata,*[38] written a few days before he died.

7. He died in the twelfth year of the reign of Gallienus.[39]

NOTES

1. Dionysius of Alexandria (fl. 247–264); see Eus., *h.e.* 6.29.4; 6.44.1–6; M. Sordi, "Dionigi d'Alessandria, Commodiano ed alcuni problemi della storia del III secolo," *Rendiconti della Pont. Accademia di Archeologia* 35 (1962–63): 123–46; for exhaustive coverage cf. W. A. Bienert, *Dionysius von Alexandrien. Das erhaltene Werk,* BGL 2 (Stuttgart, 1972), and *idem, Dionysius von Alexandrien. Zur Frage des Origenismus im dritten Jahrhundert,* PTS 21 (Berlin and New York, 1978). For a collection of texts, see *ΔΙΟΝΥ-ΣΙΟΥ ΛΕΙΨΑΝΑ. The Letters and Other Remains of Dionysius of Alexandria,* ed. C. L. Feltoe (Cambridge, England, 1904); for an Eng. trans., see *St. Dionysius of Alexandria. Letters and Treatises,* trans. C. L. Feltoe (New York: The Macmillan Company, 1918).

2. He succeeded Heraclas as head of the catechetical school in 231–232 and as bishop in 247–248.

3. DHGE 23 (1990), art., "Heraclas," 1302–3, H. Crouzel.

4. *h.e.* 6.29.4.

5. "In agreement with . . . Cyprian" was not true always; see *h.e.* 7.7.4–5. On the doctrine on baptizing heretics of Cyprian and the synod of Africa, see M. Bévenot, "Cyprian's Platform in the Rebaptism Controversy," *HeyJ* 19 (1978): 123–42; J. A. Fischer, "Die Konzilien zu Karthago und Rom im Jahr 251," *AHC* 11 (1979): 263–86; St. Cavallotto, "Il magistero episcopale di Cipriano di Cartagine. Aspetti metodologici," *DT* 91 (1988): 375–407; J. P. Burns, "On Rebaptism: Social Organization in the Third-Century Church," *JECS* 1, 4 (1993): 367–403.

6. CPG 1550; see account and long excerpt in *h.e.* 6.44.1–6; trans. Feltoe (1918), 35–43.

7. *h.e.* 6.46.5; Hippolytus presumably is a letter-carrier.

8. CPG 1556 for *Epistula ad Xistum (Sixtum II) Romanum (fragmenta);* for Greek frag., see Eus., *h.e.* 7.5.3–6 and CPG 1559: *Epistula ad Xistum (Sixtum II) Romanum.*

9. *Epistula ad Philemonem:* CPG 1557; frag. in *h.e.* 7.7.1; *Epistula ad Dionysium:* CPG 1558; *h.e.* 7.7.6–8.

10. Cf. *h.e.* 7.26.1.

11. CPG 1552; frag. in *h.e.* 6.45; trans. Feltoe (1918), 50–51; Bienert, BGL 2, 36.

12. Quotation in *h.e.* 6.45.1.

13. CPG 1563; *h.e.* 7.20.1: *To Dometius (not* Dionysius) and *To Didymus.*

14. CPG 1563–66; see Y. Tissot, "Le rapt de Denys d'Alexandrie et la chronologie de ses lettres festales," *RHPR* 77 (1997): 51–65.

15. *h.e.* 7.21.1; trans. Feltoe (1918), 70.

16. CPG 1566 and *h.e.* 7.21.2–10; a festal letter, with long and vivid description of the travails in Alexandria.

17. Cf. *h.e.* 6.46.4.

18. *h.e.* 7.22.11. Feltoe (1904), 253f., thinks it may have been addressed to one Aphrodisius.

19. CPG 1596; *h.e.* 7.22.11; ed. Feltoe (1904), 256.

20. CPG 1564; *h.e.* 7.1.10; 7.22.12; trans. Feltoe (1918), 65.

21. Cf. *h.e.* 6.39; 7.22.12.

22. For Nepos see *h.e.* 7.24.1.

23. On the earthly millennium, cf. *h.e.* 7.24.1 and 3.39.11.

24. On the Apocalypse of John, cf. *h.e.* 7.24.2–3.

25. Cf. *h.e.* 7.26.1. At an early stage Jerome himself lamented, "I am accused of the Sabellian heresy for proclaiming with unwearied voice that there are three subsistent persons, true, undiminished, and perfect" (*ep.* 17.2, trans. C. C. Mierow, ACW 33, 76), and wrote in 376 (*ep.* 15, ACW 33, 70–73, and 209–212) to Pope Damasus for doctrinal clarification; cf. T. C. Lawler, "Jerome's First Letter to Damasus," in *Kyriakon*, FS J. Quasten, 548–52.

26. *h.e.* 7.26.1. This is not separate from *Against Sabellius*.

27. *h.e.* 7.26.1; not separate from *Against Sabellius*.

28. CPG 1578; *h.e.* 7.26.1; not separate from *Against Sabellius*.

29. *h.e.* 7.26.1; not separate from *Against Sabellius*.

30. *h.e.* 6.46.2.

31. *h.e.* 6.46.2; CPG 1561 has *Epistula ad Colonem (Cononem?)*.

32. *h.e.* 6.46.2.

33. CPG 1604, 1612; *h.e.* 6.46.2.

34. CPG 1576; *h.e.* 7.26.2. Fragments in Eus., *Praep. evang.* 7.19, and in Athanasius, *De sententiis Dion. ep. Alex.* It combats Epicurean atomism. Timothy was his son.

35. *h.e.* 7.26.3.

36. CPG 1569; *h.e.* 7.26.3; Cantalamessa, *Easter*, 60–61, 158–59.

37. CPG 1584; *h.e.* 7.26.3; ed. Feltoe (1904), 208–27.

38. CPG 1708; Bienert, PTS 21, 65f. For Paul of Samosata, cf. Dr, 177–78, as well as *h.e.* 7.27.1 and 7.30.18–19.

39. = *h.e.* 7.28.3. On the reign of Gallienus, cf. Eus., *Chron.*, A.D. 269; Eus., *h.e.* 7.28.3; 7.13; 7.10.1; 7.22.12.

REFERENCES

Q 2, 101–9 — Dr, 144 — DHGE 14, 248–53 — DSp 3, 243–44 — EEC 1, 333–34, E. Ferguson — EECh 1², 238, P. Nautin — LThK 3, 401, P.-Th. Camelot — LThK 3³, 241–42, W. A. Bienert — NCE 4, 876–77, E. G. Ryan — TRE 8, 767–71, W. A. Bienert — ANRW II, 23, 1, 387–459, C. Andresen — Dihle, *Greek and Latin*, 381 — Nautin, *Lettres*, 143–65 — S. Leanza, *Orpheus* 6 (1985): 156–61

LXX. NOVATIAN THE HERESIARCH

OVATIAN, A PRIEST of the city of Rome,[1] having attempted to seize the episcopal see of Cornelius,[2] established the teachings of the Novatians, who in Greek are called Καθαρῶν, or the "pure ones,"[3] being unwilling to accept the apostates as penitents.[4] His champion was Novatus, one of Cyprian's priests.[5]

2. He wrote *On the Passover*,
On the Sabbath,
On Circumcision,
On the Priesthood,
On Prayer,
On Foods of the Jews,[6]
On Zeal,
On Attalus, and many other works[7]
and a large volume, *On the Trinity*,[8] making a sort of ἐπιτομὴν of the work of Tertullian, which many through ignorance regard as a work of Cyprian.[9]

NOTES

1. Eus., *h.e.* 6.43.1. In general the Greeks call him Novatus; in the West he is Novatian.

2. Surprisingly Jerome does not include here the episode of Novatian's illicit ordination as a bishop, provided by Eusebius, and detailed in the juicy letter from Cornelius to Fabius of Antioch, in *h.e.* 6.43.5–22 (mentioned in *DVI* 66.1).

3. Καθαροί : *h.e.* 6.43.1.

4. On the penance question cf. Eus., *h.e.* 6.43.2.

5. On Novatus cf. EECh 2, 605, E. Romero Pose.

6. *On Jewish Foods, De cibis iudaicis:* CPL 68; FOTC 67, 137–56.

7. Including perhaps his *Letters*, a copy of which Jerome had requested from Paul of Concordia (*ep.* 10), explaining, "so that, as we become acquainted with the poisons of the schismatic we may the more gladly drink of the antidote of the holy martyr Cyprian" (trans. Mierow, ACW 33, 51–52). See Q 2, 213, 226.

8. *On the Trinity:* his most famous work. See CPL 71. Text appears in CCL 4, 11–78, ed. Diercks; in *Novaciano. La Trinidad*, ed. with intro., trans., and comm. by C. Granado, Fuentes patrísticas 8 (Madrid, 1996); and in *Nova-*

tianus. De Trinitate, Text und Übersetzung, ed. and trans. H. Weyer (Düsseldorf, 1962). For an example of Novatian's dependence on Theophilus of Antioch (on whom Tertullian was also dependent), cf. R. M. Grant, *Greek Apologists,* 188–90.

9. Jerome inserts this piece of bibliographical information in *Adv. Rufinum* 2.19: "He passes to the celebrated martyr, Cyprian, and says that Tertullian's book, entitled *De Trinitate,* is read under his name at Constantinople . . . it is the book of Novatian" (trans. J. N. Hritzu, FOTC 53, 138; see n. 79 also).

REFERENCES

Q 2, 212–33 — Dr, 146 — CPL 68–74 — Cath 9, 1433–36, P.-Th. Camelot — DSp 11, 479–83, R. J. De Simone — EEC 2², 819–20, H. J. Vogt — EECh 2, 603–4, H.-J. Vogt — EECh 2, art., "Novatianists," 604, R. J. De Simone — LThK 7, 1062–64, J. Quasten — LThK 7³, 938–39, H. J. Vogt — TRE 24, 678–82, J. S. Alexander

LXXI. MALCHION THE PRESBYTER

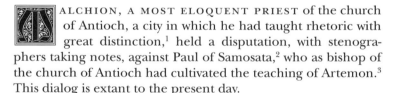ALCHION, A MOST ELOQUENT PRIEST of the church of Antioch, a city in which he had taught rhetoric with great distinction,[1] held a disputation, with stenographers taking notes, against Paul of Samosata,[2] who as bishop of the church of Antioch had cultivated the teaching of Artemon.[3] This dialog is extant to the present day.

2. In addition, another great epistle, written by him in the name of a synod, was addressed, *To Dionysius and Maximus,*[4] bishops of Rome and of the church of Alexandria.

3. He lived in the reign of Claudius and Aurelian.[5]

NOTES

1. Eus., *h.e.* 7.29.2.
2. *h.e.* 7.28.4; 7.29.2, quoted in Q 2, 140–141.
3. On Artemon cf. Q 2, 196, and *h.e.* 5.28.1–5.
4. *h.e.* 7.30.1. Part of the letter is in *h.e.* 7.30.2–17.
5. A.D. 270; *h.e.* 7.28.4.

REFERENCES

Q 2, 140–42 — EECh 1, 518, A. De Nicola — LThK 6, 1325–26, B. Kotter — LThK 6³, 1237, T. Böhm

LXXII. ARCHELAUS THE BISHOP

RCHELAUS, BISHOP of Mesopotamia,[1] composed a work in Syriac concerning the debate which he had against Mani,[2] who came from Persia. This work, in a Greek translation,[3] is in the possession of many.

2. He was well known under the emperor Probus, who was the successor of Aurelian and Tacitus.[4]

NOTES

1. He was bishop of Carcarr (Mesopotamia) in the second half of the third century.

2. On Mani, see EEC 2², 707–9, P. Perkins; LThK 6³, 1265–69, H. J. Klimkeit; TRE 22, 25–45, A. Böhlig.

3. On Hegemonius, the real author of *Acta Archelai*: EECh 1, 371, J.-M. Sauget; M. Scopello, "Vérités et contre-vérités. La vie de Mani selon les *Acta Archelai*," *Apocrypha* 6 (1995): 203–34. Text in *Hegemonius. Acta Archelai*, GCS 16, ed. C. H. Beeson. For citations from the Greek (not Syriac) original, see Epiphanius, *Panarion*, trans. F. Williams (Leiden and New York: E. J. Brill, 1987), 66, 6–7, 25–31; see also *The Panarion of St. Epiphanias Bishop of Salamis: Selected Passages*, ed. P. R. Amidon (Oxford, 1990), 232, 236; Courcelle, *LLW*, 123.

4. Probus (276–282); Aurelian (270–275); Tacitus (275–276).

REFERENCES

Q 3, 357–58 — CPG 2, 3570 — DHGE 3, 1542, P. de Labriolle — EECh 1, 71, E. Prinzivalli

LXXIII. ANATOLIUS THE BISHOP

NATOLIUS OF ALEXANDRIA, bishop of Laodicea in Syria,[1] lived in the reign of the emperors Probus and Carus.[2] He was a man of prodigious learning in arithmetic, geometry, astronomy, grammar, rhetoric, and dialectic.[3]

2. We can understand the greatness of his talent from a volume which he composed, *On the Pasch*,[4]

and from ten books, *An Introduction to Arithmetic*.[5]

NOTES

1. Eus., *h.e.* 7.32.6–20, and *Chron.*, A.D. 279.

2. *h.e.* 7.30.22. Probus (276–282) succeeded Aurelian (270–275); next reigned Carus (282–283).

3. "in . . . rhetoric": *h.e.* 7.32.6; EECh 2, art., "Rhetoric," 735–36, A. Quacquarelli.

4. *h.e.* 7.32.13–19; cf. CPG 1620.

5. *h.e.* 7.32.20; cf. CPG 1621.

REFERENCES

CPG 1620 — EECh 1, 37, M. Simonetti — Dihle, *Greek and Latin*, 402, 405, 486

LXXIV. VICTORINUS THE BISHOP

ICTORINUS, BISHOP of Poetovio,[1] did not know Latin as well as he did Greek;[2] as a result, his works, which are excellent in content, seem inferior in composition.[3]

2. His works are:

Commentaries On Genesis,[4]
On Exodus,
On Leviticus,

On Isaiah,
On Ezekiel,
On Habakkuk,
On Ecclesiastes,
On the Canticle of Canticles,
On the Apocalypse of John,[5]
Against Heresies,[6]
and numerous others.[7]

3. At the end he received the crown of martyrdom.[8]

NOTES

1. Victorinus (+304) of Poetovio, or Pettau, the first exegete to write in Latin. See M. Dulaey, *Victorin de Poetovio, premier exégète latin* (Paris, 1994). Poetovio is present-day Ptuj on the Drava in Slovenia.

2. Quasten, *Patrology*, Vol. 2, 411, notes, "The fact that his Greek was better than his Latin does not necessarily imply that he was a Greek by birth, because of the well-known mixture of languages in his native Pannonia."

3. Jerome has some good-natured remarks about him elsewhere: "Victorino martyri in libris suis, licet desit eruditio, tamen non deest eruditionis voluntas" (*ep.* 70.5, CSEL 54, 707), and "Victorinus martyrio coronatus, quod intellegit, eloqui non potest" (*ep.* 58.10, CSEL 54, 539). Both remarks are quoted in Q 2, 411, and ACW 33, 218 n. 45. Jerome also mentions Victorinus in *Against Helvidius* 17, FOTC 53, 36–37.

4. CPL 82, listed among Dubia.

5. The only work surviving from Jerome's list. See CPL 80; Q 2, 410–11; CSEL 49; PLS 1, 102–71; ANF 7, 344–60. For its chiliastic tenor, cf. M. Dulaey, "Jérôme, Victorin de Poetovio et le millénarisme," in *Jérôme entre l'Occident et l'Orient*, ed. Y. M. Duval, 83–98.

6. See Q 2, 272, 412, for this work as Victorinus's Latin translation of an appendix added to Tertullian's *De praescriptione;* CSEL 47, 213–26.

7. *Multa alia* must include *De fabrica mundi* (CPL 79; CSEL 49, 3–9; ANF 7, 341–43), surprisingly not mentioned here.

8. Most probably in the persecution of Diocletian in A.D. 304.

REFERENCES

Q 2, 411–13 — CPL 79–84 — EEC 2², 1160, M. P. McHugh — EECh 2, 867, C. Curti — LThK 6³, 1387–88, W. Geerlings — SC 423 (Paris, 1997) — Dihle, *Greek and Latin*, 390

LXXV. PAMPHILUS THE PRESBYTER

AMPHILUS, A PRIEST,[1] a close friend of Eusebius, bishop of Caesarea,[2] was on fire with such love for the sacred library,[3] that he copied with his own hand the greatest part of the volumes of Origen[4] which are contained to this very day in the library of Caesarea.

2. But I have discovered, written by his own hand, twenty-five volumes of the Commentaries of Origen *On the Twelve Prophets*,[5] which I embrace and hold on to with such joy that I believe I am in possession of the riches of Croesus.

3. If it is a joy to possess one letter of a martyr, how much more to possess so many thousands of his which he seems to me to have signed by the traces of his blood!

4. He wrote, before Eusebius wrote, a *Defense of Origen*,[6] and died at Caesarea in Palestine during the persecution of Maximinus.[7]

NOTES

1. Pamphilus was a disciple of Pierius in Alexandria; the latter was nicknamed "Origen Junior." See Q 2, 145, and *DVI* 76.1.

2. Eusebius named himself Eusebius Pamphili, i.e., the spiritual son of Pamphilus, and wrote a biography of him, now lost; see Q 3, 309–10. Nothing survives of this "special work on him" by Eusebius; cf. Eus., *h.e.* 7.32.25, quoted in Q 2, 144–45.

3. *bibliotheca: h.e.* 6.32.3; H. Y. Gamble, *Books*, 155–59, 231.

4. Cf. *h.e.* 6.32.3.

5. *In duodecim prophetas:* see Jerome, *DVI* 135.2.

6. Rufinus, Latin translation of *Apology for Origen*, PG 17, 541–616 (only Book 1); Jerome, *Adv. Rufinum* 3.12, FOTC 53, 176–79; E. Junod, "L'auteur de l'*Apologie* pour Origène traduite par Rufin: les témoignages contradictoires de Rufin et de Jérôme à propos de Pamphile et d'Eusèbe," FS H. Crouzel (Paris, 1992), 165–79.

7. He was imprisoned and died as a martyr in the seventh year of the persecution of Diocletian, on February 16, 310. See *h.e.* 7.32.25 and 8.13.6.

REFERENCES

Q 2, 121, 144–46 — Dr, 113 — Cath 10, 497–98, H. Crouzel — DSp 12, 150–53 — EEC 2², 859, E. Ferguson — EECh 2, 638, H. Crouzel — Photius, *Biblio., cod.* 118, ed. R. Henry — P. Nautin, *Origène* (Paris, 1977)

LXXVI. PIERIUS THE PRESBYTER

IERIUS, A PRIEST of the church of Alexandria,[1] in the reign of the emperors Carus and Diocletian,[2] at the same time when Theonas[3] was bishop of Alexandria, instructed the faithful with great success and reached such a pitch of eloquence in different treatises of his which survive to the present day that he was called Origen Junior.[4]

2. It is well known that he was a practitioner of extreme asceticism and voluntary poverty and was most knowledgeable in the art of dialectic,[5] and after the persecution spent the rest of his life in Rome.[6]

3. There is in existence a very long tract of his, *On the Prophet Hosea*,[7] which was delivered on the vigil of the Pasch, as the text itself makes clear.[8]

NOTES

1. Eus., *h.e.* 7.32.26–27; L. B. Radford, *Three Teachers of Alexandria: Theognostus, Pierius and Peter: A Study in the Early History of Origenism and Anti-Origenism* (Cambridge, 1908).

2. *h.e.* 7.30.22. Carus reigned, 282–283; Diocletian, 284–305.

3. *h.e.* 7.32.30. Theonas succeeded Dionysius, c. 281.

4. "Origen Junior": Q 2, 145.

5. *h.e.* 7.32.27.

6. Courcelle, *LLW*, 113, states, "He knows equally well Pierius [i.e., as Origen] . . . probably had in his possession the collection of Pierius' twelve *Logoi* that Photius still read."

7. *On the Prophet Hosea*: cf. Jerome, *ep.* 48.3, CSEL 54, 348–49, where Jerome quotes Pierius. By *tractatus* Jerome here must mean a "sermon," one for the paschal vigil.

8. Jerome read it for his own Commentary: PL 25:819B; cf. Courcelle, *LLW*, 113 n. 176.

REFERENCES

Q 2, 111–13 — Cath 11, 318, P.-Th. Camelot — EEC 2², 920, F. W. Norris — EECh 2, 687, C. Kannengiesser — LThK 8, 496, J. Quasten — NCE 11, 349, F. X. Murphy

LXXVII. LUCIAN THE PRESBYTER

UCIAN, A VERY CULTIVATED man, a priest of the church of Antioch,[1] so applied himself to the study of the Scriptures that down to this day some of the copies of the Scriptures are called after him.[2]

2. Works *On Faith*[3] are ascribed to him, and short epistles to various recipients.

3. For confessing Christ, he was put to death in Nicomedia during the persecution of Maximinus[4] and was buried at Helenopolis in Bithynia.

NOTES

1. Eus., *h.e.* 9.6.3.
2. CPG 1723; B. M. Metzger, *Chapters in the History of New Testament Textual Criticism (The Lucianic Recension of the Greek Bible)*, New Testament Tools and Studies 4 (Leiden, 1963), 1–41.
3. Cf. *h.e.* 8.13.2.
4. *h.e.* 8.13.2 and 9.6.3. For Maximinus Daia (310–313), cf. *h.e.* 9.6.4 through 9.7.15.

REFERENCES

Q 2, 142–44 — Dr, 197 — CPG 1720–1723 — EEC 2², 697, F. W. Norris — EECh 1, 507, M. Simonetti — Dihle, *Greek and Latin,* 382 — G. Bardy, *Recherches sur Saint Lucien d'Antioche et son école* (Paris, 1936)

LXXVIII. PHILEAS THE BISHOP

HILEAS, FROM THE EGYPTIAN city called Thmuis,[1] a man of noble family and not inconsiderable means, after becoming bishop, composed a most elegant book, *In Praise of Martyrs*,[2] and, after a debate against the judge who compelled him to offer sacrifice,[3] he was beheaded for Christ by the same instigator of persecution in Egypt[4] as was Lucian in Nicomedia.[5]

NOTES

1. Eus., *h.e.* 8.9.7–8; Thmuis, a town in lower Egypt.
2. CPG 1671; *h.e.* 8.10.2–10, a letter to the Thmuites.
3. *h.e.* 8.10.11–12; 8.13.7.
4. He died c. 307. See *The Acts of Phileas Bishop of Thmuis including Fragments of the Greek Psalter*, P. Chester Beatty XV (With a New Edition of P. Bodmer XX, and Halkin's *Latin Acta*), ed. with intro., trans., and comm. by A. Pietersma (Geneva, 1983).
5. For Lucian in Nicomedia, see *h.e.* 8.13.2.

REFERENCES

Q 2, 117 — CPG 1, 1671–1672 — EEC 2², 908, E. Ferguson — EECh 2, 680, V. Saxer — BHL 6799

LXXIX. ARNOBIUS THE RHETORICIAN

RNOBIUS,[1] IN THE REIGN of the emperor Diocletian,[2] taught rhetoric with great success in Sicca, Africa, and wrote volumes *Against the Pagans*[3] which enjoy wide circulation.

NOTES

1. The first entry under A.D. 327 in Jerome's *Continuation* of Eusebius's *Chronicle* (ed. Helm, 231g), trans. Donalson, 39, reads: "Arnobius was con-

sidered a distinguished rhetorician from Africa. When he was in Sicca [in Africa] instructing young men in declamation he was converted to true belief by his dreams; a pagan up to then, he did not receive the faith, that which he had always fought against, from the bishop. He spent his nights composing the most authoritative books against his former religion. Finally he obtained the covenant through certain pledges of faith, as it were." M. B. Simmons, *Arnobius of Sicca: religious conflict* (Oxford, 1995), takes this at face value, with interesting results.

2. Diocletian reigned, 284–305.

3. *Adversus nationes:* CPL 93. Text: C. Marchesi (Turin, 1953). Trans.: G. E. McCracken, *Arnobius of Sicca, The Case Against the Pagans,* ACW 7–8 (Westminster, Maryland, 1949). See also G. Gierlich, *Arnobius von Sicca. Kommentar zu den ersten beiden Büchern* (Mainz, 1985); O. P. Nicholson, "The date of Arnobius' *Adversus gentes,*" StudPat 15 (1984): 100–107; R. MacMullen, *Christianity and Paganism in the Fourth to Eighth Centuries* (New Haven: Yale University Press, 1997), 87 and 206. In the latter location, MacMullen characterizes *Adv. nat.* 2.10 as "dismissing all non-Christian religious thought as so much argy-bargy and quarrelous obfuscation" (n. 29).

REFERENCES

Q 2, 383–92 — CPL 93 — EEC 1², 119–20, M. P. McHugh — EECh 1,82, P. Siniscalco — LThK 1³, 1020, R. Kany — HLL 5, 365–75, A. Wlosok — R. M. Grant, *Greek Apologists,* 193–94

LXXX. FIRMIANUS THE RHETORICIAN, SURNAMED LACTANTIUS

IRMIANUS, ALSO CALLED Lactantius,[1] a disciple of Arnobius, summoned to Nicomedia under Diocletian, along with the grammarian Flavius,[2] whose verse compositions *On Medicinal Matters* are extant, taught rhetoric there; but because of the scarcity of pupils, in that it was a Greek city, he switched to writing.

2. We have surviving his *Symposium,*[3] which he wrote as a young man in Africa;

an Ὁδοιπορικόν, *Travel Guide,*[4] from Africa to Nicomedia, composed in hexameters;

another book entitled, *The Grammarian;*[5]

112   ST. JEROME

another fine work, *On the Anger of God;*[6]
seven books, *Divine Institutes against the Pagans;*[7]
and an' Ἐπιτομήν, *Epitome,*[8] of the same work in a book ἀκε-
φάλῳ, without a heading;
and *To Asclepiades,*[9] two books;
On Persecution,[10] one book;
To Probus,[11] four books of letters;
To Severus,[12] two books of letters;
To Demetrianus, his disciple, two books of letters;[13]
and to the same, *On the Workmanship of God, or On the Formation of Man,*[14] one book.

3. In extreme old age he became the teacher in Gaul of Caesar Crispus, son of Constantine, who was later put to death by
his father.[15]

NOTES

1. E. Heck, HLL 8, 5, 375–404. See also M. Perrin, "Jérôme lecteur de
Lactance," in *Jérôme entre l'Occident et l'Orient,* ed. Duval, 99–114.
2. Nicomedia: in Bithynia, a district, later a Roman province on the
northwest coast of Asia Minor. See R. MacMullen, *Christianity and Paganism
in the Fourth to Eighth Centuries* (New Haven: Yale University Press, 1997),
85–87 and 205 nn. 23–25. On the appointments, see Jerome, *Chron.,* A.D.
230; P. F. Beatrice, " 'Antistes philosophiae.' Ein christenfeindlicher Propa-
gandist am Hofe Diocletians nach dem Zeugnis des Laktanz," *AugR* 33
(1993): 31–48. The *grammaticus* Flavius is identified in PL 23, 687, note q,
as Fabius Flavius Clemens. Flavius is also mentioned in Jerome, *Adv. Iovinianum* 2.6.
3. Not extant.
4. Ὁδοιπορικός: W. Berschin, *Greek Letters,* 47, cites this entry as an example of Jerome ornamenting his Latin style with Greek elements.
5. Not extant.
6. *De ira Dei:* Q 2, 399; CPL 88. Text: CSEL 27, 65–132.
7. CPL 85. Text: CSEL 19, 1–672. Trans. M. F. McDonald, FOTC 49.
8. Ἐπιτομή: CPL 86. Text: CSEL 19, 673–761. See I. Opelt, art., "Epitome," RAC 5 (1962): 944–72; A. Wlosok, "Lactance lecteur d'Arnobe dans
l'*Epitome* des Institutions?" *REA* 30 (1984): 36–41. In *ep.* 70.5 (CSEL 54,
707) we read: "Septem libros adversus gentes Arnobius edidit totidemque
discipulus eius Lactantius, qui de ira quoque et de opificio dei duo volumina condidit; quos si legere volueris, dialogorum Ciceronis [*var.:* in eis]
ἐπιτομὴν repperies." This judgment, no doubt, prompted Pico della Miran-
dola and the Humanists to dub him "the Christian Cicero." But despite the
undoubted Ciceronian overtones, Jerome also thought him short on theol-

ogy, while being facile on rebuttal skills: "Lactantius, quasi quidam fluvius eloquentiae Tullianae, utinam tam nostra adfirmare potuisset, quam facile aliena destruxit" (*ep.* 58.10, CSEL 54, 539). Ironically, Lactantius seems to have got in a pre-emptive strike against just such a criticism (and that, at the expense of Tertullian and Cyprian!): "Although Tertullian handled the same material fully in that book called *The Apology;* however, because it is one thing to make answer to accusers, which consists in defense or negation alone, and another to give instruction (which we are doing) which must contain the substance of all doctrine, I did not shrink from this task, so that I might complete the material which Cyprian did not reach in that work in which, as he himself says, he tries to refute Demetrianus' 'barking and roaring against' the truth" (*Div. Inst.* 5.4, FOTC 49, 337, trans. Sr. M. F. McDonald, 337).

9. Not extant. See Q 2, 405; HLL 8, 5, 401.

10. CPL 91; Lactantius, *De Mortibus Persecutorum*, ed. and trans. J. L. Creed, OECT (Oxford, 1984).

11. CPL 89; CSEL 27, 155.

12. CPL 89; Herzog-Schmidt, HLL 8, 5, 402.

13. CPL 89; CSEL 27, 156–57; HLL 8, 5, 402.

14. *De opificio Dei:* CPL 87.

15. Crispus: PLRE 1, 233; Barnes, *C. and E.*, 220–21, 250; P. Guthrie, "The Execution of Crispus," *Phoenix* 20 (1966): 325–31. Under A.D. 328 the *Chronicle* reports, "Constantine killed his wife Fausta" (ed. Helm, 232a, trans. Donalson, 40).

REFERENCES

Q 2, 392–410 — Dr, 147–50 — CPL, 85–92 — Cath 6, 1581–83, P.-Th. Camelot — *CW* 76, 125–27, R. D. Sider — DSp 9, 47–59, E. Lamirande — EEC 2², 660–61, M. P. McHugh — EECh 1, 469–70, V. Loi — HLL 5, 570, A. Wlosok — LThK 6, 726–28, J. Martin — LThK 6³, 583–84, E. Heck — NCE 8, 308–9, J. Stevenson — TRE 20, 370–74, A. Wlosok — *Gestalten* 1, 176–88, A. Wlosok — BBKL 4, 952–65

Texts: CSEL 19 and 27

LXXXI. EUSEBIUS THE BISHOP

USEBIUS, BISHOP of Caesarea in Palestine,[1] extremely industrious in the study of the Sacred Scriptures,[2] and, with Pamphilus the martyr a diligent researcher of the sacred library,[3] published numerous works, including the following:

2. Εὐαγγελικῆς ἀποδείξεως, *Demonstratio evangelica*,[4] twenty books;

Εὐαγγελικῆς προπαρασκευῆς, *Praeparatio evangelica*,[5] fifteen books;

Θεοφανείας, *Theophany*,[6] five books;

Ecclesiastical History,[7] ten books;

Universal History of Chronological Tables,[8] and an᾽ Ἐπιτομή, *Epitome*[9] of these;

On the διαφωνία, *Discrepancies in the Gospels*,[10] ten books;

On Isaiah,[11] ten books;

and *Against Porphyry*,[12] who, as some think, was writing in Sicily at the same time,[13] twenty-five books;

On Places (Τοπικῶν),[14] one book;

Ἀπολογίας, *An Apology for Origen*,[15] six books;

three books, *On the Life of Pamphilus*;[16]

other writings, *On the Martyrs*;[17]

most learned *Commentaries on the 150 Psalms*;[18]

and many other works.[19]

3. He lived mainly in the reign of Constantine the emperor and Constantius,[20] and because of his friendship for Pamphilus the martyr was called Eusebius Pamphili.[21]

NOTES

1. For a recent over-view see H. W. Attridge and G. Hata, edd., *Eusebius, Christianity and Judaism* (Leiden and Detroit, 1992).

2. On his exegetical works see Q 3, 334–40.

3. On Pamphilus and the library, see Eus., *h.e.* 6.32.3, 7.32.25, 8.13.6; also Gamble, *Books*, 155–59.

4. CPG 3487; Q 3, 331–32.

5. CPG 3486; Q 3, 329–31.

6. CPG 3488; Q 3, 332–33.

7. CPG 3495; Q 3, 314–17.

8. CPG 3465.

9. Ἐπιτομή : a common term in Jerome's list of Varro's works; see *ep.* 33.2, CSEL 54, 254.

10. "*De Evangeliorum* διαφωνία [*or* Περὶ διαφωνίας Εὐαγγελίων], ten books" = *Quaestiones et solutiones*, CPG 3470; Q 3, 337; LThK 3, art., "Ero-

tapokriseis," 1041, H. Hunger; A. E. Johnson, "Rhetorical Criticism in Eusebius's *Gospel Questions*," StudPat 18, 1 (Kalamazoo, 1986), 33–39; G. Geraci, "L'utilizzazione dell'Antico Testamento nelle *Quaestiones et Responsiones* di Eusebio di Cesarea," *AnSE*, ser. 2 (1985): 251–55.

11. *On Isaiah:* fifteen (*not* ten) books, CPG 3468; Q 3, 338.

12. Q 3, 333.

13. See Eus., *h.e.* 6.19.1.

14. Τοπικῶν = *Onomastikon*, a gazetteer of biblical sites, CPG 3466; Q 3, 336; D. Groh, "The *Onomasticon* of Eusebius and the Rise of Christian Palestine," StudPat 18, 1 (Kalamazoo, 1986), 23–31.

15. CPG 3476; Q 2, 145–46; Q 3, 340–41.

16. Not extant; cf. Q 2, 145–46.

17. CPG 3490; Q 3, 317–19.

18. CPG 3467; Q 3, 337–38.

19. "many other works": See CPG 3469, 3475–3485, 3488, 3496–3503.

20. Constantine (306–337); Constantius (337–361).

21. See art., "Pamphilus," EECh 2, 638, H. Crouzel.

REFERENCES

Q 3, 309–345 — Dr, 188–197 — CPG 2, 3465–3507 — *TLG* 2018 — Cath 4, 702–7, G. Bardy — DHGE 15, 1437–60, J. Moreau — DSp 4, 1687–90, M. J. Rondeau and J. Kirchmyer — EEC 1², 399–402, R. Lyman — EECh 1, 299–301, C. Curti — LThK 3, 1195–97, H. Rahner — LThK 3³, 1007–9, T. D. Barnes — NCE 5, 633–36, J. Stevenson — RAC 6, 1052–88, J. Moreau — TRE 10, 537–43, D. S. Wallace-Hadrill — *Gestalten* 1, 224–35, G. Ruhbach — *Gestalten* 1, art., "Konstantin der Grosse," 189–214, T. Schleich — Dihle, *Greek and Latin*, 422–26, 473–74

LXXXII. RETICIUS THE BISHOP

ETICIUS, BISHOP of the Aedui, or more precisely of Autun,[1] was held in great esteem in Gaul in the reign of Constantine.[2]

2. His *Commentaries on the Song of Songs* are still read;[3] also another fine work, *Against Novatian*.[4]

Apart from these, I have found no other works of his.[5]

NOTES

1. Autun = Augustodunum: DHGE 5, 896–97, 907; cf. J. Régnier, *Les évêques d'Autun* (1988), 6–9.

2. For Reticius's role of mediation in Donatist affairs, cf. Eus., *h.e.* 10.5.19, as well as Barnes, *C. and E.*, 57 and 316 n. 136.

3. CPL 78; "still read": i.e., by Jerome himself; cf. *ep.* 5.2, CSEL 54, 22, in which Jerome besought Florentinus to request of Rufinus "the commentaries of bishop Reticius of Autun to have them copied. In them he has discussed *The Song of Songs* in eloquent style" (ACW 33, 37, and 196 n. 7). When he finally acquired the *commentarii* he was less enthusiastic: "cum mihi in illis multo displiceant plura, quam placeant" (*ep.* 37.4, CSEL 54, 288). Reticius was praised by Augustine in *Contra Julianum Pelagianum* 1.3.7, PL 44, 644, and *Op. imperf. contra Julianum* 1.55, PL 45, 1078.

4. CPL 77. Both works are now lost except for a fragment quoted in Peter Berengarius, *Liber apologeticus pro Abelardo.*

5. For a tear-jerking account of his death and burial, cf. Gregory of Tours, *Glory of the Confessors*, trans. R. Van Dam (Liverpool, 1988), 77–78.

REFERENCES

CPL 77–78 — Cath 12, n.s., 1174–75 — DSp 5, 789 — EECh 2, 733, V. Saxer — HLL 8, 5, 419 — LThK 8, 1258, J. A. Fischer

LXXXIII. METHODIUS THE BISHOP

ETHODIUS, BISHOP of Olympus in Lycia,[1] and later of Tyre, in a limpid and elegant style composed works, *Against Porphyry*[2] and

The Symposium of the Ten Virgins;[3]
an important work, *On the Resurrection*[4] against Origen, and another against the same author, *On the Pythoness;*[5]
a work, *On Freewill;*[6]
also a *Commentary on Genesis;*[7]
one *On the Song of Songs,*[8] and many other works[9] which are read eagerly by a wide public.

2. Toward the end of the last persecution, or, as others assert, under Decius and Valerian, he received the crown of martyrdom in Chalcis in Greece.[10]

NOTES

1. See L. G. Patterson, *Methodius of Olympus. Divine Sovereignty, Human Freedom, and Life in Christ* (Washington, D.C., 1997), esp. 6–8, 15–16.

2. Unfortunately lost; Q 2, 137; fragments in GCS 27, 509–519.

3. CPG 1810; Q 2, 130–33. Text: SC 95, ed. H. Musurillo and V.-H. Debidour (Paris, 1963). Trans.: H. Musurillo, ACW 27 (1958). See also Patterson, 64–140.

4. *On the Resurrection:* also called *Aglaophon*, after one of the interlocutors; see CPG 1812; Patterson, 141–99.

5. Lost.

6. CPG 1811; Q 2, 133; Patterson, 31–63.

7. Lost.

8. Lost.

9. CPG 1810–1830; Patterson, 200–227; see E. Prinzivalli, *L'esegesi biblica di Metodio di Olimpo* (Rome, 1985).

10. "martyrdom in Chalcis": in Euboia in 311, in the last persecution under Diocletian; Barnes, *C. and E.*, 193, 195.

REFERENCES

Q 2, 129–37 — *TLG* 2959 — CPG 1810–1830 — Cath 9, 46–48, P.-Th. Camelot — DSp 10, 1109–17, H. Musurillo — EEC 2², 747–48, F. W. Norris — EECh 1, 557, C. Riggi — LThK 7, 369, V. Buchheit — LThK 7³, 202–3, E. Prinzivalli — NCE 9, 742, H. Musurillo — Dihle, *Greek and Latin*, 382–84 — Buchheit, *Studien*, TU 69 (Berlin, 1958)

LXXXIV. JUVENCUS THE PRESBYTER

 UVENCUS, A SPANIARD[1] of very noble family, and a priest, translating into hexameter verse almost word for word the four Gospels,[2] published them in four volumes; also some other works in the same meter regarding the order of rites.

2. He lived in the reign of the emperor Constantine.

NOTES

1. See M. Flieger, *Interpretationen zum Bibeldichter Iuvencus* (Stuttgart, 1993).

2. Juvencus himself tells us this in *Evangeliorum libri iv* 4.803–6, CSEL 24,

145–46. The work consists of 3219 hexameters. See Eus., *Chron.*, A.D. 329 (ed. Helm, 232d), trans. Donalson, 40: "The priest, Juvencus, a native of Spain, expounded the Gospels in epic poetry [i.e., Vergilian hexameter]"; also Jerome's *ep.* 70 *ad Magnum* (CSEL 54, 707–8): "Iuvencus presbyter sub Constantino historiam domini salvatoris versibus explicavit nec pertimuit evangelii maiestatem sub metri leges mittere."

REFERENCES

Q 4, 265–69 — CPL 1385 — Cath 6, 1345, P.-Th. Camelot — DSp 8, 1651–52, M. C. Diaz y Diaz — EEC 1², 653, M. P. McHugh — EECh 1, 466, I. Opelt — HLL 8, 5, 331–36 — LThK 5³, 1118, W. Röttger — NCE 8, 102, E. P. Colbert

LXXXV. EUSTATHIUS THE BISHOP

EUSTATHIUS, WHO CAME from Side in Pamphylia,[1] first ruled a church of Beroea in Syria,[2] and then that of Antioch,[3] and having composed many works against the teaching of the Arians,[4] was, in the reign of Constantine, driven into exile to Trajanopolis, in Thrace,[5] where he remains buried down to the present day.

2. Works of his that survive are *On the Soul,*[6] *On the Witch of Endor against Origen,*[7] and countless epistles, which it would take too long to list in detail.

NOTES

1. Side, on the coast: *OCD*³, 1404.
2. On Beroea see DHGE 8, 887–88, R. Janin.
3. See Eus., *Chron.*, A.D. 328 (ed. Helm, 232c), trans. Donalson, 40: "twenty-third bishop of Antioch."
4. R. P. C. Hanson, "The Source and Significance of the fourth *Oratio contra Arianos* attributed to Athanasius," *VigChr* 42 (1988): 257–68.
5. See *Chron.*, A.D. 328, trans. Donalson, 40: "From the time he was driven into exile for his faith down to the present day, Arians have continued to control the church in Antioch"; also R. P. C. Hanson, "The fate of Eustathius of Antioch," *ZKG* 95 (1984): 171–79. For the cause of exile, see

Adv. Rufinum 3.42, where Jerome alludes to the stratagem of Eusebius of Nicomedia [cf. Theodoret, *h.e.* 5.20, PG 82, 966] to discredit Eustathius: "These are the tricks of the heretics, that is to say, of your masters, to resort to reviling when convicted of perfidy. It was through such an invention that Eustathius, bishop of Antioch, found out about the sons of whom he had no knowledge" (trans. J. N. Hritzu, FOTC 53, 215 and n. 86).

6. *De anima contra philosophos*, CPG 3351.

7. *De* ἐγγαστριμύθῳ: CPG 3350. J. F. Dechow, "Origen's 'heresy.' From Eustathius to Epiphanius," *Origeniana quarta* (1987), 405–9; M. Spanneut, "La Bible d'Eustathe d'Antioche," StudPat 4 [= TU 79 (Berlin, 1961)], 171–90.

REFERENCES

Q 3, 302–6 — Dr, 160, 169–70 — CPG 3350–3390 — Cath 4, 715–16, G. Bardy — DHGE 16, 13–23, M. Spanneut — DSp 4, 2, 1706–8, M. Spanneut — EEC 1², 403, R. A. Greer — EECh 1, 303, M. Simonetti — LThK 3, 1202–3, A. van Roey — LThK 3³, 1014–15, A. van Roey — NCE 5, 638, M. Spanneut — TRE 9, 543–46, R. Lorenz — Dihle, *Greek and Latin,* 549

LXXXVI. MARCELLUS THE BISHOP

ARCELLUS, BISHOP OF ANCYRA,[1] lived in the reign of the emperors Constantine and Constantius,[2] and wrote many works on different subjects, and especially *Against the Arians.*[3]

2. The books of Asterius[4] and Apollinaris against him are cited, accusing him of the heresy of Sabellius,[5] and Hilary also, in the seventh book of his *Against the Arians*[6] mentions his name as that of a heretic.

3. However, he maintained that he did not hold the doctrine of which he was accused, but belonged to the community of Julius and Athanasius, bishops of the cities of Rome and Alexandria.[7]

NOTES

1. J. T. Lienhard, "Marcellus of Ancyra in Modern Research," *TS* 43 (1982): 486–503; *idem, "Contra Marcellum": Marcellus of Ancyra and Fourth-*

Century Theology (Washington, D.C.: Catholic University of America Press, 1999).

2. Constantine (306–337); Constantius (337–361).

3. L. Barnard, "Marcellus of Ancyra and the Eusebians," *GkOrthThR* 25 (1980): 63–76; M. Simonetti, "Ancora su *Homoousios* a proposito di due recenti studi," *VetChr* 17 (1980): 85–98; *idem*, "Homoousians," and "Homoousios," EECh 1, 396; C. Luibhéid, *Eusebius of Caesarea and the Arian Crisis* (Dublin, 1981), *s.v.:* "The Polemic against Marcellus of Ancyra."

4. Asterius Sophista, *Syntagmation*, CPG 2817.

5. J. T. Lienhard, "Basil of Caesarea, Marcellus of Ancyra, and 'Sabellius'": *ChH* 58 (1989): 157–67; *idem*, "Acacius of Caesarea: *Contra Marcellum*. Historical and Theological Considerations," *CrSt* 10 (1989): 1–21.

6. Hilary, *On the Trinity*, Book 7, trans. Stephen McKenna, FOTC 25 (1954), 223–71.

7. Julius, Bishop of Rome, 337–352; Athanasius lived, 295–373; see M. Tetz, "Markellianer und Athanasios von Alexandrien. Die markellische *Expositio fidei ad Athanasium* des Diakons Eugenios von Ankyra," *ZNW* 64 (1973): 75–121; *idem*, "Zur Theologie des Markell von Ankyra, I–III," *ZKG* 75 (1964): 217–70; 79 (1968): 3–42; 83 (1972): 145–94; M. Simonetti, "Su alcune opere attribuite di recente a Marcello d'Ancira," *RSLR* 9 (1973): 313–29; F. Dinsen, *"Homoousios."* Die Geschichte des Begriffs bis zum Konzil von Konstantinopel (381) (Kiel, 1976); W. A. Bienert, "Das vornicaenische ὁμοούσιος als Ausdruck der Rechtgläubigkeit," *ZKG* 90 (1979): 151–75; G. Feige, *Die Lehre Markells von Ankyra in der Darstellung seiner Gegner, EThSt* 58 (1991).

REFERENCES

Q 3, 197–201 — Dr, 178–80 — CPG 2800–2806 — Cath 8, 403, P.-Th. Camelot — EEC 2², 713–14, R. Lyman — EECh 1, 522, C. Kannengiesser — LThK 7, 4–5, O. Perler — LThK 6³, 1302–3, W. A. Löhr — NCE 9, 1910, V. C. De Clerq — TRE 22, 83–89, K. Seibt

LXXXVII. ATHANASIUS THE BISHOP

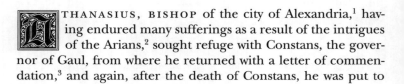THANASIUS, BISHOP of the city of Alexandria,[1] having endured many sufferings as a result of the intrigues of the Arians,[2] sought refuge with Constans, the governor of Gaul, from where he returned with a letter of commendation,[3] and again, after the death of Constans, he was put to

flight and stayed in hiding until the reign of Jovian, who restored him to his church;[4] and he died under Valens.[5]

2. Two books of his, *Against the Pagans*,[6] are known;

and one, *Against Valens and Ursacius;*
a work, *On Virginity;*[7]
and many *On the Persecutions of the Arians;*
On the Titles of the Psalms;
a history containing *The Life of Antony the Monk;*[8]
also Ἑορταστικαί, *Festal Letters;*[9] and many other works which it would take too long to enumerate.

NOTES

1. *Chron.*, A.D. 330 (ed. Helm, 232f.), trans. Donalson, 40: "At Alexandria Athanasius was ordained as the nineteenth bishop." See also C. Kannengiesser, "The Athanasian Decade, 1974–1984. A Bibliographical Report," *TS* 46 (1985): 524–41; *idem*, "Bulletin de théologie patristique: Athanase et son siècle," *RechSR* 74 (1986): 575–614; *idem*, *Arius and Athanasius* (Variorum reprints, 1991).

2. Markus Vinzent, *Pseudo-Athanasius. Contra Arianos IV. Eine Schrift gegen Asterius von Kappadokien, Eusebius von Cäsarea, Markell von Ankyra und Photin von Sirmium*, Supplements to Vigiliae Christianae 36 (Leiden: Brill, 1996).

3. Cf. *Chron.*, A.D. 346, ed. Helm, 236e, trans. Donalson, 44.

4. A. Martin, *Athanase d'Alexandrie et l'Église d'Égypte au IVe siècle (328–373)* (Rome and Paris, 1996).

5. Valens, 364–378.

6. CPG 2090; see Athanasius, *Contra Gentes*, with intro., trans., and comm. by E. P. Meijering, Philosophia Patrum 7 (Leiden: Brill, 1984); also *Athanasius. "Contra Gentes" and "De Incarnatione"*, ed. and trans. R. W. Thomson (Oxford: Clarendon Press, 1971).

7. CPG 2145.

8. CPG 2101.

9. CPG 2102.

REFERENCES

Q 3, 20–79 — Dr, 207–13 — CPG 2000–2309 — *TLG* 2035 — Cath 1, 974–80, G. Bardy — DHGE 4, 1313–40, G. Bardy — DSp 1, 1047–52, G. Bardy — EEC 1², 137–40, C. Kannengiesser — EECh 1, 93–95, G. C. Stead — LThK 1, 976–81, P.-Th. Camelot — LThK 1³, 1126–30, C. Kannengiesser — NCE 1, 996–99, V. C. De Clerq — RAC 1, 860–66, G. Gentz — TRE 4, 333–49 — Dihle, *Greek and Latin*, 409–12 — C. Kannengiesser, *Gestalten* 1 (1984), 266–83

LXXXVIII. ANTONY THE MONK

NTONY, the hermit[1] of whom Athanasius, bishop of Alexandria, composed a *Life*[2] in an excellent volume, sent seven letters[3] of apostolic sense and preaching in Coptic to various monasteries, which have been translated into Greek, the chief one of which is addressed, *To the Monks of Arsinoe*.

2. He lived in the reign of Constantine and his sons.[4]

NOTES

1. Antony (+356). See I. Gobry, *Les moines en Occident, I. De saint Antoine à saint Basile* (Paris, 1985).

2. See Q 3, 39–44; L. W. Barnard, "Did Athanasius Know Antony?" *Ancient Society* 24 (1993): 139–49.

3. Letters: PG 40, 977–100; *Epistulae VII* (*Latine*), CPG 2330; *Fragmenta epistulae* (*coptice et arabice*), CPG 2331; *Epistula ad Theodorum*, CPG 2332. See also S. Rubenson, *The Letters of Antony: Origenist Theology* (Lund, 1990); *idem*, *The Letters of St. Antony. The Monasticism and the Making of a Saint* (Minneapolis: Fortress Press, 1995); D. J. Chitty, *The Desert a City* (Oxford, 1966).

4. *Chronicon*, A.D. 356 (ed. Helm, 240b), trans. Donalson, 48: "The monk Antony died in the desert in his one-hundred-and-fifth year."

REFERENCES

Q 3, 148–53 — Dr, 316–19 — *TLG* 2035.047 (*Vita*) — CPG 2330–2338 — Cath 1, 664–66, G. Bardy — DHGE 3, 726–34, J. David — DSp 1, 702–3, G. Bardy — EEC 1², 59–60, F. W. Norris — EECh 1, 44, T. Orlandi — LThK 1, 786–88, G. J. M. Bartelink — LThK 1³, 786–88, G. J. M. Bartelink — NCE 1, 594–95, R. T. Meyer

LXXXIX. BASIL THE BISHOP

ASIL, bishop of Ancyra, by profession a physician,[1] wrote

Against Marcellus[2] and
On Virginity[3] and some other works.

In the reign of Constantius he was, together with Eustathius of Sebaste, the leader of the party of the Macedonians.[4]

NOTES

1. "a physician": R. Le Coz, "Les Pères de l'Église Grecque et la Médecine," *BLE* 98 (1997): 137ff. On Ancyra see EEC 1[2], 50, R. Lyman; EECh 1, 37, D. Stiernon.

2. J. N. Steenson, *Basil of Ancyra and the course of Nicene orthodoxy* (Ph.D. diss., Oxford, 1983).

3. CPG 2827.

4. See art., "Macedoni," EECh 1, 516, M. Simonetti. They are also called Pneumatomachians; cf. EEC 2[2], 930, F. W. Norris.

REFERENCES

Q 3, 201–3 — Dr, 184–86 — *TLG* 2084 — CPG 2, 2825–2827 — Cath 1, 1280, G. Bardy — DHGE 6, 1104–7, R. Javin — DSp 1, 1283, F. Cavallera — EEC 1[1], 169, E. Ferguson — EECh 1, 113, M. Simonetti — LThK 2, 31, O. Volk — LThK 2[3], 66–67, W. A. Löhr — NCE 2, 147–48, H. Musurillo — Dihle, *Greek and Latin*, 548–49

XC. THEODORUS THE BISHOP

THEODORUS, BISHOP of Heraclea in Thrace[1] during the reign of the emperor Constantius,[2] published

Commentaries on Matthew,[3]
On John,[4]
On the Apostle [Paul],[5]
and *On the Psalter*,[6] in an elegant and precise style that followed mainly the literal interpretation.

NOTES

1. CPG 3561–66.

2. Constantius, Emperor, 337–361.

3. CPG 3562, *in catenis;* mentioned also in Jerome, Prolog to *Hom. in Matt.*, quoted in Courcelle, *LLW*, 99 note; J. Reuss, *Matthaeus-Kommentare*, TU 61 (Berlin, 1957), 55–95.

4. CPG 3564, *Fragmenta in catenis,* J. Reuss, TU 89, 65–178.

5. CPG 3566: on 1 Cor 15.51, *in catenis;* see Courcelle, *LLW,* 118 nn. 222–224.

6. CPG 3567: *Fragmenta in Psalmos, in catenis;* see Courcelle, *LLW,* 120 n. 245.

REFERENCES

CPG 3561–3567 — LThK 4³, 1027–29, H. Crouzel

XCI. EUSEBIUS, ANOTHER BISHOP

 USEBIUS OF EMESA,[1] who had a fine rhetorical talent, composed innumerable works suited to elicit popular approval; and his historical writings, following more a literal exegesis, are most eagerly read by those who practice public speaking.[2]

2. Among these the chief are,

Against the Jews, Gentiles, and Novatians,[3]
On the Epistle to the Galatians,[4] ten books;
and brief but numerous *Homilies on the Gospels.*[5]

3. He lived in the times of the emperor Constantius and died during his reign and was buried at Antioch.[6]

NOTES

1. Bishop from 341 until sometime before 359. Emesa (Homs), on the Orontes, was a center of Syrian sun-worship.

2. Eusebius, born at Edessa, received his education at Edessa, Scythopolis, Caesarea Maritima, Alexandria, and Antioch. See M. F. Wiles, "The Theology of Eusebius of Emesa," StudPat 19 (1989), 267–80.

3. Not extant.

4. CPG 3533, *Fragmenta.*

5. Eusebius Gallicanus, *Sermones* i–xvii (CPG 3525; CPL 966). See Courcelle, *LLW,* 148 n. 51. For text see *Eusebius "Gallicanus",* ed. Glorie, CCL 101, 101A, 101B, 1970–71; A. M. Triacca, "Cultus in Eusebio Gallicano [Pseudo Eusebius]," *AFLC* 6 (1987): 207–26.

6. Eusebius had accompanied Constantius on an expedition against the Persians, c. 348.

REFERENCES

Q 3, 348–51 — CPG 3525–3543 (*Fragmenta syriaca 'XXV*, CPG 3527)— DHGE 15, 1462–63, E. M. Buytaert — DSp 4, 1690–1695, J.-M. Leroux — EECh 1, 301, M. Simonetti — LThK 3³, 1010, M. Stark — NCE 5, 636, E. des Places

XCII. TRIPHYLIUS THE BISHOP

RIPHYLIUS, bishop of Ledra, or Leucosia,[1] in Cyprus, was the most eloquent man of his time and enjoyed the most widespread fame during the reign of the emperor Constantius. I have read his *Commentaries on the Song of Songs*.[2] And he is said to have composed many other works which have not at all come into our hands.

NOTES

1. F. Halkin, "La Vie de sainte Tryphylios," *AnBoll* 66 (1948): 11–26. For Ledra (modern Nicosia) in Cyprus, see EECh, Map 23.
2. Not extant.

REFERENCES

Cath 15, 356–57

XCIII. DONATUS THE HERESIARCH

ONATUS, FROM WHOM the Donatists throughout Africa[1] got their name, during the reigns of the emperors, Constantine and Constantius,[2] asserting that the Scriptures were handed over to the pagans by our fellow Christians during the persecution,[3] deceived almost the whole of Africa, and particularly Numidia,[4] by his persuasiveness.[5]

2. Many of his works pertaining to his heresy are extant, also a volume, *On the Holy Spirit*, which is in accord with Arian teaching.

NOTES

1. Eus., *Chron.*, A.D. 328 (ed. Helm, 232b), trans. Donalson, 40: "Donatus, whose followers throughout Africa were called Donatists, won renown." Cf. J. S. Alexander, "The Motive for a Distinction between Donatus of Carthage and Donatus of Casae Nigrae," *JThS*, n.s., 31 (1980): 540–47.

2. Constantine, 306–337; Constantius, 337–361. See J.-L. Maier, *Le dossier du Donatisme, I: Des origines à la mort de Constance, II (303–361)* (Berlin, 1987).

3. W. H. C. Frend, *The Donatist Church.* Those handing over the Scriptures were the *traditores.* See also M. A. Tilley, *The Bible in Christian North Africa: The Donatist World* (Minneapolis: Fortress Press, 1997).

4. On the spread of Donatism, cf. *Chron.*, A.D. 355, ed. Helm, 239h, trans. Donalson, 47; J.-P. Brisson, *Autonomisme et christianisme dans l'Afrique romaine* (1958); and, *e contra*, A. Mandouze, *AC* 29 (1960): 61–107. See also J. E. Merdinger, *Rome and the African Church* (New Haven, 1997), 66–67, 201–4.

5. Perhaps surprisingly, there is no mention of Jerome's teacher of the same name, Donatus, the grammarian, of whom he does speak in *Adv. Rufinum* 1.17, listing him among the great commentators: "Commentarios praeceptoris mei Donati aeque in Virgilium"; on this Donatus cf. Dihle, *Greek and Latin*, 442–43; G. Brugnoli, "Donato e Girolamo," *VetChr* 2 (1965): 139–49.

REFERENCES

Q 2, 381, 382, 413 — Dr, 337 — CPL 709–724, *Scriptores Donatistae* — EEC 1², 343–47, W. H. C. Frend — EECh 1, 250, W. H. C. Frend — LThK 3, 505–6, art., "Donatisten (streit)," L. Ueding — LThK 3³, 332–34, art., "Donatismus, Donatisten," B. Kriegbaum

XCIV. ASTERIUS THE PHILOSOPHER

STERIUS, A PHILOSOPHER of the Arian sect,[1] in the reign of Constantius,[2] wrote commentaries *On the Epistle to the Romans,*
On the Gospels,[3]
and *On the Psalms,*[4]
and many other works[5] which are studiously read by those who belong to his sect.

NOTES

1. W. Kinzig, "Asterius *Sophista* oder Asterius *ignotus*? Eine Antwort," *VigChr* 45 (1991): 388–98.
2. Constantius, 337–361.
3. Neither work survives.
4. M. Richard, ed., *Asterii Sophistae Comm. in Psalmos* (Oslo, 1956); W. Kinzig, *In search of Asterius: Studies on the Authorship of the Homilies on the Psalms* (Göttingen, 1990). For excerpt from 6th Homily on Psalm 5, see R. Cantalamessa, *Easter in the Early Church,* trans. Quigley and Lienhard, 70, 166–67.
5. See CPG 2816–2819.

REFERENCES

Q 3, 194–97 — CPG 2, 2815–19 — Cath 1, 969, G. Bardy — DHGE 4, 1167–68, G. Bardy — EEC 1², 136, R. Lyman — EECh 1, 92, M. Simonetti — LThK 1³, 1101, W. Kinzig — NCE 1, 984, M. R. P. McGuire

XCV. LUCIFER THE BISHOP

UCIFER, BISHOP of Cagliari,[1] who had been sent, with Pancratius and Hilarion, clerics of the church of Rome, as a delegation in defense of the faith, by Bishop Liberius[2] to the emperor Constantius,[3] was exiled to Palestine[4] because he refused to deny the Nicene faith, under the name of Athanasius;

2. showing marvelous constancy and a spirit ready for martyrdom, he wrote a work *Against Constantius the Emperor* and sent it to him to read,[5] and not much later he returned in the time of the emperor Julian, and died in Cagliari in the reign of Valentinianus.[6]

NOTES

1. See Eus., *Chron.*, 355 A.D., ed. Helm, 239I, trans. Donalson, 47–48.

2. For Liberius, ordained the thirty-fourth bishop of Rome, cf. *Chron.*, A.D. 349, ed. Helm, 237b; LThK 6³ (1997), 894–95, G. Schwaiger.

3. EEC 1², 286–87, art., "Constantius II," R. M. Grant; EECh 1, 198, M. Forlin Patrucco; M. M. Mudd, *Studies in the Reign of Constantius II* (New York, 1989).

4. Exiled by Constantius, 355–361. The occasion was the Council of Milan; see Eus., *Chron.*, A.D. 355, ed. Helm, 239I, trans. Donalson, 47–48.

5. I. Opelt, "Formen der Polemik bei Lucifer von Calaris," *VigChr* 26 (1972): 200–226.

6. Return from exile: *Chron.*, A.D. 362, ed. Helm, 242e, trans. Donalson, 50. His death: *Chron.*, A.D. 370 (ed. Helm, 246a), trans. Donalson, 53: "like Gregory, a bishop in Spain, and Philo of Libya, he never joined himself to the Arian depravity."

REFERENCES

Q 4, 61–65 — CPL 112–118 — Cath 7, 1250–51, J. Liébaert — DSp 6, 923 — EEC 2², 697, M. P. McHugh — EECh 2, M. Simonetti — LThK 6³, 1083–84, C. Kannengiesser — LThK 2³, 882–83, art., "Cagliari," M. Lupi — HLL 8, 5, 486–91

XCVI. EUSEBIUS, ANOTHER BISHOP

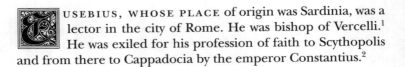

USEBIUS, WHOSE PLACE of origin was Sardinia, was a lector in the city of Rome. He was bishop of Vercelli.[1] He was exiled for his profession of faith to Scythopolis and from there to Cappadocia by the emperor Constantius.[2]

2. In the reign of the emperor Julian he was restored[3] to his church and published *Commentaries on the Psalms of Eusebius of Caesarea*[4] which he had translated from Greek into Latin. He died in the reign of Valentinianus and Valens.[5]

NOTES

1. See Ambrose, *ep.* 63; E. Milano, "Eusebio di Vercelli, vescovo metropolita. Leggenda o realtà storica?" *IMU* 30 (1987): 313–22.

2. He was exiled for opposing the condemnation of Athanasius at the synod of Milan; see *Chron.*, A.D. 355, ed. Helm, 239. Cf. L. A. Speller, "A note on Eusebius of Vercelli and the Council of Milan," *JThS* 36 (1985): 157–65.

3. *Chron.*, A.D. 369, ed. Helm, 245.

4. On translation of commentaries on Psalms, now lost, cf. Jerome, *ep.* 61.2. Three of his letters, however, are extant; see PL 12, 947–954.

5. L. S. Dattrino, "Eusebio di Vercelli, vescovo <martire>? vescovo <monacho>?" *AugR* 24 (1984): 167–87. Eus., *Chron.*, ed. Helm, 245j, gives 369 as date of his death.

REFERENCES

Q 3, 32, 337 — Q 4, 62–64 — CPL 105 — EEC 1², 403, J. T. Lienhard — EECh 1, 302, L. Dattrino — DHGE 15, 1477–83, V. C. de Clerq— LThK 3, 1200, L. Ueding — LThK 3³, 1012–13, M. Friedrowicz

For texts and studies, see L. Dattrino, *Il "De Trinitate" pseudoatanasiano* (Rome, 1976); M. Simonetti, "Qualche osservazione sul *De Trinitate* attribuito a Eusebio di Vercelli," *RiCultCM* 5 (1963): 386–93; *Eusebii Vercellensis episcopi quae supersunt. De Trinitate Libelli VII. Epistulae*, ed. V. Bulhart, CCL 9 (1957), 1–205 (*De Trinitate*).

XCVII. FORTUNATIANUS THE BISHOP

ORTUNATIANUS, AN AFRICAN by origin,[1] and bishop of Aquileia in the reign of the emperor Constantius,[2] wrote *Commentaries on the Gospels*,[3] divided in sections[4] in a concise and inelegant style;

2. and for this he is held in disdain because at first he solicit-

ed Liberius, bishop of the city of Rome, to go into exile for the
faith,[5] then broke his word and induced him to subscribe to
heresy.[6]

NOTES

1. Fortunatianus of Aquileia (d. 361) was a native of Sicca Veneria, in
Numidia.

2. Emperor, 337–361.

3. CPL 104; CCL 9, 365–70; PLS 1, 239. In *ep.* 10, a sort of prose *geneth-
liacon* to Paul, his centenarian friend in Concordia, Jerome, after much
warm-hearted flattery, shamelessly requests payment for his praise in the
form of books: "To be explicit I ask for the Commentaries of Fortunatianus
. . ."; see ACW 33, 51 and 202 n. 11. Jerome may be referring to Fortunatianus's (now lost) *Comm. on Matthew* in the Preface to his translation of
Origen's *Homilies on Luke;* cf. Lienhard, FOTC 94, 3 n. 2. See also Paul Mey-
vaert, "An unknown source for Jerome and Chromatius. Some new fragments of Fortunatianus of Aquileia?" in *Scire litteras*, FS B. Bischoff, ABAW,
N.F. 99 (Munich, 1988), 277–89.

4. On "sections," cf. Q 2, 101, on Ammonius, and Q 3, 335, on Eusebius
of Caesarea.

5. *Chron.*, A.D. 349. On Pope Liberius see HLL 8, 5, 510–16.

6. *Chron.*, A.D. 349 (ed. Helm, 237b), trans. Donalson, 45: "Liberius,
overcome by the weariness of exile, and subscribing to a heretical depravity, had entered Rome like a conqueror."

REFERENCES

Q 4, 572 — CCL 9, 365–370 — DSp 7, 2162 — EECh 1, 328, B. Studer —
EECh 1, 328, U. Dionisi — HLL 8, 5, 419–21 — Kelly, *Jerome*, 62

XCVIII. ACACIUS THE BISHOP

CACIUS,[1] WHOM, because he was blind in one eye
they nicknamed "the one-eyed," bishop of the church
of Caesarea in Palestine,[2] composed seventeen volumes
On Ecclesiastes,[3]

and six, Συμμίκτων ζητημάτων, *On Miscellaneous Questions*,[4]
and many treatises besides on various subjects.[5]

2. He was so influential in the reign of the emperor Constantius[6] that he made Felix bishop of Rome in place of Liberius.[7]

NOTES

1. Acacius was a disciple and successor (340–366) of Eusebius of Caesarea, leader of the Homoeans in the East. See Jerome, *ep.* 119.6.

2. J. M. Leroux, "Acace évêque de Césarée de Palestine (341–365)," StudPat 8, 2 [= TU 93 (Berlin, 1966)], 82–85. Elsewhere (*ep.* 34.1) Jerome mentions his work on renovating the library in Caesarea.

3. Not extant.

4. Συμμίκτων ζητημάτων (CPG 3510); cf. Jerome, *ep.* 119.6, quoted in Courcelle, *LLW*, 117 n. 213; art., "Erotapokriseis," RAC 6, 348.

5. Socrates, *h.e.* 2.4. Jerome himself in *ep.* 119.6 quotes a fragment of Acacius on 1 Cor 15:51. Epiphanius, *Pan.* 72.5–10, mentions a *Contra Marcellum* (CPG 3512); see J. T. Lienhard, "Acacius of Caesarea: *Contra Marcellum.* Historical and Theological Considerations," *CrSt* 10 (1989): 1–22; *idem*, "Acacius of Caesarea's *Contra Marcellum:* its Place in Theology and Controversy," StudPat 19 (1989), 185–88.

6. Constantius ruled, 337–361.

7. "influential": P. Nautin, art., "Felix II," DHGE 16, 887, doubts the accuracy of this. Cf. Philostorgius, *h.e.* 5.1; also, referring to the see of Jerusalem and Cyril as its proposed recipient, *Chron.*, A.D. 348 (ed. Helm, 237a), trans. Donalson, 45: "after the death [of Maximus] the see was offered to him by Acacius and other Arians."

REFERENCES

Q 3, 345–46 — Dr, 169 — CPG 3510–15 — EEC 1², 9, F. W. Norris — EECh 1, 5, M. Simonetti — LThK 1, 234, H. Rahner — LThK 1³, 285, art., "Akakios," W. A. Löhr — HLL 8, 5, 440

XCIX. SERAPION THE BISHOP

ERAPION, BISHOP of Thmuis,[1] who because of his great learning earned the surname Scholasticus,[2] was a friend of Antony[3] the hermit and published an important work, *Against Mani;*[4]

another, *On the titles of the Psalms;*[5]
and valuable letters to various recipients.[6]

And he became celebrated for his profession [of the faith] in the reign of the emperor Constantius.[7]

NOTES

1. Thmuis, in Lower Egypt, in the Nile Delta.

2. Scholasticus: Q 3, 82, glosses, "There is ample evidence of his rhetorical, philosophical and theological erudition." See also A. Globe, "Serapion of Thmuis as Witness to the Gospel Text Used by Origen in Caesarea," *NovTest* 26 (1984): 97–127.

3. Cf. Antony's instruction on his death-bed: "To Bishop Athanasius give the one sheepskin and the cloak on which I lie . . . and to Bishop Serapion give the other sheepskin," *St. Athanasius: The Life of Saint Antony*, trans. R. T. Meyer, ACW 10, 96.

4. CPG 2485; *Serapion of Thmuis Against the Manichees*, ed. R. P. Casey (Cambridge, Mass., 1931).

5. Not extant.

6. Letters: Q 3, 84; CPG 2493; *Lettres des Pères du désert: Ammonas, Macaire, Arsène, Sérapion de Thmuis*, ed. B. Outtier, A. Louf, M. van Parys, and C. A. Zirnheld (Bégrolles-en-Mauges: Abbaye de Bellefontaine, 1985). Serapion was also a recipient of letters from Athanasius (CPG 2094). Not mentioned is *The Euchologium* (CPG 2495), generally regarded as his, *pace* B. Botte, *OrChr* 48 (1964): 50–56. See also R. C. D. Jasper and G. J. Cuming, *Prayers of the Eucharist* (2nd ed., New York, 1980), 52–66 (Liturgy of St. Mark), 74–79 (Prayers).

7. "Konstans," LThK 6³, 294, K. Gross.

REFERENCES

Q 3, 80–85 — CPG 2485–95 — Cath 13, 1126–27, G. Mathon — DSp 14, 643–52, D. Dufrasne — EEC 2², 1050, E. Ferguson — EECh 2, 768, A. Hamman — *PWRE* Suppl. 8, 1260–67, H. Dörrie

C. HILARY THE BISHOP

ILARY, bishop of the city of Poitiers,[1] [in the province] of Aquitaine, was exiled to Phrygia as a result of a synod in Béziers, by a faction of Saturninus,[2] bishop of Arles.

2. He composed twelve books, *Against the Arians*;[3]

another book, *On Synods,*[4] which he addressed to the bishops of Gaul;

also *Commentaries on the Psalms,* Books One and Two: Book One, *On Psalms 51 to 62;* and [Book Two], *On Psalms 118 to the end.*[5] In this work he imitated Origen and added not a few things of his own.

3. Also belonging to him is a little work, *To Constantius,*[6] which he presented to the emperor during his rule in Constantinople.[7]

And a second, *Against Constantius,*[8] which he wrote after the emperor's death;

a book, *Against Valens and Ursacius,*[9] which contains the history of the Synod of Rimini and Seleucia;

also *To the Prefect Sallustius, or Against Dioscorus;*[10]

and *A Book of Hymns;*[11]

and *A Book On the Mysteries;*[12]

also *Commentaries on Matthew;*[13]

and *Tractates on Job,*[14] which he freely translated from the Greek of Origen;

another elegant work, *Against Auxentius;*[15]

and some *Epistles* to various recipients.

Some say that he had written *On the Canticle of Canticles,* but this work has not come to my attention.

4. He died at Poitiers in the reign of Valentinian and Valens.[16]

NOTES

1. J. Doignon, *Hilaire de Poitiers* (Paris, 1971).

2. The *Chronicon* (ed. Helm, 240c; trans. Donalson, 48) dates this exile to 356; T. D. Barnes, "Hilary of Poitiers on his Exile," *VigChr* 46 (1992): 129–40; D. H. Williams, "A Re-assessment of the Early Career and Exile of Hilary of Poitiers," *JEH* 42 (1991): 202–17.

3. *De Trinitate:* Q 4, 38–42; CPL 433; CCL 62 and 62A, ed. P. Smulders; *The Trinity,* trans. Stephen McKenna, FOTC 25 (1954). For *duodecim,* see Jerome, *ep.* 70 (CSEL 54, 707): "Hilarius, meorum temporum confessor et episcopus, duodecim Quintiliani libros et stylo imitatus est et numero."

4. *On Synods:* CPL 434, 468f., 818; Q 4, 42–43; *Sinodi e fede degli orientali,* trans. with intro. and notes by Luigi Longobardo, *Collana di testi patristici* 105 (Rome: Città Nuova, 1993).

5. *Commentaries on the Psalms:* CPL 208, 428, 592. For Hilary's *Tractates* on Psalm 63 and on Psalm 132, see PLS 1: 241–246.

6. *To Constantius:* CPL 460; Q 4, 43–44. See *Chron.*, A.D. 359.

7. This is just a repetition of *Chron.*, A.D. 359, ed. Helm, 241g.

8. CPL 461; Q 4, 44; *Contre Constance*, ed. A. Rocher, SC 334 (Paris, 1987).

9. See recent trans. by L. R. Wickham in *Hilary of Poitiers. Conflicts of Conscience in the IVth-Cent. Church* (Liverpool, 1998), which contains Hilary's *Against Valens and Ursacius* and *Letter to the Emperor Constantius*, with intro. and notes by Wickham.

10. CPL 450; cf. Jerome, *ep.* 70 (CSEL 54, 707): "brevique libello, quem scripsit *Contra Dioscorum medicum*, quid in litteris possit ostendit." But in the end, for Jerome, the achievement did not quite measure up to the potential: "Sanctus Hilarius Gallicano coturno adtollitur et, cum Graeciae floribus adornetur, longis interdum periodis involvitur, et a lectione simpliciorum fratrum procul est" (*ep.* 58, CSEL 54, 539).

11. CPL 463, 464; Q 4, 50–51.

12. CPL 427; Q 4, 49–50.

13. CPL 430; Q 4, 47–48; *Ilario di Poitiers. Commentario a Matteo*, trans. with intro. and notes by L. Longobardo (Rome: Città Nuova, 1988); see also Dihle, *Greek and Latin*, 577–78.

14. "*Tractates on Job*, which he freely translated from the Greek of Origen": now lost; CPL 429; Q 4, 51. Jerome in *ep.* 57.6 praises Hilary's translations: "Hilary the confessor who has turned some homilies on Job and several treatises on the Psalms from Greek into Latin; yet has not bound himself to the drowsiness of the letter or fettered himself by the stale literalism of inadequate culture. Like a conqueror he has led away captive into his own tongue the meaning of his originals" (NPNF 6, ser. 2, 114–15).

15. CPL 462; Q 4, 44–45.

16. For death see *Chron.*, A.D. 367, ed. Helm, 245e, trans. Donalson, 53.

REFERENCES

Q 4, 48–61 — CPL 427–464 — Dr, 213–19 — Cath 5, 731–34, P.-Th. Camelot — DHGE 24, 459–61, R. Aubert — DSp 7, 1, 466–99, C. Kannengiesser — EEC 1², 527–28, M. T. Clark — EECh 1, 381–82, M. Simonetti — HLL 8, 5, 447–80 — LThK 5, 337–38, A. Antweiler — LThK 5³, 100–102, M. Durst — NCE 6, 1114–16, S. J. McKenna — RAC 15, 139–67, J. Doignon — TRE 15, 315–22, H. C. Brennecke — Dihle, *Greek and Latin*, 547–48 — W. Berschin, *Greek Letters*, 45–46, 295 n. 20

CI. VICTORINUS THE RHETORICIAN

ARIUS VICTORINUS, an African[1] by birth, taught rhetoric at Rome in the reign of the emperor Constantius,[2] and in extreme old age converted to the Christian faith[3] and wrote books *Against the Arians*,[4] extremely obscure and written in a dialectical style, which only experts understand,[5] also, *Commentaries on the Apostle [Paul].*[6]

NOTES

1. Under A.D. 354 (ed. Helm, 239e), Jerome's *Chronicon* notes: "The rhetorician Victorinus and the grammarian Donatus, my teacher (*praeceptor meus*), were considered outstanding men (*insignes habentur*) at Rome. One of them, Victorinus, was even honored with a statue in the Forum of Trajan" (trans. Donalson, 47). For more on Donatus, cf. Jerome, *Comm. in Eccl.* 1.9–10.

2. Constantius, 337–361.

3. Cf. Augustine, *Conf.* 8.2.3: "When I mentioned [to Ambrose] that I had read some books of the Platonists, which Victorinus (at one time a rhetorician in the city of Rome, who had, I heard, died a Christian) had translated into Latin" (trans. V. J. Bourke, FOTC 21, 198). The passage goes on to describe Victorinus's conversion very movingly.

4. *Adversus Arium:* CPL 95; Victorinus's theological works listed at Q 4, 70; *Marius Victorinus: Traités théologiques sur la Trinité*, ed. P. Henry and P. Hadot, SC 68–69 (Paris, 1960); trans. M. T. Clark, FOTC 69; see also P. Hadot, *Marius Victorinus. Recherches sur sa vie et ses oeuvres* (Paris, 1971).

5. *more dialectico:* cf. M. P. Corsini, "Il *Timeo* di Platone negli scritti teologici di Mario Vittorino. L'interpretazione aritmo-geometrica," *AMATosc* 59 (1996): 61–133; M. T. Clark, "The Neoplatonism of Marius Victorinus," StudPat 11 [= TU 108 (Berlin, 1972)], 13–19; Jerome, *Prol. Ep. ad Gal.* (PL 26: 308): "because he was immersed in secular literature he was totally ignorant of Sacred Scripture and nobody, however eloquent, can expatiate well on what he does not know."

6. Exegetical works listed: Q 4, 73. *Comm. in ep. Pauli*, on Galatians, Ephesians, and Philippians: CPL 98; text in PL 8, 1145–1294. Cf. Courcelle, *LLW*, 127 n. 305: Jerome, *Prol. Ep. ad Gal.* (PL 26: 308): "Non quod ignorem C. Marium Victorinum, qui Romae me puero [= in my boyhood] rhetoricam docuit, edidisse Commentarios in Apostolum."

REFERENCES

Q 4, 69–79 — CPL 94–99 — Cath 8, 695–97, P.-Th. Camelot — DSp 10, 616–23, A. Solignac — EEC 2², 1159–60, M. P. McHugh — EECh 1, 525–26, M. Simonetti — LThK 7, 90–91, A. Stuiber — LThK 6³, 1387–88, W. Geerlings — NCE 9, 231, P. Hadot — HLL 8, 5, 342–55 — Kelly, *Jerome*, 10–14

CII. TITUS THE BISHOP

 N THE REIGN of the emperors Julian and Jovian,[1] Titus, bishop of Bostra,[2] wrote [two] spirited works *Against the Manicheans*[3] and some others.[4]

2. He died during the reign of Valens.[5]

NOTES

1. For Julian, see *Chron.*, A.D. 361 (ed. Helm, 242b), trans. Donalson, 50: "Julian was the thirty-sixth ruler of the Romans. He reigned for one year and eight months." For Jovian, see *Chron.*, A.D. 363 (ed. Helm, 243b), trans. Donalson: "Jovian was the thirty-seventh ruler of the Romans. He reigned for eight months."

2. Bostra: DHGE 9, 1399–1405, C. Korolevsky; LThK 2³, 624–25, E. A. Knauf-Belleri.

3. *Against the Manichees:* CPG 3575; J. Ries, "Introduction aux études manichéens," *EThL* 33 (1957): 453–82, and 35 (1959): 362–409; LThK 6³, 1265–69, H. J. Klimkeit; TRE 22, 25–45, art., "Mani, Manichäismus," A. Böhlig; EECh 1, 519, C. Riggi.

4. See CPG 3576–3578.

5. Valens reigned, 364–378.

REFERENCES

Q 3, 359–62 — CPG 3575–3581 — DSp 15, 999–1006, A. Solignac — EEC 2², 1135, F. W. Norris — EECh 2, 843, E. Cavalcanti — LThK 10, 212, A. Van Roey — NCE 14, 181, P. Canivet

CIII. DAMASUS THE BISHOP

AMASUS, BISHOP of the city of Rome,[1] had a splendid talent for composing verses[2] and published many short compositions in hexameters.[3]

He was close to eighty years old when he died, during the reign of the emperor Theodosius.[4]

NOTES

1. A rather frigid entry from his one-time secretary and confidante. Damasus was Pope from Oct. 1, 366, until Dec. 11, 384; see *Chron.*, A.D. 365, ed. Helm, 244e, trans. Donalson, 52.

2. What did Jerome really think about Damasus? Is *ep.* 22.28 (*auriscalpium matronarum*, "an ear-pick of matrons") a thinly veiled attack by a disgruntled former secretary? Praising his poetic talent in the circumstances sounds like a variant on Nero fiddling as Rome was burning. See P. Nautin, "Le premier échange epistolaire entre Jérôme et Damase," *Freiburger Zeitschrift für Philosophie und Theologie* 30 (1983): 331–34. On *epp.* 15 and 16, see J. E. Merdinger, *Rome and the African Church*, 92–93, 366–84.

3. *Epigrammata:* CPL 1635; A. Ferrua, *Epigrammata Damasiana* (Rome, 1942); G. Bernt, *Das lateinische Epigramm im Übergang von der Spätantike zum frühen Mittelalter* (Munich, 1968).

4. He died on Dec. 11, 384, almost eighty. Jerome had entertained hopes of succeeding him, but had slipped considerably in the polls since the heady days described in *ep.* 45.3: "Before I became acquainted with the family of the saintly Paula, all Rome resounded with my praises. Almost everyone concurred in judging me worthy of the episcopate [*omnium paene iudicio dignus summo sacerdotio decernebar*]; Damasus, of blessed memory, spoke no words but mine" (CSEL 54, 325; trans. in NPNF 6, ser. 2, 59). There appears not a word about Damasus's liturgical reforms, on which cf. M. H. Shepherd, Jr., "The liturgical reform of Damasus I," *Kyriakon*, FS J. Quasten, Vol. 2, 847–63.

REFERENCES

Q 3, 206 — Q 4, 273–78 — CPL 1632–1636 — Cath 3, 429–31, G. Bardy — DHGE 14, 48–53, A. Van Roey — EEC 1², 316–17, M. P. McHugh — EECh 1, 218–20, C. Pietri — LThK 3, 136–37, O. Perler — LThK 2³, 1385, J. Speigl — NCE 4, 624–25, M. R. P. McGuire — ODP, 32–34 — PL 13, 375–414 — PLS 1, 314–423 — Kelly, *Jerome*, 80–90 — C. Pietri, *Roma Christiana (311–440)* (Rome, 1976), chap. 6–10

CIV. APOLLINARIS THE BISHOP

POLLINARIS, BISHOP of Laodicea in Syria,[1] son of a priest,[2] in his youth devoted himself chiefly to the study of grammar, but later turned to the Sacred Scriptures,[3] writing innumerable volumes.[4]

He died in the reign of Theodosius.[5]

2. Thirty volumes of his entitled, *Against Porphyry,* are extant,[6] which are particularly appreciated among his other works.

NOTES

1. E. Mühlenberg, *Apollinaris von Laodicea,* FKDG 23 (Göttingen, 1969).

2. Cf. Dihle, *Greek and Latin,* 605: "His eponymous father is even said to have written tragedies, dramatic pieces, meant for reading, about Biblical subjects." In the same work Dihle, 429, 604–605, deals with a side to Apollinaris completely neglected here: "long poetical works for Christian schools. He recast stories from the Old Testament in Homeric hexameters, but also in the form of tragedies and comedies after the manner of Euripedes and Menander and as Pindaric odes."

3. E. Mühlenberg, "Zur exegetischen Methode des Apollinaris von Laodicea," *Christliche exegese zwischen Nicaea und Chalcedon,* ed. J. van Oort and U. Wickert (Kampen, 1992), 132–47; E. Mühlenberg, "Apollinaris von Laodicea und die origenistische Tradition," *ZNTW* 76 (1985): 270–83.

4. See *Chron.,* A.D. 365 (ed. Helm, 244b), trans. Donalson, 52: "composed a great number of works on our religion." For details, cf. Q 3, 377–78. See also Courcelle, *LLW,* 49 and n. 9; A. Tuilier, "Le sens de l'Apollinarisme dans les controverses théologiques du IVe siècle," StudPat 13 [= TU 116] (1975), 295–305; E. Cattaneo, *Trois homélies pseudo-Chrysostomiennes sur la Pâque comme œuvre d'Apollinaire de Laodicée. Attribution et étude théologique* = ThH 58 (Paris, 1981); "Apollinare, Epiphanio, Gregorio di Nazianio, Gregorio di Nissa e altri," *Su Cristo. Il Grande Dibattio nel Quarto Secolo,* ed. Enzo Bellini (Milan, 1978), esp. 15–107.

5. He must have died c. 390.

6. Jerome, *Praef. in Danielem prophetam* (CCL 75A, 771): "I asserted that Porphyry had spoken at length against this prophet and I introduced as witnesses to this fact Methodius, Eusebius, and Apollinaris who answered his nonsense in many thousand verses." *Ep.* 70 (CSEL 54, 703) is more specific: "Scripserunt contra nos Celsus atque Porphyrius: priori Origenes, alteri Methodius, Eusebius et Apollinaris fortisssime responderunt; quorum Origenes octo scripsit libros [= *Contra Celsum*]; Methodius usque ad decem milia procedit versuum [cf. *supra, DVI* 83]; Eusebius [*DVI* 81.2] et Apollinaris viginti quinque et triginta volumina condiderunt." In *ep.* 84

Jerome is more critical: "Apollinaris is the author of a most weighty book against Porphyry . . . yet . . . has mutilated Christ's incarnate humanity" (NPNF 6, ser. 2, 176).

REFERENCES

Q 3, 377–83 — Dr, 220–24 — *TLG* 2074 — CPG 2, 3645–95 — Cath 1, 706–7, G. Bardy — DHGE 3, 962–82, R. Aigrain — EEC 1², 79–81, C. Kannengiesser — EECh 1, 58–59, C. Kannengiesser — LThK 1, 714, H. de Riedmatten — LThK 1³, 826–28, C. Kannengiesser — NCE 1, 667–68, J. Bentivegna — RAC 1, 520–22, G. Genz — TRE 3, 362–71, E. Mühlenberg

CV. GREGORY THE BISHOP [OF ELVIRA]

REGORY, A NATIVE of Baetica in Spain,[1] was bishop of Elvira[2] and up to extreme old age composed different tracts in a middle style[3]

and an elegant composition *On Faith*.[4]
He is said to be still alive.[5]

NOTES

1. See *Chron.*, A.D. 370.
2. Bishop of Elvira, c. 359. He was anti-Arian.
3. *mediocris = stylus medius*. See E. Auerbach, *Literary Language and its Public in Late Latin Antiquity and in the Middle Ages*, trans. R. Manheim (New York: Pantheon Books, 1965), 33–39, 190–91, 194.
4. *De fide orthodoxa*, CPL 551, formerly assigned to Phoebadius (*infra*, *DVI* 108), is his; see M. Simonetti, *Gregorio di Elvira, La fede* (Turin, 1975). The work is found in CCL 69, 217–47, ed. V. Bulhart and J. Fraipont (Turnholt, 1967).
5. He may have still been alive in 403; see EECh 1, 363.

REFERENCES

Q 4, 84–89 — CPL 546–557 — Cath 5, 253–54, G. Jacquemet — DHGE 21, 1501 — DSp 6, 923–27 — EEC 1², 491, M. P. McHugh — EECh 1, 363, M. Simonetti — LThK 4, 1193–94, H. Rahner — LThK 4³, 1000, A. Viciano — NCE 6, 790, F. J. Buckley

CVI. PACIAN THE BISHOP

ACIAN, BISHOP of Barcelona[1] in the Pyrenean mountains, a man of sober eloquence, and distinguished both for his mode of conduct and for his speech, wrote various works, including

Cervus[2] and

Against the Novatians,[3] and died in extreme old age in the reign of the emperor Theodosius.[4]

NOTES

1. See FOTC 99, trans. C. Hanson (1998), 1–94.
2. *Cervus* (or *Cervulus*): written to dissuade the faithful from participating in pagan New Year celebrations.
3. *Against the Novatians:* CPL 561, *Epistulae iii ad Sympronianum;* see EECh 2, 604, art., "Novatianists," R. J. De Simone.
4. Theodosius reigned, 379–395.

REFERENCES

Q 4, 135–38 — CPL 561–563 — Cath 10, 376–77, J. Liebaert — DSp 12, 1, 17–20, A. Solignac — EEC 2², 846, M. P. McHugh — EECh 2, 628, M. Simonetti — LThK 7, 1332–33, K. Baus — NCE 10, 854, S. J. McKenna — J. Matthews, *Western Aristocracies* (1995), 133

CVII. PHOTINUS THE HERESIARCH

HOTINUS, a native of Galatia,[1] a disciple of Marcellus[2] and ordained bishop of Sirmium,[3] endeavored to revive the Ebionite[4] heresy and, after he was expelled from his church by the emperor Valentinianus, wrote numerous volumes, among which the most significant are his books, *Against the Pagans* and *To Valentinianus*.

NOTES

1. *Chron.*, ed. Helm, 248d. On Galatia see DHGE 19, 714–31, R. Janin (+) and D. Stiernon.

2. Cf. *DVI* 86.

3. See art., "Sirmium," NCE 13, 260, P. Joannou.

4. On the Ebionite heresy, cf. *DVI* 9.1 (John the Evangelist) and 54.6 (Origen). In the Arian controversy he championed Eunomius.

REFERENCES

Cath 11, 229, P.-Th. Camelot — EEC 2², 919–20, F. W. Norris — EECh 2, 685–86, M. Simonetti — LThK 8, 483, B. Kotter

CVIII. PHOEBADIUS THE BISHOP

HOEBADIUS, BISHOP of Agen in Gaul,¹ published a volume, *Against the Arians.*² Other works of his are said to exist which I have not read.

2. He survives in extreme old age to the present day.³

NOTES

1. P. P. Glässer, *Phoebadius von Agen* (Ph.D. diss., Augsburg, 1978). See also Cath 1, 203–5, art., "Agen," E. Jarry; 11, 139–41, art., "Phébad," R. Darricau.

2. *Contra Arianos*, ed. A. Durengues (Agen, 1927); CCL 64 (1985), 5–52, R. Demeulenaere; CPL 473.

3. *usque hodie:* i.e., until 393.

REFERENCES

Q 4, 83–84 — CPL 473 — EECh 2, 685, M. Simonetti — LThK 8, 480, J. A. Fischer — NCE 1, 200–201, E. P. Colbert

CIX. DIDYMUS THE BLIND

IDYMUS OF ALEXANDRIA,[1] while still quite young, became blind[2] and as a result never learned the alphabet. He presented to all an extraordinary proof of his talent by acquiring complete mastery of dialectic and geometry, which particularly needs[3] the sense of sight.

2. He wrote very many distinguished works:

Commentaries on all the Psalms;[4]
Commentaries on the Gospels of Matthew and John;[5]
two books, *On Dogma* and *Against the Arians;*[6]
one book, *On the Holy Spirit,*[7] which I have translated into Latin;
eighteen books, *On Isaiah;*[8]
three books of *Commentaries on Hosea,*[9] dedicated to me;[10]
five books, *On Zechariah,*[11] at my request;
Commentaries on Job,[12]

and numerous other works,[13] to give an account of which would be a work in itself.

3. He is still living and is already over eighty-three years old.

NOTES

1. Didymus of Alexandria, the Blind (+ c. 398).
2. *a parva aetate: Chron.*, A.D. 372 (ed. Helm, 246e; trans. Donalson, 54) specifies that because he lost his eyesight in the fifth year after his birth, he was wholly illiterate and therefore used secretaries; cf. Palladius, *Hist. Laus.* 4.
3. Following the reading of Cer.-Gast.
4. *Commentarii in psalmos:* CPG 2550, 2551; A. Kehl, "Der Psalmenkommentar von Tura," *Quaternio* IX (Cologne, 1964); (i) on Ps. 20–21: *Didymus der Blinde Psalmenkommentar,* I. Ps. 20–21, ed. L. Doutreleau, A. Gesche, and M.Gronewald, PTA 7 (1969); (ii) on Ps. 22–26.10, ed. M. Gronewald, PTA 4 (1968); (iii) on Ps. 29–34, ed. A. Gesche, M. Gronewald, PTA 8 (1969); (iv) on Ps. 35–39, ed. *idem,* PTA 6 (1969); (v) on Ps. 40–44.4, ed. *idem,* PTA 12 (1970). See also E. Mühlenberg, *Psalmenkommentare aus der Katenenüberlieferung,* Bd. 1 (Berlin, 1975); A. Gesche, "L'âme humaine de Jesus dans la christologie du IVe siècle. Le témoignage du Comm. sur les Psaumes découvert à Toura," *RHE* 54 (1959): 385–425.; P. Photiades, "Notes sur un

commentaire paleochrétien [pap. In Psalmos]," *NDid* 12 (1962): 49–53; reprint, *Oikoumene* (1964), 55–59; E. Prinzivalli, "Didimo il Cieco e l'interpretazione dei Salmi," (Rome: L'Aquila, 1988); T. W. Mackay, "Didymos the Blind on Psalm 28 (LXX): Text from Unpublished Leaves of the Tura Commentary," StudPat 20 (1987), 40–48; J. M. Olivier, *RHT* 18 (1988): 233–41.

5. CPG 2557; cf. D. Lührmann, "Das Bruchstück aus dem Hebräer-Evangelium bei Didymus von Alexandrien," *NovTest* 29 (1987): 265–79.

6. CPG 2571; on *Against Eunomius* see Q 3, 88, and A. Dihle, *Greek and Latin*, 502, 549–50. For the lost dogmatic work, *Dialexis Montanistae et orthodoxi*, see CPG 2572; G. Ficker, *ZKG* 26 (1905): 447–63.

7. CPG 2544; see *DVI* 135.4 and n. 28; L. Doutreleau, "Vie et survie de *De spiritu sancto*, du IVe siècle à nos jours," *Les mardis de Dar-El-Salam* 46–47 (1959): 35–92; *idem*, "Le *De spiritu sancto* de Didyme et ses éditeurs," *Rech-SR* 51 (1963): 383–406; *idem*, "Étude d'une tradition manuscrite: Le *De Spiritu Sancto* de Didyme," in *Kyriakon*, FS J. Quasten, Vol. 1, 352–89; C. Noce, ed., *Didimo il Cieco, Lo Spirito Santo*, CTP 89 (Rome, 1990); E. Staimer, *Die Schrift "De Spiritu Sancto" von Didymus dem Blinden von Alexandrien. Eine Untersuchung zur altchristlichen Literatur- und Dogmengeschichte* (Munich, 1960).

8. *Fragmenta in Isaiam:* CPG 2547; see SC 83, 122ff.

9. CPG 2564.

10. In *ep.* 50, *To Domnio,* Jerome claims him as his teacher: "having Gregory of Nazianzus and Didymus as my catechists in the Holy Scriptures" (NPNF 6, ser. 2, 80). See also Jerome, *ep.* 84: "I went on to Alexandria and heard Didymus. And I have much to thank him for: for what I did not know I learned from him, and what I knew already I did not forget. So excellent was his teaching . . . Does a certain person dare to bring forward against me the letter I wrote to Didymus calling him my master? It is a great crime, it would seem, for me a disciple to give to one both old and learned the name of master" (NPNF 6, ser. 2, 176).

11. CPG 2549; L. Doutreleau, *Didyme l'Aveugle. Sur Zacharie,* SC 83–85 (Paris, 1962).

12. CPG 2553; *Komm. zu Hiob. I. Kap. 1–4,* ed. A. Henrichs (1968); *II. Kap. 5,1–6,28* (1968); *III. Kap. 7,20c–11,* ed. U. Hagedorn and L. Koenen (1968).

13. *infinita alia: Contra Manichaeos,* CPG 2545; *On the Trinity,* CPG 2570; *Commentarii in Octateuchum et Reges,* CPG 2546; *Fragmenta in Ieremiam in catenis,* CPG 2548; *Commentarii in Ecclesiasten,* CPG 2555; *Kommentar zum Ecclesiastes. 1/1. Kap. 1,1–2,14,* ed. G. Binder and L. Liesenborghs, PTA 25 (1979); *1/2 Erl.,* ed. G. Binder, PTA 26 (1980); *II. Kap. 3–4,12,* ed. M. Gronewald, PTA 22 (1977); *III. Kap. 5 u. 6,* ed. L. Koenen and J. Kramer, PTA 13 (1970); *IV. Kap. 7–8,18,* ed. J. Kramer and B. Krebber, PTA 16 (1972); *V. Kap. 9,8–10,20,* ed. G. Binder and M. Gronewald, PTA 24 (1979); *VI. Kap. 11–12,* ed. L. Koenen, G. Binder, and L. Liesenborghs, PTA 9 (1969). See also M. Simonetti, "Lettera e allegoria nell'esegesi veterotestamentaria di Didimo," *VetChr* 20 (1983): 341–89; M. Diego Sanchez, "El Commentario al Ecclesiastes de Didimo Alejandrino," *Teresianum* 41

(1990): 231–42; A. I. C. Heron, *Studies in the Trinitarian writings of Didymus the Blind; his authorship of the "Adversus Eunomium IV–V" and the "De Trinitate*," (Ph.D. diss., Tübingen University, 1972); L. Béranger, "Sur deux énigmes du *De Trinitate* de Didyme l'Aveugle," *RechSR* 51 (1963): 255–67; A. Heron, "Some sources used in the *De Trinitate* ascribed to Didymus the Blind," in *The Making of Orthodoxy*, FS H. Chadwick, ed. R. Williams (Cambridge, 1989), 173–81; M. Bogaert, "Fragment inédit de Didyme l'Aveugle en traduction latine ancienne," *RBén* 73 (1963): 9–16; F. Dolbeau, "Deux opuscules latines relatifs aux personnages de la Bible et anterieurs à Isidore de Seville," *RHT* 16 (1986): 83–139.

REFERENCES

Q 3, 85–100 — Dr, 259 — *TLG* 2102 — CPG 2, 2544–72 — Cath 3, 759–60, G. Bardy — *CW* 76, 316–17, T. Halton — DHGE 14, 416–27, A. Van Roey — DSp 3, 868–71, G. Bardy — EEC 1², 329–30, A. Heron — EECh 1, 235–36, P. Nautin — LThK 3, 373–74, A. Van Roey — LThK 3³, 212–13, B. Kramer — NCE 4, 861, P. Roche — TRE 8, 741–46, B. Kramer

CX. OPTATUS THE BISHOP

PTATUS, AN AFRICAN, bishop of Milevis,[1] on the Catholic side,[2] under the emperors Valentinianus and Valens,[3] wrote six books against the calumny of the Donatist party,[4] in which he asserted that the accusation against the Donatists had been falsely turned against our side.[5]

NOTES

1. Milevis is in the highlands of Numidia.

2. Cf. J. E. Merdinger, "Optatus Reconsidered," StudPat 22 (1989), 294–99; *eadem, Rome and the African Church*, 50–60.

3. Valentinianus was Emperor in the West, 364–375, while his brother, the Arian Valens, 364–378, was Emperor in the East.

4. "adversus Donatianae partis calumniam": not an exact title; cf. Q 4, 122; CPL 244; *Optat. De schismate Donatistarum*, ed. C. Ziwsa, CSEL 26 (Vienna, 1893); *The Work of St. Optatus, Bishop of Milevis, Against the Donatists*, trans. with notes by O. R. Vassall-Phillips (London, 1917); *Ottato di Milevi, La vera Chiesa, (Libri VII)*, ed. L. Dattrino (Rome, 1988). Number of books:

septem, not *sex, pace* Jerome! Cf. A. C. De Veer, "À propos de l'authenticité du livre VII d'Optat di Milève," *REAug* 7 (1961): 389–91.

5. Jerome chooses to ignore the main thrust of Optatus's work: Peter is *principium nostrum,* and the *cathedra Petri* is the premier see of the West. Also there is no mention of Optatus's *On the origin of human souls;* see *ep.* 144 of Jerome (= Augustine, *ep.* 202A).

REFERENCES

Q 4, 122–27 — CPL 244–49 — Cath 10, 103–5, P.-Th. Camelot — EEC 2², 830–31, F. W. Norris — EECh 2, 612–13, F. Scorza Barcellona — LThK 7, 1180–81, A. Stuiber — NCE 10, 706–7, A. Stuiber — TRE 25, 300–302, B. Kriegbaum — Dihle, *Greek and Latin,* 542–43 — SC 412 — PLS 1: 287–302

CXI. ACILIUS SEVERUS THE SENATOR

CILIUS SEVERUS, OF SPANISH origin, and from the well-known family of Severus to whom Lactantius directed two books of letters, wrote compositions in prose and verse, a sort of Ὁδοιπορικόν, an itinerary,[1] a work containing the whole course of his life which he called Καταστροφήν or Πεῖραν.[2]

He died in the reign of the emperor Valentinianus.[3]

NOTES

1. Cf. *DVI* 80.2 for the same term.
2. Not extant. See HLL 8, 5, 211.
3. Emperor in the West, 364–375.

REFERENCES

EECh 1, 8, V. Saxer — PWK 2, 2003

CXII. CYRIL THE BISHOP

YRIL, BISHOP of Jerusalem,[1] many times excommunicated from his church[2] but finally reinstated under the
emperor Theodosius,[3] held the episcopacy uninter-
ruptedly for eight years.[4]

2. His Κατηχήσεις, *Catecheses*,[5] which he composed in his
youth, are still extant.

NOTES

1. F. Cardman, "Fourth-Century Jerusalem: Religious Geography and
Christian Tradition," in *Schools of Thought in the Christian Tradition*, ed. P.
Henry (Philadelphia, 1984).

2. "many times": the details are spelled out in *Chron.*, A.D. 348, ed. Helm,
237a, trans. Donalson, 45. And Q 3, 362, relates: "He was expelled three
times from his see. He was first deposed at a council in Jerusalem in 357
and took refuge in Tarsus. After he was restored by the council at Seleucia
in the next year, Acacius banished him again in 360, but he was allowed to
return to his see in 362 on Julian's accession. Though Acacius died in 366,
Cyril's longest exile was yet to come. In 367 the emperor Valens deprived
him once more of his diocese, which he did not regain until eleven years
later (378) after the ruler's death."

3. Theodosius reigned, 379–395.

4. "eight years": see P. Nautin, "La date du *De viris illustribus* de Jérôme
de la mort de Cyrille de Jérusalem et de celle de Grégoire de Nazianze,"
RHE 56 (1961): 33–35.

5. Κατηχήσεις: see most recently G. Maestri and V. Saxer, *Cirillo e Gio-
vanni di Gerusalemme, Catechesi prebattesimali e mistagogiche* (Milan, 1994);
Eng. trans. by Leo P. McCauley and Anthony A. Stephenson, FOTC 61 and
64; A. Pauli, *Saint Cyrille de Jérusalem catéchese, Lex orandi* 29 (Paris, 1959); C.
Renoux, "La lecture biblique dans la liturgie de Jérusalem," in *Le monde
grec et la Bible*, ed. C. Mondésert, 171–93; A. A. Stephenson, "The Lenten
Catechetical Syllabus in Fourth-Century Jerusalem," *TS* 15 (1954): 103–
16; R. Gregg, "Cyril of Jerusalem and the Arians," in *Arianism* (Cambridge,
Mass., 1985), 85–105.

REFERENCES

Q 3, 362–76 — Dr, 247–50 — *TLG* 2110 — CPG 3585–3588 — Cath 3,
412–14, G. Bardy — DHGE 13, 1181–85, G. Bardy — DSp 2, 2, 2683–87,
G. Bardy — EEC 1², 312–13, F. W. Norris — EECh 1, 215, M. Simonetti —

LThK 6, 709–10, O. Perler — LThK 2³, 1370, S. Heid — NCE 5, 576–78, A. A. Stephenson — TRE 8, 261–66, E. J. Yarnold

CXIII. EUZOIUS THE BISHOP

UZOIUS[1] AS A YOUNG man was educated at Caesarea at the school of the rhetor Thespesius,[2] and had Gregory of Nazianzus, a bishop,[3] as a fellow student. He later became bishop of the same city of Caesarea, after great endeavors to preserve the holdings of the library of Origen and Pamphilus[4] which had greatly deteriorated. Finally he was excommunicated from the church in the reign of the emperor Theodosius.[5]

2. Diverse and numerous works of his[6] are in circulation and it is very easy to get to know them.

NOTES

1. Euzoius was a moderate Arian who baptized Constantius on his deathbed.

2. For the rhetor Thespesius, cf. "Thespesius 2," *PLRE* 1, 910.

3. See F. W. Norris, *Faith Gives Fullness to Reasoning: The Five Theological Orations of Gregory of Nazianzen* (Leiden, 1991), 3 and n. 18. Gregory wrote Epitaph 4 for Thespesius.

4. *bibliotheca:* Courcelle, *LLW*, 104; H. Y. Gamble, *Books,* 154–60 (*DVI* 113, *not* 112!); and on the phrase *in membranis instaurare,* Gamble, *op. cit.,* 159, where it is explained as a conversion from papyrus to parchment; cf. Barnes, *C. and E.,* 347 n. 21.

5. For his earlier associations with Arius, see Barnes, *C. and E.,* 229, 238.

6. Cf. Q 3, 348: "all [his works] have disappeared, and even their titles are unknown." Jerome had easy access to his works in the library of Caesarea.

REFERENCES

Q 3, 348 — EECh 1, 305, M. Simonetti — Kelly, *Jerome,* 135

CXIV. EPIPHANIUS THE BISHOP

EPIPHANIUS, BISHOP of Salamis in Cyprus, wrote *Against All Heresies*[1] and many other works[2] which are eagerly read by the more learned for their content and by the less sophisticated for their literary form.[3]

2. He is alive at the present day and even in extreme old age is still publishing various works.[4]

NOTES

1. *Against all Heresies:* a generic title embracing the *Panarion,* or *Medicine Chest* (CPG 3745); *The Panarion of St. Epiphanius, Bishop of Salamis: Selected Passages,* trans. P. R. Amidon (New York: Oxford University Press, 1990) [Omits the Refutations]; also *The Panarion of Epiphanius of Salamis,* Book 1 [Sections 1–46] and Books 2–3 [Sections 47–80; *De fide*], trans. F. Williams (Leiden and N.Y.: E. J. Brill, 1987–1994). See also *Su Cristo,* ed. Bellini, 193–265; R. M. Hübner, "Die Hauptquelle des Epiphanius (*Panarion haer.* 65) über Paulus v. Samosata," *ZKG* 90 (1979): 201–20; G. Vallée, *A Study in Anti-Gnostic Polemics. Irenaeus, Hippolytus and Epiphanius* (Waterloo, Ontario, 1981); A. Pourkier, *L'hérésiologie chez Épiphane de Salamine,* CAnt 4 (1992).

2. *Ancoratus:* CPG 3744; *Epistula ad Hieronymum* [Latin]: CPG 3755 (*ep.* 91 in Jerome's correspondence; trans. in NPNF 6, ser. 2, 184–85). See J. F. Dechow, *Dogma and Mysticism in Early Christianity. Epiphanius of Cyprus and the Legacy of Origen,* PatMS 13 (1988); E. A. Clark, *The Origenist Controversy. The Cultural Construction of an Early Christian Debate* (Princeton, 1992); P. Devos, "*Mega Sabbaton* chez saint Epiphane," *AnBoll* 108 (1990): 293–306.

3. Jerome was especially impressed by Epiphanius's erudition, asking, "Must he be charged with a crime for knowing Greek, Syriac, Hebrew, Egyptian, and, in part measure, also Latin?" in *Adv. Rufinum* 2.22 (trans. Hritzu, FOTC 53, 141).

4. Jerome translated into Latin a letter of his addressed to John of Jerusalem, contained in Jerome's correspondence as *ep.* 51, trans. in NPNF 6, ser. 2, 83–89.

REFERENCES

Q 3, 384–96 — Dr, 253–56 — *TLG* 2021 — CPG 2, 3744–3807 — Cath 4, 320–21, G. Bardy — DHGE 15, 617–31, P. Nautin — DSp 4, 1, 854–61 — EEC 1², 380–81, F. W. Norris — EECh 1, 281–82, C. Riggi — LThK 3, 944–46, R. Gögler — LThK 3³, 723–25, W. A. Bienert — NCE 5, 478–79, P. Canivet — RAC 5, 909–27, W. Schneemelcher — Dihle, *Greek and Latin,* 593

CXV. EPHREM THE DEACON

PHREM, DEACON of the church of Edessa,[1] composed many works in Syriac[2] and came to enjoy such prestige that his works are read publicly after the Scripture readings in some churches.[3]

2. I read in Greek his work, *On the Holy Spirit,*[4] which he had translated from the Syriac, and even in translation[5] I could recognize the acuteness of his sublime genius.

3. He died in the reign of the emperor Valens.[6]

NOTES

1. S. Brock, "Syriac Studies 1971–1980, a Classified Bibliography," *PdO* 10 (1981–82): 291–412; S. Brock, *The Harp of the Spirit,* Studies Supplementary to Sobornost, no. 4, 2nd ed. (St. Alban and St. Sergius, 1985).

2. *Ephrem the Syrian Hymns,* trans. K. E. McVey, Classics of Western Spirituality (New York, 1989); *St. Ephrem the Syrian: Selected Prose Works,* trans. Edward G. Mathews, Jr., and Joseph P. Amar, ed. Kathleen McVey, FOTC 91 (1994).

3. Jerome does not seem to be aware of Ephrem's hymns, which were used in the liturgy.

4. No longer extant.

5. For translations of Ephrem, cf. DSp 4, 1, 800–822 ("Les versions"), D. Hemmerdinger-Iliadou and J. Kirchmeyer.

6. Valens, Emperor in the East, 364–378.

REFERENCES

DSp 4, 1, 788–822, E. Beck, J. Kirchmeyer, and D. Hemmerdinger-Iliadou — EEC 1², 376–77, K. McVey — EECh 1, 276–77, F. Rilliet — LThK 3, 926–29, E. Beck — LThK 3³, 708–10, W. Cramer — NCE 5, 463–64, É. des Places — TRE 9, 755–62 — Dihle, *Greek and Latin,* 574

CXVI. BASIL, ANOTHER BISHOP

ASIL, BISHOP of Caesarea in Cappadocia,[1] which was formerly called Mazaca, composed excellent works: *Against Eunomius;*[2]

a work, *On the Holy Spirit;*[3]
nine *Homilies on the Hexameron,*[4]
an Ἀσκητικόν;[5] and other various short works.[6]

2. He died in the reign of the emperor Gratian.[7]

NOTES

1. A rather curt entry; in the *Chron.* under A.D. 376 (ed. Helm, 248e), we read what may be the reason for his antipathy: "Basil of Caesarea the bishop of Cappadocia was a famous man. By the one fault of pride he ruined his many good qualities of chastity and talent" (trans. Donalson, 55–56).

2. Q 3, 209–210; Dr, 229; text in SC 299; for *Against Eunomius* cf. Dihle, *Greek and Latin,* 549, who dates it to 364; the work contains five books, the last two of which belong to Didymus.

3. Q 3, 210–11; Dr, 230–31. Text: SC 17, 1968², ed. B. Pruche.

4. Q 3, 210–11.

5. "an Ἀσκητικόν": PG 31; Q 3, 210–11; LThK 2³, 71–72, K. S. Frank. See also K. Suso Frank, "Monastische Reform im Altertum. Eustathius von Sebaste und Basilius von Caesarea," *Reformatio ecclesiae* (1979), 33–50.

6. For listing see CPG 2835–3005.

7. Gratian reigned, 375–383. Basil died on January 1, 379. The 1600th anniversary in 1979 was the occasion of two important Congresses: *Basilio di Cesarea: la sua età, la sua opera e il Basilianesimo in Sicilia. Atti del Congresso internazionale I e II* (Messina, 1979 and 1983); P. J. Fedwick, ed., *Basil of Caesarea: Christian, Humanist, Ascetic,* 2 vols. (Toronto, 1981). See also J. Gribomont, *Saint Basile, Évangile et Église. Mélanges,* 2 vols. (Abbaye de Bellefontaine, 1984); *Mémorial Dom Jean Gribomont* = SEAug 27 (1988).

REFERENCES

Q 3, 204–36 — Dr, 225–31 — *TLG* 2040 — CPG 2835–3005 — DSp 1, 1273–83, G. Bardy — EEC 1², 169–72, F. W. Norris — EECh 1, 114–15, J. Gribomont — LThK 2³, 67–69, C. Kannengiesser — NCE 2, 143–46, 148–49, J. Gribomont — TRE 5, 301–13, W.-D. Hauschild — Dihle, *Greek and Latin,* 511, 549 — *Gestalten* 11, 7–19, W.-D. Hauschild

CXVII. GREGORY, ANOTHER BISHOP

REGORY OF Nazianzus, a bishop, a man of outstanding eloquence,[1] was my teacher, and I learned the Scriptures at his school.[2] He composed all his works in about thirty thousand verses[3] and they include the following:

2. *On the death of his brother, Caesarius;*[4]

Περὶ φιλοπτωχίας, *On the Love of Poverty,*[5]
In Praise of the Maccabees;[6]
In Praise of Cyprian;[7]
The Praises of Athanasius;[8]
The Praises of Maximus the Philosopher upon his return from exile, to whom some gave the pseudonym Hero,[9]

because there is another satirical book by the same Maximus, as if it were not permissible to praise and criticize the same person, depending on the circumstances;

3. and a book in hexameter verse, *On Virginity and Marriage,* in which the pair debate each other;

two books, *Against Eunomius;*[10]
one book, *On the Holy Spirit;*[11]
one book, *Against Julian the Emperor.*[12]

4. He followed the oratorical style of Polemon[13] and ordained another bishop in his own place while he was still alive.[14] He embarked on the monastic life and died almost three years ago, in the reign of the emperor Theodosius.[15]

NOTES

1. P. Gallay, *Grégoire de Nazianz* (Paris, 1993); F. Trisoglio, "San Gregorio di Nazianzo scrittore e teologo in quaranta anni di ricerche (1925–1965)," *RSLR* 8 (1972): 341–74; *idem, San Gregorio di Nazianzo in un quarantennio di studi (1925–1965),* Rivista Lasalliana 40 (Turin, 1974); *idem, San Gregorio di Nazianzo, l'uomo attraverso all'oratore* (Genoa, 1987); A. Benoit, *Saint Grégoire de Nazianze, archévêque de Constantinople et docteur de l'Église. Sa vie, ses oeuvres et son époque* (Marseille and Paris, 1876; reprint, Hildesheim, 1973).

2. *praeceptor meus:* Jerome declares, "Could I not have mentioned in that

letter [*ep.* 83] Gregory, a very eloquent man? Who among the Latins is his equal? I glory and exult in him as my master" (*Adv. Rufinum* 1.13, trans. Hritzu, FOTC 53, 76). Jerome was in Constantinople from 379 to 381. He gives a good example of Gregory's style as *praeceptor* in *ep.* 52 (CSEL 54, 429): the elegantly playful reply (*eleganter lusit*) Gregory gave him when he too eagerly asked for an explanation of δευτερόπρωτον in Luke (Lk 6.1). See C. Moreschini, "*Praeceptor meus:* Tracce del'insegnamento di Gregorio di Nazianzo in Gerolamo," *Jérôme entre l'Occident et l'Orient,* ed. Duval, 129–38. On Gregory and Scripture, see P. Gallay, "La Bible dans l'oeuvre de Grégoire de Nazianz le Théologien," *Le monde grec ancien et la Bible,* ed. Mondésert, 313–34; for Philo's influence, F. Trisoglio, ANRW II, 21, 1, 588–730.

3. *triginta milia versuum:* see *Saint Gregory of Nazianzus: Three Poems,* trans. D. Meehan, with notes by T. Halton, FOTC 75 (1987); on his poetry, see Dihle, *Greek and Latin,* 572; RAC 12 (1983), 793f.; Q 3, 244–46.

4. *On the death of his brother, Caesarius* = *or.* 7. Text: SC 405, 180–245, ed. M.-A. Calvet-Sebasti. Trans.: Leo P. McCauley, FOTC 22, 5–25. And, in the same volume, *On St. Basil the Great,* 27–99; *On his sister, St. Gorgonia,* 101–18; *On his Father,* 119–56. See also C. Nardi, "Echi dell' Orazione funebre su Basilio di Gregorio Nazianzo nel *De Sacerdotio* di Giov. Crisostomo," *Prometheus* 2 (1976): 175–84.

5. Περὶ φιλοπτωχίας, *On the Love of Poverty* = *or.* 14. Text: PG 35: 857–909.

6. *The Praises of the Maccabees* = *or.* 15. Text: PG 35: 911–934.

7. *The Praises of Cyprian* = *or.* 24. Text: SC 284, 40–85.

8. *The Praises of Athanasius* = *or.* 21. Text: SC 270, 86–193.

9. *The Praises of Maximus the Philosopher* = *or.* 25. Text: SC 284, 156–205. See Norris, *Faith Gives Fullness,* 8 and n. 42, and 10 n. 51, citing J. Mossay, "Note sur Héron-Maxime, écrivain ecclésiastique," *AnBoll* 100 (1982): 229–36. The pseudonym, Hero, occurs in *or.* 25; see D. R. Dudley, *A History of Cynicism* (London, 1937). See also *DVI* 127.

10. "two books, *Against Eunomius*" = *or.* 28–29; Norris, *Faith Gives Fullness,* 224–61.

11. "one book, *On the Holy Spirit*" = *or.* 31; Norris, *Faith Gives Fullness,* 279–99. See also *Grégoire de Nazianze, Les 5 Discours sur Dieu,* trans. and notes by P. Gallay, intro. and comm. by A.-G. Hamman, *Les Pères dans la foi* 61 (Paris, 1995).

12. "one book, *Against Julian the Emperor*" = *or.* 4–5: SC 309, ed. J. Bernardi (Paris, 1983); *Gregorio di Nazianzo Contro Giuliano l'Apostata. Orazione IV,* ed. L. Lugaresi, Bibliotheca patristica 23 (Florence, 1993); A. Kurmann, *Gregor von Nazianz. Oratio IV gegen Julian;* C. Moreschini, "L'opera e la personalità dell' imperatore Giuliano nelle due 'Invectivae' di Gregorio Nazianzo," *Forma futuri,* FS M. Pellegrino (Turin, 1975), 416–30.

13. "the oratorical style of Polemon" (*Polemonis dicendi* χαρακτῆρα): On Polemon, a celebrated Greek, see *Polemonis Declamationes quae exstant duae,* ed. H. Hinck (Leipzig, 1873). Polemon is also mentioned in Eus., *Chron.,* A.D. 132, ed. Helm, 200, where he is linked with Favorinus. Socrates, *h.e.*

4.26 (NPNF 2, ser. 2., 110), names Himerius and Prohaeresius as Gregory's teachers at Athens.

14. "another bishop": i.e., Nectarius, Bishop of Constantinople, 381–397; cf. EECh 2, 584, D. Stiernon.

15. Gregory died three years before *DVI* was written. His retirement in Arianzum (383–389) produced most of his 244 extant letters and much of his poetry. On the poetry cf. Dihle, *Greek and Latin*, 604. For the final phase of his life, see J. Plagnieux, "Saint Grégoire de Nazianze," *Théologie de la vie monastique* (Paris, 1961), 115–130. On Jerome's dating of his death, see P. Nautin, "La date du *De viris illustribus* de Jérome, de la mort de Cyrille de Jérusalem et de celle de Grégoire de Nazianze," *RHE* 56 (1961): 33–35.

REFERENCES

Q 3, 236–54 — *TLG* 2022 — CPG 3010–3125 — DHGE 22, 15–18, J. Mossay — DSp 6, 932–71, J. Rousse — EEC 1², 491–95, F. W. Norris — EECh 1, 361–62, J. Gribomont — *LCI* 6, 444–50, U. Knoben — LThK 4³, 1004–7, B. Coulie — NCE 6, 791–94, J. T. Cummings — RAC 12, 793–863, B. Wyss — TRE 14, 164–73, J. Mossay — Dihle, *Greek and Latin*, 486–87, 510–11, 519–20, 551–52

CXVIII. LUCIUS THE BISHOP

UCIUS, A BISHOP of the Arian party, governed the church of Alexandria after Athanasius,[1] until Theodosius, after he became emperor, expelled him.[2]

2. His annual letters, *On the Pasch*,[3] survive, and a few treatises of ὑποθέσεων,[4] various subjects.

NOTES

1. Athanasius died, May 2, 373.

2. Q 3, 162, noting that Macarius, the Egyptian monk, was in turn exiled by Lucius.

3. *solemnis* = annual; CPG 2535, *Sermo in pascha* (*fragmentum*).

4. Courcelle, *LLW*, 123 n. 288, cites Epiphanius, *Adv. haer.* 3.2.68 (PG 42: 201A) as the probable source of Jerome's information.

Q 3, 162 — EECh 1, 509, E. Prinzivalli

CXIX. DIODORE THE BISHOP

IODORE, BISHOP of Tarsus,[1] while still a priest at Antioch achieved great fame. Works of his that are extant include his *Commentaries on the Apostle Paul*[2] and many others,[3] which reflect the method of Eusebius of Emesa,[4] for, while he followed his meaning, he could not imitate his style because he had no knowledge of secular literature.[5]

NOTES

1. L. Abramowski, "Le prétendue condemnation de Diodore de Tarsé en 449," *RHE* 60 (1965): 64ff.; J. R. Pouchet, " Les rapports de Basile de Césarée avec Diodore de Tarse," *BLE* 87 (1986): 243–72.
2. CPG 3819.
3. His works included the following:
Fragmenta in Octateuch, CPG 3815;
Fragmenta in Reges, I, II, CPG 3816;
Fragmenta in Exodum (Latin), CPG 3817;
Fragmenta in Psalmos, CPG 3818, for the text of which see CCG 6 (Ps. 1–50), ed. J. M. Olivier (Turnholt, 1980); *Biblical Interpretation in the Early Church*, ed. K. Froehlich, Sources of Early Christian Thought 5 (Philadelphia: Fortress Press, 1985), 82–94; J. M. Olivier, "Un fragment palimpseste du Commentaire de Diodore de Tarse sur les Psaumes (Vindob. Theol. Gr. X)," *RHT* 18 (1988): 233–41.
4. Eusebius of Emesa: *DVI* 91.
5. Jerome criticizes Marius Victorinus for the opposite reason. Courcelle, *LLW*, 119, has a more personal explanation.

REFERENCES

Q 3, 397–401 — Dr, 267–70 — *TLG* 4134 — DHGE 14, 496–504, L. Abramowski — DSp 3, 986–93, G. Bardy — EEC 1², 331–32, R. Greer — EECh 1, 236–37, M. Simonetti — LThK 3³, 238, C. Kannengiesser — NCE 4, 875, F. A. Sullivan — TRE 8, 763–67, C. Schäublin — Rebenich, 107

CXX. EUNOMIUS THE HERESIARCH

UNOMIUS, BISHOP of the Arian faction in Cyzicus,[1] lapsed into such open blasphemy in his own heresy as to proclaim in public what the others were covering up. He is said to live still[2] in Cappadocia and to write many works[3] against the Church.

2. Responses to him have been produced by Apollinaris, Didymus, Basil of Caesarea, Gregory Nazianzus, and Gregory of Nyssa.[4]

NOTES

1. *Chron.*, A.D. 373, trans. Donalson, 54: "Eunomius, a disciple of Aetius of Constantinople, won notoriety." Cyzicus: on the Sea of Marmara.

2. Q 3, 307: "He lived until 394 in Halmyris in Moesia, Caesarea in Cappadocia and in near-by Dacora."

3. R. P. Vaggione, *Eunomius. The Extant Works*, OECT (Oxford, 1987); L. R. Wickham, "The Date of Eunomius' *Apology*," *JThS* 20 (1969): 231–40; M. van Esbroeck, "Amphiloque d'Iconium et Eunome: l'homelie CPG 3238," *AugR* 21 (1981): 517–39; M. Wiles, "Eunomius: Hair-Splitting Dialectician or Defender of the Accessibility of Salvation?" in *The Making of Orthodoxy*, FS H. Chadwick (1989), 157–72.

4. Responses: for that of Basil of Caesarea, see B. Sesboué, *L' "Apologie" d'Eunome de Cyzique et le "Contre Eunome" de Basile* (Rome, 1980); for that of Gregory of Nyssa, see *Gregorii Nysseni Opera*, ed. W. Jaeger, *Contra Eunomium Libri*, 2 vols. (Leiden, 1960); M. van Esbroeck, "L'aspect cosmologique de la philosophie d'Eunome pour la réprise de l'*Hexaemeron* basilien par Grégoire de Nysse," in *El "Contra Eunomium 1" en la producción literaria de Gregorio de Nisa. VI Coloquio Internacional sobre Gregorio de Nisa*, ed. L. F. Mateo-Seco and J. L Bastero (1988), 203–16; M. S. Troiano, "Cappadoci e la questione dell'origine dei nomi nella polemica contro Eunomio," *VetChr* 17 (1980): 313–46.

REFERENCES

Q 3, 306–309 — Dr, 228–30 — *TLG* 2017.030 — CPG 2, 3455–60 — DHGE 15, 1399–1405, M. Spanneut — EEC 1², 399, R. P. Vaggione — EECh 1, 297, M. Simonetti — LThK 3³, 989–90, F. X. Risch — NCE 5, 631, V. C. de Clerq — RAC 6, 936–47, L. Abramowski — TRE 10, 525–28, A. M. Ritter — Dihle, *Greek and Latin*, 548–50

CXXI. PRISCILLIAN THE BISHOP

■RISCILLIAN, BISHOP of Avila,[1] who, at the instigation of the faction of Hydatius and Ithacius, was killed at Trier by Maximus[2] the tyrant, published many works, some of which survive to the present day.[3]

2. To this day he is accused by some of being a follower of the heresy of Gnosticism, that is, of Basilides and Marcion, about whom Irenaeus wrote,[4] although others defend him as not sharing the views that are ascribed to him.[5]

NOTES

1. Sulpicius Severus, *Chron.* 2.46–51; H. Chadwick, *Priscillian of Avila* (Oxford, 1976); J. E. Merdinger, *Rome and the African Church*, 145–46, 174–76; J. Matthews, *Western Aristocracies*, 134 n. 1, 166f.

2. Hydatius was bishop of Merida; Ithacius, bishop of Ossonuba. Priscillian was condemned by the Emperor Magnus Maximus, usurper of Gaul, in A.D. 385 for allegedly practicing magic and fornicating with some of his followers; cf. Dihle, *Greek and Latin*, 436, 540; H. Chadwick, "Magnus Maximus and the Persecution of Heresy," *Bull. J. Rylands Lib.* 66, 1 (Manchester, 1983): 13–43. On Hydatius: C. Molè, "Uno Storico del V secolo, il Vescovo Idazio," *Siculorum Gymnasium* 27, 2 (1974): 279–351; 28, 1 (1975): 58–139. See also V. C. de Clerq, "Ossius of Cordova and the Origins of Priscillianism," StudPat 1 (= TU 63 [Berlin, 1957]), 601–6.

3. CPL 785–796.

4. Irenaeus, *Adv. haer.* 1.24 (Basilides), 1.27 (Marcion); cf. ACW 55, 84–87, 91–92.

5. Jerome is much more negative about him in *ep.* 133: "Then there is Priscillian in Spain, whose infamy makes him as bad as Manichaeus . . . . But why do I speak of Priscillian who has been condemned by the whole world?" (NPNF 6, ser. 2, 273–74). Cf. A. Ferreiro, "Jerome's Polemic against Priscillian in his Letter to Ctesiphon (133, 2)," *REA* 39 (1993): 309–32. Priscillian's defenders included St. Martin of Tours.

REFERENCES

Q 4, 126–130 — CPL 785–787 — Cath 11, 1039–41, P.-Th. Camelot — DSp 12, 2, 2353–69, H. Chadwick — EEC 2², 949–50, P. M. Bassett — EECh 2, 711–12, M. Simonetti — NCE 11, 790–91, J. N. Hillgarth — Dihle, *Greek and Latin*, 540–41 — Rebenich, 209, 213, 214, 217

CXXII. LATRONIANUS

ATRONIANUS, WHO ORIGINATED from the province of Spain,[1] was a man of great learning and worthy to be compared with the ancients as a composer in verse. He, too, was put to death at Trier, along with Priscillian, Felicissimus, Julian, and Euchrotia, authors of the same faction.

2. Works of this talented man survive, published in a variety of meters.[2]

NOTES

1. Hispania, the peninsula of Spain, was divided into the two Roman provinces of Hispania Citerior (later Tarraconensis) and Hispania Ulterior (later Baetica); cf. J. Matthews, *Western Aristocracies*, 149–50, 166.
2. Nothing survives.

REFERENCES

Q 4, 142 — Rebenich, 213, 215, 270

CXXIII. TIBERIANUS

IBERIANUS FROM BAETICA [in Spain],[1] to dispel a suspicion which associated him with the heresy of Priscillian,[2] wrote an *Apology* in a turgid and well-ordered style;[3] but, after the murder of his followers, he got tired of his life in exile, weakened in his resolution and, to use the words of Holy Scripture, "like a dog, returned to his vomit,"[4] and entered into a matrimonial union with his daughter, who was a virgin consecrated to Christ.

NOTES

1. The province of Baetica in southern Spain now comprises Andalusia and part of Granada; Tacitus, *Hist.* 1.53.

2. Cf. *DVI* 121.

3. The *Apologeticum* is lost.

4. Prv 26.11; 2 Pt 2.22. The phrase was also applied by Jerome to Jovinianus; cf. *Adv. Iovinianum* 1.39, NPNF 6, ser. 2, 378.

REFERENCES

CPL 470

CXXIV. AMBROSE THE BISHOP

MBROSE, BISHOP of Milan,[1] continues writing down to the present day.[2] Concerning him I postpone judgment in that he is still alive[3] lest I get blamed for flattery, on the one hand, or, on the other, for telling the truth.[4]

NOTES

1. See N. B. McLynn, *Ambrose of Milan: Church and Court in a Christian Capital* (Berkeley, 1994).

2. "usque in praesentem diem scribit": cf. *Prol.* (to *DVI*) 5: "qui usque hodie scriptitant." Is he already thinking of Ambrose and sharpening his rapier? For Ambrose's writings, see F. Braschi and A. Zani, "Guida ai testi di Sant'Ambrogio," *Theologia* 22, 3 (1997): 291–315.

3. "de quo quia superest": Withholding judgment because the person is still alive, while understandable as a principle of literary criticism, is conveniently forgotten elsewhere, as, for example, in regard to the other Ambrose (*DVI* 126): "usque hodie superest," and Epiphanius (*DVI* 114): "scripsit *Adversus omnes haereses* . . . . Superest usque hodie." This wait-and-see principle of literary criticism can also be glimpsed in *ep.* 58, to Paulinus of Nola, where, after a series of thumb-nail cameos on Tertullian, Cyprian, Victorinus, Lactantius, Arnobius, and Hilary, he concludes: "taceo de ceteris vel defunctis vel adhuc viventibus, super quibus in utramque partem post nos alii judicabunt" (CSEL 54, 539). If only he had been magnanimous enough to repeat the advice he had given to Eustochium in *ep.* 22, where he shows perfect familiarity with at least *De virginibus, libri tres*, dedicated by Ambrose to his sister, Marcellina, in A.D. 377: "Lege . . . et Ambrosii nostri quae nuper ad sororem scripsit opuscula, in quibus tanto se fudit eloquio ut, quidquid ad laudem virginum pertinet, exquisierit, ordinarit, expresserit" (CSEL 54, 174–75).

4. G. Nauroy, "Jérôme lecteur et censeur de l'exégèse d'Ambroise," *Jérôme entre l'Occident et l'Orient*, ed. Duval, 173–203; S. M. Oberhelman, "Jerome's earliest attack on Ambrose," *TAPA* 121 (1991): 377–401.

REFERENCES

Q 4, 144–80, M. G. Mara — Dr, 39–40 — CPL 123–165 — DHGE 2, 1091–1108, P. de Labriolle — DSp 1, 425–28, G. Bardy — EEC 1², 41–44, L. J. Swift — LThK 1³, 495–97, C. Jacob — NCE 1, 372–75, M. R. P. McGuire — TRE 2, 362–86, E. Dassmann

CXXV. EVAGRIUS THE BISHOP

VAGRIUS, BISHOP of Antioch,[1] a man of keen and extraordinary intelligence, while still a priest read to me tractates on diverse ὑποθέσεων, subjects, which he had not yet published,[2] and he translated, from Greek to Latin, Athanasius's *Life of Blessed Antony*.[3]

NOTES

1. Evagrius of Antioch, c. 320–c. 394; not to be confused with Evagrius Ponticus (c. 345–c. 399), excluded probably because of his Origenist leanings and because Rufinus was his pupil.

2. Jerome had enjoyed the hospitality and encouragement of Evagrius during a period of illness prior to his departure to the desert in Chalcis, and used him as a conduit for his mail after arriving there. Writing to Damasus in Rome in 376 (*ep.* 15.5), Jerome requests, "and, lest the obscurity of the place in which I dwell should baffle the letter carriers, deign to direct your epistle to the priest Evagrius whom you know very well" (ACW 33, 73). See also *ep.* 1.15: "our friend Evagrius" (ACW 33, 27 and 189 n. 22); *ep.* 7.2: "the letter was brought to me through the instrumentality of the holy Evagrius in that part of the desert which draws a vast line of demarcation between the Syrians and the Saracens" (ACW 33, 41).

3. Evagrius replaced an earlier (c. 365), crudely literal Latin translation with his own newer (c. 370) version following classical principles; cf. W. Berschin, *Greek Letters* (1988), 48–49 [see also, *loc. cit.*, 57–58], quoting the interesting *Prolog* in which Evagrius defends his procedures, later reproduced by Jerome in his *ep.* 57, *ad Pammachium de optimo genere interpretandi*. For the *Life of Antony:* PG 26, 835–976; PL 73, 125–170; on which see R. T.

160 ST. JEROME

Meyer, ACW 10, 14 and 104 nn. 45–49. St. Augustine, *Conf.* 8.6, was told about this work by the African Ponticianus.

REFERENCES

Q 3, 40 — Q 4, 206–7, 214 — Dr, 317–19 — Cath 4, 74 — EECh 1, 305, J. Gribomont — LThK 3, 1140, A. Van Roey — LThK 3³, 1027, M. Fiedrowicz — Rebenich, 52–75 — Cer.-Gast., 10

CXXVI. AMBROSE, THE DISCIPLE OF DIDYMUS

AMBROSE OF ALEXANDRIA,[1] a disciple of Didymus,[2] wrote a long, drawn-out work against Apollinaris, *On Dogmas*, and also *Commentaries on Job*, as someone told me lately. He is still alive.

NOTES

1. Jerome here is our only source of information.
2. Didymus: see *DVI* 109.

REFERENCES

DHGE 2, 1108, S. Salaville — EECh 1, 28, E. Prinzivalli — LThK 1³, 493–94, W. A. Bienert

CXXVII. MAXIMUS, AT FIRST PHILOSOPHER, THEN BISHOP

MAXIMUS THE PHILOSOPHER, born in Alexandria,[1] was ordained bishop of Constantinople,[2] and then exiled.[3] He wrote a distinguished volume against the Arians, entitled *De fide*,[4] which he presented to the emperor Gratian in Milan.[5]

NOTES

1. Cf. *DVI* 117. Maximus claimed to be a Cynic philosopher converted to Christianity.

2. He beguiled Gregory Nazianzus (*Orationes* 25 and 26).

3. He had been secretly ordained by night in the Anastasia. The Council of Constantinople (381) declared (Canon 4) that he had never been a bishop. Cf. Theodoret, *h.e.* 5.8.4, NPNF 3, ser. 2, 136.

4. He was congratulated for so doing in Athanasius, *Epistula ad Maximum Philosophum*. His work is lost. See J. Mossay, "Note sur Héron-Maxime, écrivain ecclésiastique," *AnBoll* 100 (1982): 229–236.

5. Gratian, Emperor of the West, 375–383, had his court at Milan.

REFERENCES

Q 3, 61 — EECh 1, 549, C. Gianotto — Dihle, *Greek and Latin*, 486–87

CXXVIII. GREGORY, ANOTHER BISHOP

REGORY, BISHOP of Nyssa,[1] brother of Basil of Caesarea,[2] a few years ago read to me and to Gregory of Nazianzus[3] his books, *Against Eunomius*,[4] and he is said to have written and to continue writing many other works.[5]

NOTES

1. On Nyssa cf. EECh 2, 608, M. Forlin Patrucco.

2. On Macrina, their sister, see LThK 6³, 1230, O. Volk.

3. At Constantinople.

4. *Contra Eunomium*, CPG 3135; text: *Gregorii Nysseni Opera* I and II, ed. W. Jaeger. See also *Gregorio di Nissa Teologia Trinitaria Contro Eunomio Confutazione della Professione di Fede di Eunomio*, ed. C. Moreschini (Milan, 1994), 5–588; *Gregor von Nyssa. Contra Eunomium, 1–146*, trans. with intro. and comm. by J.-A. Röder (Frankfurt and New York, 1993); L. F. Mateo-Seco and J. L. Bastero, *El "Contra Eunomium I" en la producción literaria de Gregorio de Nisa* (Pamplona, 1988); S. G. Hall, "Translator's Introduction. Gregory Bishop of Nyssa. A refutation of the first book of the two published by Eunomius after the decease of holy Basil," in *El "Contra Eunomium I"* (1988), 21–135; B. Pottier, *Dieu et le Christ selon Grégoire de Nysse* (Turnhout, 1994) [a study of *C. Eun.* and trans. of excerpts from Eunomius]; H. R. Drobner, "Die biblische Argumentation Gregors von Nyssa im ersten Buch 'Contra Eunomium,'" in *El "Contra Eunomium I"* (1988), 285–301; R. Winling,

"Mort et Résurrection du Christ dans les traités *Contre Eunome* de Grégoire de Nysse," *RSR* 64 (1990): 127–40; J. L. Bastero, "Los titulos cristologicos en el *Contra Eunomium* 1 de San Gregorio de Nisa," in *El "Contra Eunomium I"* (1988), 407–19; M. R. Barnes, "The Polemical Context and Content of Gregory of Nyssa's Psychology," *Medieval Philosophy and Theology* 4 (1994): 1–24.

5. *alia multa:* one would have expected at least a nod in the direction of his extensive exegetical work; cf. Q 3, 263–269. See C. Fabricius and D. Riddings, "A computer-made concordance to the works of Gregory," in *El "Contra Eunomium I"* (1988), 431–33; R. E. Heine, trans., *Gregory of Nyssa's Treatise on the Inscriptions of the Psalms* (Oxford); S. Hall, ed., *Gregory of Nyssa, Homilies on Ecclesiastes* (Berlin and New York, 1993); P. Huybrechts, "Le 'Traité de la virginité' de Grégoire de Nysse. Idéal de vie monastique ou idéal de vie chrétienne?" *NRTh* 115 (1993): 227–42; *Gregorio de Nisa. Sobre la vida de Moisés,* trans. with intro. and notes by L. F. Mateo-Seco (Madrid, 1993); *Gregorio de Nisa. Commentario al Cantar de los Cantares,* ed. T. H. Martín (Salamanca, 1993); E. Peroli, *Il Platonismo e l'antropologia filosofica di Gregorio de Nisa* (Milan, 1993).

REFERENCES

Q 3, 254–96 — Dr, 231–36 — *TLG* 2017 — CPG 2, 3135–3226 — DHGE 22, 20–24, P. Maraval — DSp 6, 971–1011, M. Canévet — EEC 1², 495–98, D. L. Balás — EECh 1, 363–65, J. Gribomont — LThK 4³, 1007–8, W. D. Hauschild — NCE 6, 794–96, R. F. Harvanek — RAC 12, 863–95, H. Dörrie — TRE 14, 173–81, D. L. Balás — Dihle, *Greek and Latin,* 550–51 — *Gestalten* 2, 37–47, art., "Makrina," F. van der Meer — *Gestalten* 2, 49–62, E. Mühlenberg

For bibliography see M. Altenberger and F. Mann, *Bibliographie zu Gregor von Nyssa. Editionen, Übersetzungen, Literatur* (Leiden, 1988); E. Moutsoula, (bibl. to 1968); M. M. Bergadá (Buenos Aires, 1970).

CXXIX. JOHN THE PRESBYTER

OHN, A PRIEST of the church of Antioch,[1] a disciple of Eusebius of Emesa[2] and of Diodore,[3] is said to have composed many works; the only one of which I have read is Περὶ ἱερωσύνης, *On the Priesthood.*[4]

NOTES

1. John [Chrysostom]: As Quasten points out (Q 1, 2): "the whole work [*DVI*] betrays the sympathies and antipathies of Jerome, as, for instance, the sections dealing with St. John Chrysostom and St. Ambrose indicate." See also J. N. D. Kelly, *Golden Mouth. The Story of John Chrysostom. Ascetic, Preacher, Bishop* (Ithaca, N.Y., and London, 1995); D. Attwater, *St John Chrysostom, Pastor and Preacher* (London, 1959); Chr. Baur, *John Chrysostom and His Time*, 2 vols.: Vol. 1, *Antioch*, and Vol. 2, *Constantinople*, trans. from German by M. Gonzaga (Westminster, Md., 1961); A.-J. Festugière, *Antioche païenne et chrétienne: Libanius, Chrysostome et les moines de Syrie* (Paris, 1959); J. Liebeschuetz, *Antioch: City and Imperial Administration in the Later Roman Empire* (Oxford, 1972); F. W. Norris, "Antioch-on-the-Orontes as a Religious Center. I. Paganism before Constantine," ANRW II, 18, 4 (Berlin, 1990), 2322–79; H. Tardif, *Jean Chrysostome, Église d'Hier et d'Aujourd'hui* (Paris, 1963); R. L. Wilken, *John Chrysostom and the Jews: Rhetoric and Reality in the Late Fourth Century* (Berkeley, CA, 1983).

2. Eusebius of Emesa: see *DVI* 91.

3. Diodore: see *DVI* 119.

4. *De sacerdotio libri VII* (CPG 4503).

REFERENCES

Q 3, 424–82 — Dr, 274–83 — CPG 4305–5197 — *TLG* 2062 — Cath 6, 498–511, D. Stiernon — DHGE 15, 1336–1337, G. Garitte — EEC 1², 622–24, R. Wilken — EECh 1, 440–42, A. M. Malingrey — LThK 5³, 889–92, P. Klasvogt — RAC 6, 844–47, H. G. Beck — RAC Lief. 139/140 (1997), 426–503, R. Brändle — TRE 17, 118–27, J.-M. Leroux — *Gestalten* 2, 125–44, P. Stockmeier — K. H. Uthemann, BBKL 3, 305–26

CXXX. GELASIUS THE BISHOP

 ELASIUS,[1] WHO SUCCEEDED Euzoius as bishop of Caesarea in Palestine,[2] is said to have composed certain works in an accurate and precise style,[3] but refrained from publishing them.[4]

NOTES

1. Gelasius succeeded Acacius; cf. *DVI* 98.

2. See EECh 1, 305, M. Simonetti; DHGE 12, 206–9, art., "Césarée."

3. For his works, cf. CPG 3520–3521.

4. Gelasius is nowadays credited with several works seemingly unknown to Jerome: see *Fragmenta Dogmatica: Expositio Symboli*, CPG 3520; and *Historia Ecclesiastica*, for which see CPG 3521; Photius, *Bibl. cod.* 89; J. Schamp, "The Lost Ecclesiastical History of Gelasius of Caesarea: Towards a Reconsideration," *PBR* 6 (1987): 146–52; *idem*, "Gélase ou Rufin. Un fait nouveau sur des fragments oubliés de Gélase de Césarée (CPG 3521)," *Byzantion* 57 (1987): 360–90, which reexamines the problem of the relationship betweeen the *History* of Gelasius and that of Rufinus, on the basis of the testimony of Photius (15, 88, 89, 102).

REFERENCES

Q 3, 347–48 — Cath, 300–301, P. Nautin — CPG 3520–3521 — DHGE 20, 299–301, C. Curti — EEC 1², 455, F. W. Norris — EECh 1, 379, C. Curti — LThK 4³, 401, K.-H. Uthemann — NCE 6, 317, V. C. de Clerq

CXXXI. THEOTIMUS THE BISHOP

HEOTIMUS, BISHOP of Tomi in Scythia, has published short treatises in the form of dialogues[1] and in the old style of *incisi*.[2]

I hear that he has composed other works besides.

NOTES

1. "breves commaticosque tractatus": TLL 3, 1822, *s.v. commaticus*, gives Jerome the lion's share of references, including *ep.* 112.4 and *Praef. in Vulg. XII Prophetae* ("Osee commaticus est et quasi per sententias loquens"). See also Liddell, Scott, Jones, *s.v.*, κομματικός, "consisting of short clauses" [i.e., *cola*], citing Lucian, *Bis Acc.* 28 (μικρὰ καὶ κ., as here) and Hermogenes, *Id.* 1.9; Philostratos, *VS* 2.29, has the substantive, κομματίας, "one who speaks in short clauses." See also M. Guignet, *St. Grégoire de Nazianze et la rhétorique* (Paris), 82f., and his distinction between "style périodique and style kommatique," quoted in C. Milovanic-Barham, "Three Levels of Style in Augustine of Hippo and Gregory of Nazianzus," *Rhetorica* 11 (1993): 1–26; also D. A. Russell, *Criticism in Antiquity* (Berkeley, 1981), 129–47.

2. Cf. Ceresa-Gastaldo, who translates *per incisi*, citing E. Arns, *La technique du livre d'après saint Jérôme* (Paris, 1953), 115.

REFERENCES

EECh 2, 833, G. Ladocsi

CXXXII. DEXTER, SON OF PACIAN, NOW PRAETORIAN PREFECT

EXTER, SON OF PACIAN,[1] of whom we have already spoken, a man of social distinction and a devotee of the Christian faith,[2] is said to have composed a *Universal History*[3] dedicated to me, which I have not yet read.

NOTES

1. Pacian: see *DVI* Preface and 106.
2. In *Adv. Rufinum* 23 we are told that Dexter was in charge of the praetorian guard.
3. No trace left.

REFERENCES

Q 4, 135 — EECh 1, 232–33, U. Dionisi — LThK 3, 316, H. Rahner — LThK 3³, 175, C. Brever-Winkler — *PLRE* 1, 251 — Rebenich, 214

CXXXIII. AMPHILOCHIUS THE BISHOP

MPHILOCHIUS, BISHOP of Iconium, lately read to me a book, *On the Holy Spirit*,[1] arguing that He is God and that He is to be worshipped, and that He is omnipotent.[2]

NOTES

1. The reading occurred at the Council of Constantinople in 381; cf. Courcelle, *LLW,* 121. Nothing of it survives.

2. Basil dedicated his own *On the Holy Spirit* to him. Amphilochius is sometimes described as the fourth great Cappadocian.

REFERENCES

Q 3, 296–300 — Dr, 224–25, 230 — *TLG* 2112 — CPG 3230–3254 — EEC 1², 46, M. P. McHugh — EECh 1, 32, S. J. Voicu — LThK 1³, 540–41, H.-C. Brennecke — Rebenich, 121

For the works of Amphilochius, see *Amphilochii Iconiensis Opera*, C. Datema, ed., CCG 3 (Turnhout-Leuven, 1978).

CXXXIV. SOPHRONIUS

OPHRONIUS, an extremely learned man while still a youth, composed *Praises of Bethlehem*[1] and, more recently, a distinguished volume, *On the Destruction of Serapis*.

2. Besides, he has translated into most elegant Greek a work of my own, *To Eustochium, On Virginity*,[2]

and the *Life of Hilarion*, the monk,[3]

also, the *Psalter* and the *Prophets*, which have been translated by me from the Hebrew into Latin.

NOTES

1. Cf. A. Pollastri, EECh 2, 787: "juvenile works in Greek, now lost."
2. = *ep.* 22 of Jerome.
3. See CPG 3630 and *DVI* 135 n. 32 (*infra*); trans. of *Life of Hilarion* in NPNF 6, ser. 2, 303–15. The Greek version of *DVI* was not his; cf. Ceresa-Gastaldo, 44–45.

REFERENCES

CPG 3630–36

CXXXV. JEROME THE PRESBYTER

JEROME, SON OF EUSEBIUS,[1] born in the town of Stridon which, overrun by the Goths, was once a border town between Dalmatia and Pannonia,[2] up to the present year, that is, the fourteenth year of the reign of Theodosius,[3] has written the following works:[4]

2. *The Life of Paul the Monk;*[5]
Letters to Various Recipients, one book;[6]
A Letter of consolation to Heliodorus;[7]
The Disputation between a follower of Lucifer and an Orthodox;[8]
The Chronicle of Universal History;[9]
twenty-eight *Homilies of Origen on Jeremiah and Ezekiel,*[10] which I have translated from Greek into Latin;
On the Seraphim;[11]
On the Hosanna;[12]
On the two sons, the frugal and the prodigal;[13]
On Three Questions of the Old Law;[14]
two *Homilies on the Canticle of Canticles;*[15]

3. *Against Helvidius, on the Perpetual Virginity of Mary;*[16]
To Eustochium, on the Preservation of Virginity;[17]
To Marcella, one book of letters;[18]
A Letter of Consolation to Paula on the death of her daughter;[19]
Commentary on Paul's epistle, To the Galatians,[20] three books;
Commentary on Paul's epistle, To the Ephesians,[21] three books;
On the Epistle to Titus, one book;[22]
On the Epistle to Philemon, one book;[23]
Commentaries on Ecclesiastes;[24]

4. *Hebrew Questions on Genesis,* one book;[25]
On Places, one book;[26]
On Hebrew Names, one book;[27]
On the Holy Spirit by Didymus, one book,[28] which I have translated into Latin;
thirty-nine *Homilies on Luke;*[29]

On the Psalms, from the Tenth to the Sixteenth, seven treatises;[30]
On a Captive Monk[31] [Malchus];
The Life of blessed Hilarion.[32]

5. I have translated the New Testament, faithful to the Greek;[33]

I have translated the Old Testament in accordance with the Hebrew;[34]

however, the number of letters to Paula and Eustochium, because they are written daily, is uncertain.[35]

6. I have written, besides, *Explanations of Micah,* two books;[36]
On Nahum, one book;[37]
On Habakkuk, two books;[38]
On Zephaniah, one book;[39]
On Haggai, one book;[40]

and many others on the work of the Prophets which I have on hand, and are not yet finished.[41]

NOTES

1. Sophronius Eusebius Hieronymus: Ἱερώνυμος, "having a holy name."

2. Stridon = Emona and present-day Ljubljana/Laibach in Slovenia. Pannonia belongs to modern Hungary. See I. Fodor, "Le lieu d'origène de S. Jérôme," *RHE* 81 (1986): 498–500; A. D. Booth, "The date of Jerome's birth," *Phoenix* 33 (1979): 346–52; A. Grilli, "San Gerolamo. Un dalmata e i suoi correspondenti," *Antichità altoadriatiche* 26 (1985): 297–314; R. Bratok, "Die Geschichte des frühen Christentums im Gebiet zwischen Sirmium und Aquileia im Licht der neueren Forschungen," *Klio* 72 (1990): 508–50. On Goths, see P. J. Heather, *Goths and Romans 332–489* (Oxford, 1991).

3. See P. Nautin, "La date du *De uiris inlustribus* de Jérôme, de la mort de Cyrille de Jérusalem, et de celle de Grégoire de Nazianze," *RHE* 56 (1961): 33–35.

4. *Opera omnia:* PL 22–30; PLS 2, 18–328; P. Nautin, "La liste des oeuvres de Jérôme dans le *De uiris inlustribus,*" *Orpheus,* n.s., 5 (1984): 319–34. The text of *DVI* used here is the recent *Gerolamo Gli Uomini Illustri,* ed. Aldo Ceresa-Gastaldo, Biblioteca Patristica 12 (Florence: Nardini Editore, 1988), 230–33.

5. CPL 617. A. Dihle, *Greek and Latin,* 415–16, observes, "The hermit Paul seems to be Hieronymus's invention: the author describes him as the teacher of the monastic father Antonius, and this is an altogether blatant give-away of Hieronymus's attempt to outdo the famous life of Antonius written by the great Athanasius." See *Saint Jérôme, Vivre au désert: Paulus, Malchus, Hilarion,* trans. J. Miniac (Grenoble, 1992); *Vita Pauli eremitae,* R.

Degòrski (Rome, 1987); M. S. Gonzáles, "Análisis literario de tres Vitae de san Jerónimo," *EClás* 28 (1986): 105–20; E. Coleiro, "St. Jerome's Lives of the Hermits," *VigChr* 11 (1957): 161–78.

6. Probably *epp.* 1–17. For text of his *Letters*, see I. Hilberg, ed., CSEL 54–56 (1910–1918), and the recently issued Index volume; ACW 33 (*epp.* 1–22), trans. C. C. Mierow. Still useful is J. Duff, *The Letters of St. Jerome. A selection to illustrate Roman Christian Life in the 4th Century* (Dublin, 1942).

7. = *ep.* 14; for trans. see ACW 33, 59–69, and Notes, 205–9. On *ep.* 60, also addressed to Heliodorus, see J. H. D. Scourfield, *Consoling Heliodorus. A Commentary on Jerome, Letter 60* (Oxford, 1993), and J. Duff, *The Letters*, 136–46 and 303–5.

8. *Altercatio:* CPL 608; PL 23: 155–182; Q 4, 238–39; *ALGP* 14–16 (1977–79), 217–44.

9. CPL 615C; Q 4, 227. Based on Eusebius, *Chronicle* (ed. Helm, GCS 24; Eng. trans., M. D. Donalson), on which see Q 3, 311–13. See also G. Brugnoli, "Curiosissimus excerptor," in *Gerolamo e la biografia letteraria* (Genoa, 1989), 23–43; G. Brugnoli, "Questioni biografiche, 1: le *De viris illustribus* di Girolamo," *GiornItalFil* 40 (1988): 279–82.

10. In all, as Jerome tells us in his *Adv. Rufinum* 1.8, "I had translated into Latin seventy of Origen's books . . . and many of his commentaries," (trans. J. N. Hritzu, FOTC 53, 68); see also Hritzu, *op. cit.*, 48 n. 4: "About the year 380, St. Jerome translated at Constantinople nine of Origen's homilies on Isaia, fourteen on Jeremia, thirty-nine homilies on St. Luke." Text of *In Hieremiam* in CSEL 59, ed. S. Reiter (1913), and CCL 74, ed. M. Adriaen and F. Glorie (1960). Text of *In Ezechielem:* CCL 75, ed. F. Glorie (1964).

11. *On the Seraphim* [Is 6.1–9] = *ep.* 18A, *To Damasus;* see ACW 33, 79–96, and notes, 214–21. This appears to be the earliest of Jerome's Biblical works. In *ep.* 84 (NPNF 6, ser. 2, 176), he writes: "In the portion of Isaiah which describes the crying of the two seraphim, [Origen] explains these to be the Son and the Holy Ghost; but have not I altered this hateful explanation into a reference to the two testaments?" See P. Nautin, "Le *De Seraphim* de Jérôme et son appendice *Ad Damasum*," in *Roma renascens*, FS I. Opelt (Frankfurt, Berne, and New York, 1988), 257–93.

12. = *ep.* 20, to Pope Damasus.

13. *On the Prodigal Son* (Lk 15.11–32) = *ep.* 21, *To Damasus;* see ACW 33, 109–33, and Notes, 224–32.

14. = *ep.* 36. The three passages are Gn 4.15, 15.16, and 27.21.

15. Q 4, 229–30. For the two homilies on Canticles, see *Origène: Homélies sur le Cantique des Cantiques*, SC 37 (Paris, 1953). For Origen's commentaries on the Canticles, see *Origène: Commentaires sur le Cantique des Cantiques*, ed. L. Breesard, H. Crouzel, and M. Borret, SC 375/376 (Paris, 1992).

16. See "On the Perpetual Virginity of the Blessed Mary against Helvidius," in *Saint Jerome: Dogmatic and Polemical Works*, trans. J. N. Hritzu, FOTC 53, 3–43; D. G. Hunter, "Helvidius, Jovinian and the Virginity of Mary in late fourth-century Rome," *JECS* 1 (1993): 47–71. For a novel, more benign than usual, interpretation of *Adv. Iovinianum*, cf. J. Oppel, "Saint Jerome and the history of sex," *Viator* 24 (1993): 1–22.

17. *To Eustochium = ep.* 22; see ACW 33, 134–79, and notes, 232–48. *Ep.* 22 has been the subject of much recent work, especially by N. Adkin in *RSLR* 28 (1992): 461–71; *VigChr* 46 (1992): 141–50; *Hermes* 121 (1993): 100–108; and *Symbolae Osloenses* 68 (1993). For psychoanalytical probings see B. Feichtinger, "Der Traum des Hieronymus—ein Psycho-gramm," *VigChr* 45 (1991): 54–77; P. Cox Miller, "The blazing body: ascetic desire in Jerome's letter to Eustochium," *JECS* 1 (1993): 21–45.

18. *To Marcella:* 19 letters; Labourt, II, puts the number at 22; see also Cer.-Gast., 342. On *ep.* 46 see ACW 33, 185 n. 2.

19. *Consolatoriam ad Paulam = ep.* 39.

20. *Commentarii in iv epistulas Paulinas:* CPL 591; PL 26: 307–618.

21. *ad Ephesios:* About this work he tells us, in *Adv. Rufinum* 1.16: "In my *Commentary to the Ephesians*, I followed as my models, to be sure, Origen and Didymus and Apollinaris (who hold doctrines that are certainly contradictory) in such a way that I did not lose sight of the truth of my faith. What is the function of commentators?" (trans. Hritzu, FOTC 53, 79). On the answer to this, see J. T. Cummings, "St. Jerome as translator and as exegete," StudPat 12 (= TU 115), 279–82. See also E. A. Clark, "The Place of Jerome's Commentary on Ephesians in the Origenist Controversy: the Apokatastasis and Ascetic Ideals," *VigChr* 41 (1987): 154–71; *eadem, The Origenist Controversy.*

22. *Ad Titum:* CPL 591.

23. *Ad Philemonem:* CPL 591.

24. *In Ecclesiasten:* CPL 583; Q 4, 232–33; CCL 72, ed. M. Adriaen (1959), 147–361. See S. Leanza, "Sul Commentario all'*Ecclesiaste* di Girolamo. Il problema esegetico," *Jérôme entre l'Occident et l'Orient,* ed. Duval, 267–82.

25. *Quaestiones in Genesim:* CPL 580; CCL 72, ed. P. de Lagarde, G. Morin, and M. Adriaen (1959); A. Kamesar, *Jerome, Greek Scholarship and the Hebrew Bible: a Study of the "Quaestiones in Genesim,"* (Oxford, 1993); C. T. R. Hayward, "Some observations on St. Jerome's Hebrew *Questions on Genesis* and the Rabbinic Tradition," *Proc. Ir. Bib. Assoc.* 13 (1990): 58–76; *Saint Jerome's Hebrew Questions on Genesis,* trans. with intro. and comm. by C. T. R. Hayward (Oxford: Clarendon Press, 1995).

26. *De locis:* CPL 581a; Q 4, 228.

27. *Hebraica nomina:* CPL 581; CCL 72, ed. P. de Lagarde, G. Morin, and M. Adriaen (1959).

28. Cf. *DVI* 109: "[Didymus] conscripsit . . . et *De Spiritu Sancto* librum unum quem ego in Latinam verti." In *Adv. Rufinum* 3.28 Jerome says, "My master and yours [i.e., Didymus] dictated for me at my request three books of commentaries on the Prophet Osee" (trans. Hritzu, FOTC 53, 199).

29. CPG 1451; text: GCS, *Origenes Werke* 9, ed. Max Rauer (Berlin, 1959); SC 87, Rauer's text with French trans., intro., and notes by Crouzel, Fournier, and Périchon (Paris, 1962); Eng. trans. by J. T. Lienhard, *Origen: Homilies on Luke, Fragments on Luke,* FOTC 94 (Washington, D.C., 1996).

30. *On the Psalms:* CCL 72, 163–245, ed. P. de Lagarde, G. Morin, and M. Adriaen (1959); *Origene-Girolamo, 74 omelie sul Libro dei salmi,* ed. G. Coppa (1992); H. de Sainte-Marie, *Collectanea Biblica Latina* 11 (Rome, 1954); G.

Q. A. Meershoek, "Le latin biblique d'après saint Jérôme," *Latinitas Christianorum Primaeva* 20 (Nijmegen, 1966); V. Peri, *Omelie origeniane sui Salmi. Contributi all'identificazione del testo latino* = StT 289 (1980); C. Estin, "Les psautiers de Jérôme à la lumière des traductions juives antérieures," *Collectanea Biblica Latina* 15 (Rome, 1984); P. Jay, "Jérôme à Bethléem. Les *Tractatus in Psalmos*," *Jérôme entre l'Occident et l'Orient*, ed. Duval, 367–80.

31. *De captivo monacho:* i.e., Malchus; see Ceresa-Gastaldo, 232, *app. crit.;* C. C. Mierow, "Sancti Eusebii Hieronymi Vita Malchi Monachi captivi," in *Classical Essays Presented to J. A. Kleist* (St. Louis, 1946), 31–60. Malchus was a monk captured by the Saracens.

32. *Vita Hilarionis/Epitaphium sanctae Paulae:* see Ch. Mohrmann, A. A. R. Bastiaensen, J. W. Smit, L. Canali, and C. Moreschini, edd., Vite dei Santi 4 (Verona, 1975), 69–237, 291–369; S. González Marin, "Análisis literario de tres 'Vitae,'" *EClás* 28 (1986): 105–20.

33. *Nova Vulgata Bibliorum Sacrorum editio* (Vatican City, 1979); H. F. D. Sparks, "Jerome as Biblical Scholar," Cambridge History of the Bible 1 (1970), 510–41; T. Stramare, ed., *La Bibbia "Vulgata" dalle origini ai nostri giorni*, Collectanea Biblica Latina 16 (Rome, 1987); G. Q. A. Meershoek, *Le latin biblique d'après saint Jérôme, Latinitas Christianorum Primaeva* (Nijmegen, 1966); C. Nardi, *Vivens homo* 4 (1993): 127–61.

34. On *iuxta Hebraicum* see S. Rebenich, "Jerome: the *vir trilinguis* and the *Hebraica veritas*," *VigChr* 47 (1993): 50–77.

35. Actually only three letters to Paula are published (*epp.* 30, 33, 39) and two to Eustochium (*epp.* 22, 31); *cotidie scribuntur* probably explains *incertus numerus.*

36. Q 4, 234–35; *In Prophetas minores:* CCL 76–76A, ed. M. Adriaen (1969–70); *In Michaeam:* CCL 76, 421–524.

37. *In Naum:* CCL 76A, 525–78.

38. *In Abacuc:* CCL 76A, 579–654.

39. *In Sophoniam:* CCL 76A, 655–711.

40. *In Aggaeum:* CCL 76A, 713–46.

41. "Many others" would include *In Zachariam*, CCL 76A, 747–900; *In Malachiam*, CCL 76A, 901–942; *In Danielem*, CCL 75A, ed. F. Glorie (1964); *Comm. On Prophet Osee*, CCL 76, 1–158; cf. *DVI* 109: "[Didymus] *In Osee* ad me scribens commentariorum libros tres." See also *Adv. Rufinum*, ed. P. Lardet, CCL 79 (1982), and ed. *idem*, SC 303 (1983); also, *Homiliae:* G. Morin, CCL 78 (1958); Eng. trans. M. L. Ewald, FOTC 48 and 57 (1964, 1966).

REFERENCES

Q 4, 195–247 — Dr, 285–95 — CPL 580–623 — DSp 8, 901–18, J. Gribomont — Cath 6, 702–6, P. Antin — EEC 1², 606–9, M. P. McHugh — EECh 1, 430–31, J. Gribomont — LThK 5, 326–29, P.-Th. Camelot — LThK 5³, 91–93, M. Durst — NCE 7, 872–74, F. X. Murphy — RAC 15, 117–39, H. Hagendahl and J. H. Waszink — TRE 15, 304–15, P. Nautin

APPENDICES & INDICES

APPENDIX 1. JEROME'S BIBLIOGRAPHY
OF ORIGEN

[From *Ep.* 33.4–5, *To Paula*, CSEL 54, 255–59]

But why, you ask me, have I thus mentioned Varro and the man of brass (i.e., Chalcenter). Simply to bring to your notice our Christian man of brass, or rather, man of adamant [*Adamantius*]—Origen, I mean—whose zeal for the study of Scripture has fairly earned for him this latter name. Would you learn what monuments of his genius he has left us? The following list displays them.

In Genesim libros XIII,	CPG 1410
Mistarum omeliarum libros II,	CPG 1412
In Exodum excerpta,	CPG 1413
In Leuiticum excerpta,	CPG 1415
Stromatum libros X,	CPG 1483
In Isaiam libros XXXVI,	CPG 1435
item In Isaiam excerpta,	CPG 1436
In Osee de Effraim librum I,	
In Osee commentarium,	CPG 1443
In Iohel libros II,	CPG 1444
In Amos libros VI,	
In Ionam librum I,	
In Micheam libros III,	
In Naum libros II,	
In Abacuc libros III,	
In Sophoniam libros II,	
In Aggeum librum I,	
In principio Zachariae libros II,	
In Malachiam libros II,	
In Hiezechiel libros XXVIIII,	CPG 1440
In Prouerbia libros III,	CPG 1430
In Ecclesiasten excerpta,	CPG 1431
In Canticum Canticorum libros X	CPG 1433

et alios tomos II, quos super scripsit
in adulescentia,   CPG 1434
In Lamentationes Hieremiae tomos V,   CPG 1439
item Monobibla, Periarchon libros IIII,   CPG 1482
De resurrectione libros II
et alios De resurrectione dialogos II,   CPG 1478
De Prouerbiorum quibusdam quaestionibus librum I,   CPG 1430
Dialogum aduersus Candidum Valentinianum,
De martyrio librum;   CPG 1475

de nouo testamento:

In Matheum libros XXV,   CPG 1450
In Iohannem libros XXXII,   CPG 1453
In partes quasdam Iohannis excerptorum librum I,
In Lucam libros XV,   CPG 1452
In epistulam Pauli apostoli ad Romanos libros XV,   CPG 1457
In epistulam ad Galatas libros XV,   CPG 1459
In epistulam ad Ephesios libros III,   CPG 1460
In epistulam ad Philippenses librum I,
In epistulam ad Colossenses libros II,   CPG 1461
In epistula ad Thessalonicenses I libros III,   CPG 1462
In epistula ad Thessalonicenses II librum I,   CPG 1463
In epistula ad Titum librum I,   CPG 1464
In epistula ad Philemonem librum I;   CPG 1465

rursus omeliarum in uetus testamentum:

In Genesi omeliae XVII,   CPG 1411
In Exodo omeliae VIII,   CPG 1414
In Leuitico omeliae XI,   CPG 1416
In Numeris omeliae XXVIII,   CPG 1418
In Deuteronomio omeliae XIII,   CPG 1419
In Iesu Naue omeliae XXVI,   CPG 1420
In libro Iudicum omeliae VIIII,   CPG 1421
De pascha omeliae VIII,   CPG 1480
In primo Regnorum libro omeliae IIII   CPG 1423
In Iob omeliae XXII,   CPG 1424
In Paroemias omeliae VII,   CPG 1430
In Ecclesiasten omeliae VIII,   CPG 1431
In Cantico Canticorum omeliae II,   CPG 1432

In Isaiam omeliae XXXII,	CPG 1437
In Hieremiam omeliae XIIII,	CPG 1438
In Hiezechiel omeliae XII;	CPG 1441
In Psalmos	CPG 1425

omeliae in nouum testamentum:

In euangelium κατὰ Ματθαῖον omeliae XXV,	CPG 1450
In euangelium κατὰ Λουκᾶν omeliae XXXVIIII	CPG 1451
In Actus apostolorum omeliae XVII,	CPG 1456
In epistula ad Corinthios II omeliae XI,	cf. CPG 1458
In epistula ad Thessalonicenses omeliae II,	CPG 1462
In epistula ad Galatas omeliae VII,	CPG 1459
In epistula ad Titum omelia I,	CPG 1464
In epistula ad Hebraeos omeliae XVIII;	CPG 1466
De pace omelia I,	
Exhortatoria ad Pioniam, De ieiunio,	
De monogamis et trigamis omeliae II,	
In Tarso omeliae II,	
Origenis, Firmiani et Gregorii, item excerpta Origenis	
et diuersarum ad eum epistularum libri II—epistula +	
esifodorum super causa Origenis in libro IIº—,	
Epistularum eius ad diuersos libri VIIII,	CPG 1490–
	1496
Aliarum epistularum libri II,	
item Epistula pro apologia operum suorum libri II	

Videtisne et Graecos pariter et Latinos unius labore superatos? quis enim umquam tanta legere potuit, quanta ipse conscripsit? pro hoc sudore quid accepit praemii? damnatur a Demetrio episcopo; exceptis Palaestinae et Arabiae et Phoenices atque Achaiae sacerdotibus in damnationem eius consentit orbis; Roma ipsa contra hunc cogit senatum non propter dogmatum novitatem, non propter heresim, ut nunc aduersum eum rabidi canes simulant, sed quia gloriam eloquentiae eius et scientiae ferre non poterant et illo dicente omnes muti putabantur.

APPENDIX 2. WRITINGS OF TERTULLIAN
"Scripsit multa volumina" (*DVI* 53)

Ad martyras (To the Martyrs)
    CPL 1
    Q 2, 290–92
    CCL 1, 1–8, E. Dekkers
Ad nationes (To the Heathen)
    CPL 2
    Q 2, 255–56
    CCL 1, 9–75, J. G. P. Borleffs
    Le premier livre 'Ad Nationes' de Tertullien, with intro., text, trans.,
        comm. by A. Schneider (Ghent, 1968)
Apologeticum (Apology)
    CPL 3
    Q 2, 256–64
    CCL 1, 77–171, E. Dekkers
    FOTC 10, 7–126, trans. Sr. E. J. Daly
De testimonio animae (The Testimony of the Soul)
    CPL 4
    Q 2, 264–66
    CCL 1, 173–83, R. Willems
    Tertullian. La Testimonianza Dell'Anima, ed. C. Tibiletti
        (Florence, 1984)
De praescriptione haereticorum (On the Prescription of Heretics)
    CPL 5
    Q 2, 269–73
    CCL 1, 185–224, R. F. Refoulé
    R. F. Refoulé and P. de Labriolle, *Tertullien, Traité de la prescription
        contre les hérétiques,* with intro., crit. text, notes by R. F. Refoulé;
        trans. P. de Labriolle, SC 46 (Paris, 1957)
    [Tertullianus] L'Apologetico. La prescrizione contro gli eretici, trans.,
        intro., and notes by Igimo Giordani (Roma: Citta Nuova,
        1967)

C. Munier, "Analyse du traité de Tertullien *De praescriptione haereticorum*," *RSR* 59 (1985): 12–32

De spectaculis (*The Shows*)
CPL 6
Q 2, 292–94,
CCL 1, 227–53, E. Dekkers
Tertullien. Les Spectacles (De Spectaculis), M. Turcan, SC 332 (Paris, 1986)

De oratione (*Concerning Prayer*)
CPL 7
Q 2, 296–98,
CCL 1, 257–74, G. F. Diercks

De baptismo (*On Baptism*)
CPL 8
Q 2, 278–81
CCL 2, 275–95, J. G. P. Borleffs, SC 35
Tertullianus, Quintus Septimius Florens. De Baptismo, ed. with comm. by B. Luiselli, *CSLP* 32 (Turin and Paravia, 1960; 2nd ed., Paravia, 1968)
Tertullian's Homily on Baptism, ed. and trans. with intro. and comm. by E. Evans (London, 1964)
Tertulliano. Il battesimo, ed. P. A. Gramaglia (Rome, 1980)

De patientia (*Concerning Patience*)
CPL 9
Q 2, 298–99
CCL 1, 299–317, J. G. P. Borleffs
SC 310, J.-C. Fredouille

De paenitentia (*Concerning Repentance*)
CPL 10
Q 2, 299–302
CCL 1, 321–40, J. G. P. Borleffs
SC 316, C. Munier
ACW 28, 14–37, W. P. Le Saint

De cultu feminarum (*On the Dress of Women*)
CPL 11
Q 2, 294–96
CCL 1, 343–70, A. Kroymann
SC 173, M. Turcan
ANF 4, 14–26

Ad uxorem (To His Wife)
    CPL 12
    Q 2, 302–4
    CCL 1, 373–94, A. Kroymann
    SC 273, C. Munier
    ACW 13, 1–36
    ANF 4, 39–49
    Il matrimonio nel cristianesimo preniceno. Ad uxorem, De exhortatione
        castitatis, De monogamia di Tertulliano, ed. P. A. Gramaglia
        (Rome, 1988)

Adversus Hermogenem (Against Hermogenes)
    CPL 13
    Q 2, 276
    CCL 1, 395–435, A. Kroymann
    Quinti Septimii Florentis Tertulliani. Adversus Hermogenem liber, ed. J.
        H. Waszink, Str Pat 5 (Utrecht and Antwerp, 1956)
    Tertullian. The Treatise against Hermogenes, trans. and annot. by J. H.
        Waszink, ACW 24 (London, 1956)

Adversus Marcionem (Against Marcion)
    CPL 14
    Q 2, 273–76
    CCL 1, 437–726, A. Kroymann
    Tertullien. Contre Marcion, 3 vols.; Vol. 3: intro., crit. text, trans.,
        notes, and index by R. Braun, SC 399 (Paris, 1994)

Opera Montanistica

De pallio (Concerning the Pallium)
    CPL 15
    Q 2, 315–17
    CCL 2, 731–50, A. Gerlo
    CSLP 59, ed. and trans. J. Marra
    ANF 4, 5–12

Adversus Valentinianos (Against the Valentinians)
    CPL 16
    Q 2, 277–78
    CCL 11, 751–78, A. Kroymann
    Tertullien. Contre les Valentiniens, 2 vols.; Vol. 1 (SC 280): intro.,
        crit. text, trans. by J.-C. Fredouille; Vol. 2 (SC 281): comm. and
        index (Paris, 1980–81)

Tertullianus. Adversus Valentinianos, ed. A. Marastoni (Padua, 1971)
Tertulliani Adversus Valentinianos, text, trans., and comm. by M. T.
   Riley (Ph.D. diss., Stanford University, 1971)

De anima (On the Soul)
   CPL 17
   Q 2, 287–90
   CCL 2, 779–869
   M. Tertulliano. De anima, J. H. Waszink, M. Menghi, M. Vegetti
      (Venice, 1988), 36–220
   *Index verborum et locutionum quae Tertulliani De anima libro
      continentur*, J. H. Waszink (Bonn, 1935; repr., Hildesheim, 1971)

De carne Christi (On the Flesh of Christ)
   CPL 18
   Q 2, 282–83
   CCL 11, 871–917, A. Kroymann
   Tertullien. La chair du Christ, ed. and trans. J. P. Mahé, 2 vols., SC
      216, 217 (Paris, 1975)

De resurrectione mortuorum (On the Resurrection of the Dead)
   CPL 19
   Q 2, 283–84
   CCL 2, 919–1012, J. G. P. Borleffs
   Tertullien. La résurrection des morts, trans. M. Moreau, with intro.,
      analysis, and notes by J. P. Mahé, *Les Pères dans la foi* series (Paris,
      1980)
   *Q. Septimii Florentis Tertulliani De Resurrectione Carnis Liber.
      Tertullian's Treatise on the Resurrection*, ed. with intro., trans., and
      comm. by E. Evans (London, 1960)

De Exhortatione Castitatis (Exhortation to Chastity)
   CPL 20
   Q 2, 304–5
   CCL 2, 1015–35, A. Kroymann
   SC 319, C. Moreschini, J.-C. Fredouille
   ANF 4, 50–58
   ACW 13, 37–64, trans. W. P. Le Saint

De corona (The Chaplet)
   CPL 21
   Q 2, 307–9
   CCL 2, 1037–65, A. Kroymann, J. Fontaine
   Tertullien. De Corona, ed. with intro. and comm. by J.
      Fontaine (Paris, 1966)
   De Corona, ed. F. Ruggiero (Milan, 1992)

Scorpiace
  CPL 22
  Q 2, 281–82
  CCL 11, 1067–97, A. Reifferscheid and G. Wissowa
  T. D. Barnes, "Tertullian's *Scorpiace*," *JThS* 20 (1969): 105–32

De idololatria (*Concerning Idolatry*)
  CPL 23
  Q 2, 310–11
  CCL 2, 1099–1124, A. Reifferscheid and G. Wissowa
  CSEL 20, 30–58
  ANF 3, 61–76
  Q. S. F. Tertulliani De Idololatria, Pars I, cc. 1–9, ed. P. G. van der Nat
    (Leyden, 1960)
  De idololatria, ed. J. H. Waszink and J. C. M. Van Winden
    (Leyden, 1987)

Ad Scapulam (*To Scapula*)
  CPL 24
  Q 2, 266–68
  CCL 11, 1125–32, E. Dekkers
  Ad Scapulam, ed. with intro., trans., and notes by P. A. Gramaglia
    (Rome, 1980)

De fuga in persecutione (*Concerning Flight in Persecution*)
  CPL 25
  Q 2, 309–10
  CCL 2, 1133–55, J. J. Thierry.
  CSLP 59, ed. J. Marra (Turin, 1954)
  ANF 4, 116–26

Adversus Praxean (*Against Praxeas*)
  CPL 26
  Q 2, 284–86
  CCL 11, 1157–1205, A. Kroymann and E. Evans
  Q. S. F. Tertulliano. Contra Prassea, crit. ed. with intro., Ital. trans.,
    notes, and indices by G. Scarpat (Turin, 1985)

De virginibus velandis (*Veiling of Virgins*)
  CPL 27
  Q 2, 306–7
  CCL 2, 1207–26, E. Dekkers and G. F. Diercks
  ANF 4, 27–38
  De virginibus velandis, ed. E. Schulz-Flügel (Göttingen, 1977)

De monogamia (*On Monogamy*)
  CPL 28
  Q 2, 305–6
  CCL 2, 1229–53, E. Dekkers
  ANF 4, 59–73
  ACW 13, 65–108, trans. W. P. Le Saint
  De monogamia, ed. Mattei, *Corona Patrum* (Turin, 1993)
  P. A. Gramaglia, *Il matrimonio nel cristianesimo preniceno. Ad uxorem, De exhortatione castitatis, De monogamia di Tertulliano* (Rome, 1988)

De ieiunio adversus psychicos (*On Fasting*)
  CPL 29
  Q 2, 266–68
  CCL 2, 1255–77, A. Reifferscheid and G. Wissowa
  CSEL 20, 274–97
  ANF 4, 102–15

De pudicitia (*On Modesty*)
  CPL 30
  Q 2, 312–15
  CCL 2, 1281–1330, E. Dekkers
  CSEL 20, 219–73
  SC 394, 395, C. Munier and C. Micaelli
  ANF 4, 74–101
  ACW 28, 41ff., trans. W. P. Le Saint

De fato aliaque fragmenta
  CPL 31
  Q 2, 318
  CCL 2, 1331–33, A. Harnack
  L. M. Perez del Valle, "Providencia, destino y liberdad en el *De Fato* de Tertuliano," *Helmantica* 21 (1970): 79–113

Adversus Apelliacos
  CPL 31a
  Q 2, 318
  CCL 2, 1333–34, A. Harnack
  J. P. Mahé, "Le traité perdu de Tertullien *Adversus Apelleiacos* et la chronologie de sa triade anti gnostique," *REAug* 16 (1970): 3–24

De exstasi (*Concerning Ecstasy*)
  CPL 31b
  CCL 2, 1334–35

De censu animae contra Hermogenem
 CPL 31c
 CCL 2, 1335–36

Ad amicum philosophum de angustiis nuptiarum
 CPL 31d
 CCL 2, 1336
 C. Tibiletti, "Un opuscolo perduto di Tertulliano *Ad amicum philosophum*," *AtTor* 80 (1962–63): 95ff.

De paradiso
 CPL 31e
 Q 2, 318
 CCL 2, 1336

Spuria

De Execrandis Gentium Deis
 CPL 35
 CCL 11, 1411–1415, R. Willems

Carmen adversus Marcionem
 CPL 36
 CCL 11, 1417–1430, R. Willems

Dubia

Adversus Iudaeos (*Against the Jews*)
 CPL 33

APPENDIX 3. WRITINGS OF CYPRIAN
"Huius ingenii superfluum est indicem texere" (*DVI* 67)

Ad Donatum
 CPL 38
 Q 2, 346–47
 CCL 3A, 1–13, M. Simonetti
 SC 291, Molager
 FOTC 36, 5–21, trans. R. J. Deferrari
Ad Quirinum (*Testimoniorum libri adversus Iudaeos*)
 CPL 39
 Q 2, 362–63
 CCL 3A, 3–179, Weber
De habitu virginum
 CPL 40
 Q 2, 347–48
 FOTC 36, 25–52, trans. Sr. A. E. Keenan
De catholicae ecclesiae unitate
 CPL 41
 Q 2, 349
 CCL 3, 249–68, M. Bévenot
 FOTC 36, 91–121, trans. Deferrari
De lapsis
 CPL 42
 Q 2, 348–49
 CCL 3, 221–42
 FOTC 36, 55–88, trans. Deferrari
De dominica oratione
 CPL 43
 Q 2, 353–55
 CCL 3A, 87–113, C. Moreschini
 FOTC 36, 123–59, trans. Deferrari
De mortalitate
 CPL 44
 Q 2, 356–58

CCL 3A, 15–32, M. Simonetti
FOTC 36, 193–221, trans. Deferrari

Ad Fortunatum (*De exhortatione martyrii*)
CPL 45
Q 2, 361–62
CCL 3, 183–213
FOTC 36, 311–44, trans. Deferrari

Ad Demetrianum
CPL 46
Q 2, 355–56
CCL 3A, 33–51, M. Simonetti
FOTC 36, 161–91, trans. Deferrari

De opere et eleemosynis
CPL 47
Q 2, 358–59
CCL 3A, 53–72, M. Simonetti
FOTC 36, 223–53, trans. Deferrari

De bono patientiae
CPL 48
Q 2, 359–60
CCL 3A, 115–33, C. Moreschini
FOTC 36, 255–87, trans. Sr. G. E. Conway

De zelo et livore
CPL 49
Q 2, 360–61
CCL 3A, 73–86, M. Simonetti
FOTC 36, 289–308, trans. Deferrari

Epistulae
CPL 50
Q 2, 364–67
CCL 3A, 55–72, M. Simonetti
FOTC 51, trans. Sr. R. B. Donna
ACW 43–44, 46–47, trans. G. W. Clarke

Epistula ad Silvanum et Donatianum
CPL 51
Q 2, 346–47

APPENDIX 4. WORKS OF AMBROSE OF MILAN
"De quo, quia superest, meum iudicium subtraham" (*DVI* 124)

Exegetica

Exameron	CPL 123	Q 4, 153–54
	FOTC 42, 3–283, J. J. Savage	
De paradiso	CPL 124	Q 4, 154–55
	FOTC 42, 287–356, J. J. Savage	
De Cain et Abel	CPL 125	Q 4, 155
	FOTC 42, 359–437, J. J. Savage	
De Noe (et arce)	CPL 126	Q 4, 155
De Abraham	CPL 127	Q 4, 156
De Isaac vel anima	CPL 128	Q 4, 156–57
De bono mortis	CPL 129	Q 4, 157–58
	CSEL 32/1 (1896), C. Schenkl	
De Iacob et vita beata	CPL 130	Q 4, 158–59
De Ioseph	CPL 131	Q 4, 159
De patriarchis	CPL 132	Q 4, 159
De fuga saeculi	CPL 133	Q 4, 158
De interpellatione Iob et David	CPL 134	Q 4, 161–62
De apologia prophetae David	CPL 158	Q 4, 162–63
Apologia David altera	CPL 158	Q 4, 162–63
De Helia et ieiunio	CPL 137	Q 4, 160
De Nabuthae historia	CPL 138	Q 4, 160–61
De Tobia	CPL 139	
	CSEL 32/2 (1897), C. Schenkl	
Expositio evangelii secundum Lucam	CPL 143	
	CSEL 32/4 (1902), C. and H. Schenkl	
	CCL 14 (1957), M. Adriaen [with frgg. *Exp. Is.*]	

Expositio de psalmo CXVIII	CPL 141
	CSEL 62 (1913), M. Petschenig
Expositio super psalmos XII	CPL 140
	CSEL 64 (1919), M. Petschenig
	SC 45 and 52, G. Tissot
De apologia prophetae David	SC 239 (1977), P. Hadot and
	M. Cordier

Opera moralia et ascetica

De officiis ministrorum	CPL 144	Q 4, 166–67
De virginibus	CPL 145	Q 4, 167–68
De viduis	CPL 146	Q 4, 168
De virginitate	CPL 147	Q 4, 168
De institutione virginis	CPL 148	
Exhortatio virginitatis	CPL 149	

Opera dogmatica

De fide	CPL 150	Q 4, 169
	CSEL 78 (1962), O. Faller	
De spiritu sancto	CPL 151	Q 4, 169–70
	SC 179 (1971), R. Gryson	
	FOTC 44, 31–214, trans. R. J.	
	Deferrari	
De incarnatione	CPL 152	Q 4, 170
	CSEL 79 (1964), O. Faller	
	FOTC 44, 217–62, trans.	
	Deferrari	
Explanatio symboli	CPL 153	Q 4, 170–71
De sacramentis	CPL 154	Q 4, 172–73
	FOTC 44, 265–328, trans.	
	Deferrari	
De mysteriis	CPL 155	Q 4, 171
	FOTC 44, 3–28, trans. Deferrari	
De paenitentia	CPL 156	Q 4, 173

Orationes

De excessu fratris [*Satyri, lib. ii*]	CPL 157 Q 4, 174 FOTC 22, 159–259, trans. J. J. Sullivan and M. R. P. McGuire
De obitu Valentiniani	CPL 158 Q 4, 174–75 FOTC 22, 263–99, trans. R. J. Deferrari
De obitu Theodosii	CPL 159 Q 4, 175 CSEL 73 (1955), O. Faller FOTC 22, 303–32, R. J. Deferrari

Epistulae

CPL 160   Q 4, 176–77
CSEL 82/1 [1–35], O. Faller
CSEL 82/2 [36–69], M. Zelzer
FOTC 26, Letters 1–91, trans.
   Sr. M. Melchior Beyenks

Hymni

CPL 163   Q 4, 177–79
J. Fontaine (Paris, 1992)

Epigrammata

CPL 164

Life of Ambrose

Vita Ambrosii by Paulinus
of Milan
	ViSa 3, ed. Ch. Mohrmann,
	   A. A. R. Bastiaensen, L. Canali,
	   C. Carena (1975)
	W. Berschin, "La Vita S. Ambrosii
	   e la letteratura biografica
	   tardoantica," *Aevum* 67 (1993):
	   181–87

APPENDIX 5. THE CHRONOLOGICAL FRAMEWORK

The dates are taken from Michael Grant, *The Emperors of the Roman Empire*, and J. N. D. Kelly, *Dictionary of the Popes*.

Emperors

GAIUS CALIGULA (37–41)
  Philo (*DVI* 11)

CLAUDIUS (41–54)

NERO (54–68)
  Simon Peter (*DVI* 1), James (*DVI* 2), Paul (*DVI* 5),
  Mark (*DVI* 8), Seneca (*DVI* 12)

VESPASIAN (69–79)

TITUS (79–81)

DOMITIAN (81–96)
  John (*DVI* 9)

NERVA (96–98)
  John (*DVI* 9)

TRAJAN (98–117)
  John (*DVI* 9), Clement of Rome (*DVI* 15),
  Ignatius of Antioch (*DVI* 16)

HADRIAN (117–138)
  Quadratus (*DVI* 19), Aristides (*DVI* 20), Agrippa (*DVI* 21),
  Hegesippus (*DVI* 22)

ANTONINUS PIUS (138–161)
  Polycarp (*DVI* 17), Justin Martyr (*DVI* 23),
  Gaius of Rome (*DVI* 59)

MARCUS AURELIUS ANTONINUS VERUS (161–180)
AND LUCIUS AURELIUS VERUS (161–169)
  Justin (*DVI* 23), Melito of Sardis (*DVI* 24),
  Theophilus of Antioch (*DVI* 25),

Apollinaris of Hieropolis (*DVI* 26),
Dionysius of Corinth (*DVI* 27), Pinytus of Crete (*DVI* 28),
Tatian (*DVI* 29), Philip of Crete (*DVI* 30), Musanus (*DVI* 31),
Miltiades (*DVI* 32), Bardesanes (*DVI* 33)

COMMODUS (180–192) AND SEVERUS 193–211
Irenaeus (*DVI* 35), Miltiades (*DVI* 39),
Serapion of Antioch (*DVI* 41),
Apollonius, senator (*DVI* 42)

SEPTIMIUS SEVERUS (193–211) AND CARACALLA (211–217)
Pantaenus (*DVI* 36), Rhodo (*DVI* 37), Bacchylus (*DVI* 44),
Polycrates (*DVI* 45), Heraclitus (*DVI* 46),
Maximus (*DVI* 47), Candidus (*DVI* 48), Apion (*DVI* 49),
Sextus (*DVI* 50), Tertullian (*DVI* 53)

MARCUS AURELIUS ANTONINUS, OR ELAGABALUS (218–222)
Julius Africanus (*DVI* 63)

CLAUDIUS AND AURELIUS (221–222)
Malchion (*DVI* 71)

ALEXANDER, SON OF MAMMAEA (222–235)

GALLUS AND VOLUSIANUS (251–253)
Cornelius of Rome (*DVI* 66), Origen (*DVI* 54),
Novatian (*DVI* 70)

DECIUS (249–251) AND VALERIAN (253–259)
Hippolytus (*DVI* 61), Alexander of Cappadocia (*DVI* 62),
Methodius of Olympus (*DVI* 83)

VALERIAN (253–259) AND GALLIENUS (253–268)
Cyprian (*DVI* 67), Pontius, deacon (*DVI* 68),
Dionysius of Alexandria (*DVI* 69)

CLAUDIUS GOTHICUS (268–270) AND AURELIAN (270–275)
Malchion of Antioch (*DVI* 71)

PROBUS (276–282) AND CARUS (282–283)
Archelaus (*DVI* 72), Anatolius (*DVI* 73)

DIOCLETIAN (284–305)
Pierius (*DVI* 76), Arnobius (*DVI* 79)

MAXIMINUS (308–314)
Pamphilus (*DVI* 75), Lucian of Antioch (*DVI* 77),
Phileas (*DVI* 78)

CONSTANTINE (306–337) AND SONS (337–361)
Lactantius (*DVI* 80), Juvencus (*DVI* 84), Antony (*DVI* 88)

CONSTANTINE AND CONSTANTIUS
  Eusebius of Caesarea (*DVI* 81),
  Reticius of Autun (*DVI* 82), Marcellus of Ancyra (*DVI* 86)

CONSTANTIUS (337–361)
  Eustathius of Side (*DVI* 85), Basil of Ancyra (*DVI* 89),
  Theodorus of Heracleia (*DVI* 90),
  Eusebius of Emesa (*DVI* 91), Triphylius (*DVI* 92),
  Asterius (*DVI* 94), Fortunatianus (*DVI* 97),
  Acacius (*DVI* 98), Serapion of Thmuis (*DVI* 99),
  Victorinus Afer (*DVI* 101)

JULIAN (361–363)

JOVIAN (363–364)

VALENTINIANUS I (364–375) AND VALENS (364–375)
  Acilius Severus (*DVI* 111), Lucifer of Cagliari (*DVI* 95),
  Eusebius of Vercelli (*DVI* 96),
  Hilary of Poitiers (*DVI* 100), Photinus (*DVI* 107),
  Optatus of Milevis (*DVI* 110)

VALENS in East (364–375)
  Athanasius (*DVI* 87), Titus of Bostra (*DVI* 102),
  Ephrem (*DVI* 115)

GRATIAN OF MILAN (367–383)
  Basil of Caesarea (*DVI* 116)

MAXIMUS AT TREVES (383–388)
  Priscillian (*DVI* 121), Latronianus (*DVI* 122),
  Tiberianus (*DVI* 123)

THEODOSIUS (379–395)
  Pacian (*DVI* 106), Gregory Nazianzus (*DVI* 117),
  Lucius of Alexandria (*DVI* 118)

HONORIUS (395–423)
  John Chrysostom (*DVI* 129)

APPENDIX 6. *VIRI ILLUSTRES*
(alphabetically arranged)

*BBKL = Biographisch-Bibliographisches Kirchenlexikon, ed. F. W. Bautz (Hamm, Westf.: Verlag Traugott Bautz, 1970–1998).

INDEX OF PROPER NAMES

(in Introduction and Jerome's Text)

INDEX OF GREEK TERMS

(Chapter and paragraph numbers refer to text of DVI.)

INDICES TO THE FATHERS OF THE CHURCH
SERIES, VOLUMES 1–100, AND TO THE
MEDIAEVAL CONTINUATION, VOLUMES 1–5
Listed Alphabetically by Author

Fathers of the Church

INDEX TO THE SERIES 207

THE DIDACHE OR TEACHING OF THE TWELVE APOSTLES: *1*

LETTER TO DIOGNETUS: *1*

ENNODIUS
Life of St. Epiphanius (*Vita Epiphanii*): *15*

ST. EPHREM
Selected Prose Works: *91*

EUGIPPIUS
The Life of St. Severin (*Commemoratorium de vita s. Severini*): *55*

EUSEBIUS PAMPHILI
Ecclesiastical History (*Historia ecclesiastica*), Books 1–5: *19;* Books 6–10: *29*

FRUCTUOSUS OF BRAGA
General Rule for Monasteries (*Regula monastica communis*): *63*
Monastic Agreement (*Consensoria monachorum*): *63*
Pact (*Pactum*): *63*
Rule for the Monastery of Compludo (*Regula monachorum Complutensis*): *63*

FULGENTIUS
Selected Works: *95*

ST GREGORY NAZIANZEN
Concerning Himself and the Bishops (*De se ipso et de episcopis*): *75*
Concerning His Own Affairs (*De rebus suis*): *75*
Concerning His Own Life (*De vita sua*): *75*
Four Funeral Orations: *22*

ST. GREGORY OF NYSSA
On the Christian Mode of Life (*De instituto christiano*): *58*
Life of Gregory the Wonderworker (*De vita Gregorii Thaumaturgi*): *98*
The Life of St. Macrina (*Vita Macrinae*): *58*
On Perfection (*De perfectione et qualem oporteat esse Christianum*): *58*
On the Soul and the Resurrection (*Dialogus de anima et resurrectione*): *58*
On Virginity (*De virginitate*): *58*
On What It Means to Call Oneself a Christian (*Quid nomen professione Christianorum sibi velit*): *58*

ST. GREGORY THE GREAT
Dialogues (*Dialogorum libri IV*): *39*

ST. GREGORY THAUMATURGUS
Address of Thanksgiving to Origen (*Oratio prosphonetica ac panegyrica in Origenem*): *98*
Canonical Epistle: *98*
Metaphrase on the Ecclesiastes of Solomon: *98*
To Philagrius [Evagrius], on Consubstantiality: *98*

80

INDEX TO THE SERIES

InPraiseofPurity(De bono pudicitiae): 67
The Spectacles (De spectaculis): 67
The Trinity (De Trinitate): 67

ORIGEN
Commentary on the Gospel of John Books 1–10: *80;* 13–32: *89*
Homilies on Exodus (*In Exodum homiliae*): *71*
Homilies on Genesis (*In Genesim homiliae*): *71*
Homilies on Jeremiah (*In Ieremiam homiliae*): *97*
Homily on I Kings 28 (*In I Reg. 28 homiliae*): *97*
Homilies on Leviticus (*In Leviticum homiliae*): *83*
Homilies on Luke (*In Lucam homiliae*): *94*

OROSIUS OF BRAGA (PAULUS OROSIUS)
Book in Defense against the Pelagians (*Liber apologeticus*): *99*
Inquiry or Memorandum to Augustine on the Error of the Priscillianists
    and Origenists (*Consultatio sive commonitorium Orosii ad Augustinum de
    errore Priscillianistarum et Origenistarum*): *99*
The Seven Books of History against the Pagans (*Historiarum adversus
    paganos libri septem*): *50*

PACIAN OF BARCELONA
On Baptism (*De baptismo*): *99*
Letters 1, 2, 3: *99*
On Penitents (*De paenitentibus*): *99*

PAPIAS
The Fragments: *1*

PASCHASIUS OF DUMIUM
Questions and Answers of the Greek Fathers: *62*

PAULINUS (OF MILAN)
Life of St. Ambrose (*Vita s. Ambrosii*): *15*

ST. PETER CHRYSOLOGUS
Letter to Eutyches (*Epistula ad Eutychen*): *17*
Selected Sermons (*Sermones*): *17*

ST. POLYCARP
The Letter to the Philippians: *1*

PONTIUS
Life of St. Cyprian (*Vita Caecilii Cypriani*): *15*

POSSIDIUS
Life of St. Augustine: *15*

PROSPER OF AQUITAINE
Grace and Free Will (*De gratia Dei*): *7*

Mediaeval Continuation